Light on the Human Heart

Light on the Human Heart

Where Christian Faith and Psychology Meet

Colin Patterson

WIPF & STOCK · Eugene, Oregon

LIGHT ON THE HUMAN HEART
Where Christian Faith and Psychology Meet

Copyright © 2022 Colin Patterson. All rights reserved. Except for brief quotations in critical publications or reviews, no part of this book may be reproduced in any manner without prior written permission from the publisher. Write: Permissions, Wipf and Stock Publishers, 199 W. 8th Ave., Suite 3, Eugene, OR 97401.

Wipf & Stock
An Imprint of Wipf and Stock Publishers
199 W. 8th Ave., Suite 3
Eugene, OR 97401

www.wipfandstock.com

PAPERBACK ISBN: 978-1-6667-3833-9
HARDCOVER ISBN: 978-1-6667-9888-3
EBOOK ISBN: 978-1-6667-9889-0

JULY 14, 2022 10:33 AM

Unless otherwise indicated, all Scripture quotations are from The ESV® Bible (The Holy Bible, English Standard Version®), copyright © 2001 by Crossway, a publishing ministry of Good News Publishers. Used by permission. All rights reserved.

Excerpt from THE NEW JERUSALEM BIBLE, copyright (c) 1985 by Darton, Longman & Todd, Ltd. and Doubleday, a division of Penguin Random House LLC. Reprinted by permission.

To Tim, Naomi, Stephen, Philip and Michael

Contents

Preface | ix

PART I | DISCERNING THE HUMAN HEART

1 WHAT IS IN THE HEART OF MAN? | 3
2 DOMINANCE | 10
3 DOMINANCE: EXTENDING THE PICTURE | 35
4 ATTACHMENT | 49
5 ATTACHMENT AND DOMINANCE | 74
6 SOCIAL RECIPROCITY | 83
7 MATING | 101
8 MATING—FURTHER DIMENSIONS OF THE MOTIVE | 115
9 CONSCIENCE | 127
10 CONSCIENCE AND AUTHORITY | 151
11 HUMAN MOTIVATION AND HISTORICAL FORCES | 164
   CONCLUSION TO PART I | 175

Part II | Wider Perspectives

Some Implications for Faith: An Introduction | 179

12 "Lord, I believe in You—help me in my unbelief!" | 181

13 Meeting the Lord in Prayer— | 194

14 Seeking a More Real Hope of Eternal Life | 204

15 Why Do I Struggle with Belief in Hell? | 217

16 Marriage: "Love and Truth Walk Together" | 225

17 Is There a Distinctively Christian Approach to Politics? | 242

18 "Love One Another with Brotherly Affection" | 259

19 Contemporary Christian Mission: Its Failures and Possibilities | 268

Conclusion | 279

Bibliography | 287

Index | 293

Preface

THIS IS A BOOK about human beings, how we tick, what the inner forces are that impel us to act. It is written by a Christian and mainly for Christians, but I hope that it will be read with interest by believers of other religions and perhaps also by nonbelievers. It aims to shed some light on how the often-hidden parts of our mind lead us to think and feel and act as we do.

The field of psychology has an inherent interest for most people. We know that there is more to us than we are aware of, and discovering details of this "more" is something that fascinates us. What are the deepest sources of my desires and yearnings? What is it that pushes me to have the attitudes I do? But more than that, we are also interested in other people. We want to figure out what it is—deep down—that other people are aiming at. I hope the information in this book will be useful in shedding some light on these matters.

Of the books I have read dealing with the psychology of everyday life, many have enthused me initially and some have even had a long-term impact on how I live my life. But overall, I have also found them somewhat unsatisfying. In pondering why this was so, I decided that, for all their value, their main limitation is that they focused too much on our *thinking* as the main driver of our actions. Their emphasis was upon how we humans seek after things like achievement, meaning, or love as if we can and do control our thinking and thus our lives according to such abstract concepts. Yet, these books did not really explain *why* we should be like that. Why those goals and values and not others? In this work, I have aimed to make up for what has seemed to me to be the missing dimension in books of this kind by focusing on the deeper, non-rational elements of the mind.

Yet, I am not simply interested in writing something that will feed the reader's curiosity. I have a deeper concern that has to do with something we find when we read Jesus' teaching about the life of faith. Towards the end of a segment of teaching called the Sermon on the Plain found in Luke 6, Jesus talks about good actions only issuing from a good heart. Then he goes on to say that only when we build our foundation, that is, the core of our self, on Jesus' teaching will we be able to withstand the difficulties and crises that will come our way (Luke 6:43–49). We find similar teaching elsewhere in the Gospels. What is common to such passages is Jesus' idea that we need to cultivate our heart, our inner self, if we are to receive his word (seed) and allow it to grow so as to produce a good life. Understanding our heart a bit more, seeing how it can push us in false ways, finding out how we can strengthen it and make it more prepared to hear Jesus' words to us; this is what I hope the reader will be able to do in working through this book.

To pursue these aims, I will focus on two main questions: (a) What are the underlying psychological forces which drive our everyday thinking and feeling? and (b) are there pointers gained from being aware of these forces which we can use to change our life for the better? Now, when I use the word "better," I am assuming that there is some way of knowing which lives are better than others. As a Christian, of course, I look to the Christian faith to guide me in figuring out what it means to live a good life or to make my life better. I myself belong to the Catholic Church; however, if you are a believer who takes seriously the Scriptures as the word of God, you will find little in what I have written about the faith that you will not be able to agree with.

I write as a theologian who in previous employment practiced as a psychologist. The book seeks to draw upon my training and experience in both fields, but in the end my main concern is with the faith and how we are to express it in our lives. To put this another way, I would say that psychology by itself is not enough. It needs to be viewed in the light of the Scriptures before it can be fully useful. So, what I write from a purely scientific point of view about our psychology I will then put through the sieve of the biblical witness to interpret it, or to give it a moral direction that can then make it helpful to our lives. What do the Scriptures say about this aspect of human psychology? In what situations is it helpful for the believer? In what circumstances do we need to be careful of it?

I ought to say a word about what the book does not aim to do. Although it gives the reader a framework for understanding the mind, it is not a how-to manual. There is much material in it which, if you put it all together, will give you a general grasp of how we humans work, and because I connect this picture with the faith, throughout the book you will find ideas that you will be able to apply to your own life. But I do little of that work for you. That is something you, who are the expert in your own life, are most suited to do. Perhaps the best way to do this is by talking things over with other believers. After all, they can often see things about you that you do not notice, and their own experience can be useful to you as well.

The reader will notice that this book has two parts. In part I, following an introductory chapter which explains the idea of a motive, each of the next nine chapters gives a brief sketch of aspects of the key motives or drivers of our human psychology. Within each chapter there follows a scriptural evaluation of that motive, and finally I offer a few reflections on some immediate questions that the material raises for Christian life. Part I concludes with a chapter which describes how the way we have lived out our motives over recent generations has changed. That is, we humans are not unchanging creatures, but people who live in shifting and developing cultures that have important effects on how we think and act.

Part II is made up of eight essays dealing with such matters as Christian faith, prayer, marriage and family, politics, church life, and mission. In each of these, I endeavour to bring the understandings derived from part I and apply them to issues that I imagine will be of interest to Christians. This gives me an opportunity to illustrate how light can be shed on the questions I address by thinking about them in terms of the deeper forces that drive us humans. Rather than just considering one or two motives at a time, as in part I, here I take account of all those which are relevant to the question I consider. My hope is that this will help the reader understand better the framework of ideas I have described throughout the book.

I have written this book using non-technical language as far as I can manage. The theologian and the psychologist will probably want more in the way of references than I have provided. But I have limited myself to referencing works of a more general nature relating to each of the motives I consider, and also to particular research that I mention in the text. These limits serve to keep the focus of the book on the lay rather than the academic reader. I have considered elsewhere some of the questions raised in this book as part of the work of scholarly research and the interested reader should consult my other more technical writings.[1]

This book is in part the fruit of many discussions over the years which I was able to have with my colleagues at the John Paul II Institute for Marriage and Family in Melbourne. The focus of the institution and of my own work there is reflected in the emphasis I have placed on the broad themes of Christian marriage and family life. The material on the mating motive found in chapters 7 and 8, in particular, owes much to conversations with Conor Sweeney and Adam Cooper. I have also benefitted from feedback from members of the Australian Confraternity of Catholic Priests in relation to the ideas I present in chapters 17 and 19.

In terms of the writing and revision of the work, I thank Conor Sweeney and Tim Patterson for helpful comments they provided on parts of the text. Finally, I owe again a large debt of gratitude to my brother, Don Patterson, who read the whole book in draft form, parts of it multiple times, and not only picked up many grammatical and stylistic errors but provided useful information in improving its readability.

I have dedicated the book to my children, Tim, Naomi, Stephen, Philip and Michael, who are now all married with children of their own. Since their early years as young children and teenagers, and still to this day, as I watch them dealing with the issues that life has presented to them, they have been for me a continuing source of inspiration, challenge, reflection, and, above all, thankfulness to the Lord. As my wife and I often tell them, having five children has been by far the best thing we have ever done!

---

1. Patterson, *Chalcedonian Personalism*; "The World of Honour and Shame in the New Testament"; "A Cultural Evolutionary Approach to Modernity."

Part I

Discerning the Human Heart

1

What Is in the Heart of Man?

The Mystery of the Human Heart

WHAT IS MAN THAT YOU, Lord, are mindful of him? (cf. Ps 8:4) The "surface" of a man is that which he speaks and does, those things about him that others can hear and see. Mostly we understand these things. If we did not, we would not be able to get along together very well. But if we analyze them in more detail, we often find ourselves perplexed or at least uncertain, and we can appreciate the truth of the word that God spoke to the prophet Samuel, *"The Lord sees not as man sees; man looks on the outward appearance, but the Lord looks on the heart"* (1 Sam 16:7).

A part of that mystery is not knowing the reasons for someone's actions. A woman's irritable response to a friend's question might be because she has just come from having an argument with her husband and she decides that she is not going to suppress her feelings now. Or she might think of her friendship with this person as a bit of a drain on her time, and she wants to send a hint that they should reduce their contact. In recognizing her friend's annoyance, the other woman might not know its reasons and perhaps might even have no idea where to look for a reason.

But there is another, deeper part of this mystery of understanding another's actions and words that has to do with knowing what it is he or she is aiming at, what is the unconscious goal, and beneath that, what is the motive behind the words spoken or the things done. We recall how the apostle Paul, in his letter to the Philippians, remarks that while he is in prison, the gospel continues to be proclaimed by believers, yet *"some indeed preach Christ from envy and rivalry, but others from good will"* (Phil 1:15). Here, Paul was confident that the different motives for the same action of preaching the gospel were clear enough. But often this is not the case, and we find ourselves puzzled because we can often imagine more than one motive for any given word or deed, and we do not know which is the real one or what is going on at the unconscious level.

The people in ancient times had little sense of an unconscious mind, that is, a part of the human psyche which was not accessible to the consciousness of the individual. Typically, they thought that if a person would only look inside his heart, he would be able to discern the true wellsprings of what he said or did.[1] The past century or more has, however, opened up for us the existence of processes operating in the human mind which are not normally available at all to our internal gaze. Indeed, we now believe that many of an individual's actions arise from a whole array of operations of which he or she is not aware.[2] No wonder we are often mysteries not only to others but even to ourselves!

Humans and Other Animals

Regarding motives, the question arises, then, if we cannot discern these hidden processes by ourselves, how is it possible to make progress in understanding the deepest motives for our actions? The way forward seems blocked to us. Yet, there are approaches which have borne fruit. One of the most helpful techniques available to us is that of comparing ourselves as humans with other animals. We have evolved from earlier species which are the common forebears of ourselves and the animal species alive today, especially primates. And since the behavior of these animals is much simpler than that of our own, we have been able to recognize in them

---

1. Perhaps we can recognize a vague awareness of this hidden dimension in a passage such as Proverbs 16:2: "*All the ways of a man are pure in his own eyes, but the Lord weighs the spirit.*"

2. The literature relating to this question is vast. In relation to psychological research, currently, some of the most commonly used techniques for accessing unconscious process are those which rely upon a process called "priming." In this technique, ideas are introduced into a subject's mind without their awareness, and later their responses to some task are assessed to see if this idea, present but unconscious, affects their behavior. Often this is found to be the case.

fundamental motives which are just like what we see in ourselves. In fact, we can look at animals less sophisticated than non-human primates, such as mice and birds, and find the early forms of more developed motives. As we will see below, almost all the basic motives that drive our human thoughts, words, and actions are to be found in similar form in lower animals. Some have their beginnings hundreds of millions of years ago; others are of much more recent origin.

Yet, we must keep in mind that our human behavior is often extraordinarily complex. Why a person does something can depend, for example, on the mere intonation of a single word uttered by one with whom he is talking. Or consider the reason a chess grandmaster moves a pawn in a particular state of play. This might depend on a single sentence he read forty years ago. So, it is certainly the case that we cannot hope ever to be able to know the full story of any human action. However, this must not discourage us in the search for a general understanding of why humans do what they do.

One of the things that make us humans so complicated is the fact that we live in sophisticated and complex societies. We know that cultures vary enormously between themselves, even in an age when cultures are borrowing so much from each other. In their efforts to make sense of this complexity, scientists have noted in recent decades that the processes observed in biological evolution appear to be paralleled in the way cultures develop. In biology, random genetic variations that occur when new offspring are conceived become the material that a species' environment works upon to determine which variants are helpful for survival and which have no effect or even harm the chances of survival. Those genes that lead to survival more often continue in future generations, while those which are harmful are bred out. If the latter dominate, however, then a species might soon become extinct. Similarly in a culture, we find a process of variation and testing for survival. But what is worked on is not something biological but rather the core elements of culture, that is, ideas, practices, institutions, and manners. Some of these are widely adopted because they confer significant advantages on a culture, while others are discarded as unhelpful or harmful. Thus, the beneficial elements can be preserved through the centuries and thus become a fixed part of a culture, just like successful genes. Some cultures, for example, wean infants early, while other cultures encourage mothers to breastfeed well into the second or even third year of their child's life. How a culture "decides" on matters like this depends on what works within that culture.

So, the biological model of evolution has been helpful in thinking about what has now come to be called "cultural evolution."[3] There are, naturally, important differences between the two kinds of analysis, yet the similarities have been useful for scientists in their efforts to understand human behavior. For, just as the study of animal evolution has assisted scientists in understanding human motives from a biological point of view, so too has the examination of the varieties of human cultural evolution added another dimension to their knowledge.

Drawing this material together, we can conclude with the idea that the sources of human behavior are primarily three: there are the last two I mentioned, that is, motives which we share with many other animals and which emerged through biological evolution, and, within those core motives, *human cultures* develop a vast number of ways of achieving the fundamental goals which those motives seek for. But there are also the particular histories of individuals and of those with whom they interact, and these generate the conscious *reasons for acting* which also have a profound impact on the actual shape of a person's thoughts, words and deeds. As I noted above, we cannot hope to fathom the intricacies of this last category, but we can gain much from a knowledge of the first and second sources.

With this background in place, let us now consider human motivation. Which are the most important motives? How do they affect the way we think, speak, and act?

Human Motivation

Motives are central to human actions. In the book of Revelation, Christ reminds the church at Thyatira: "*It is I who test motives and thoughts and repay you as your deeds deserve*" (Rev 2:23, NJB). Here we can see that our dignity as humans rests, in part, on our accountability before God, and to render account means to give reasons for what we do. For the most part, we humans act *for reasons*. We carry out conscious actions with a purpose or a goal in mind.[4] It is also the case that the goal of one action

---

3. Here I treat cultural and biological evolution as distinct categories; however, it is now well recognized that there is a measure of overlap between them. The case for such an overlap is made in Henrich, *The Weirdest People*. The qualification does not affect the point I make here.

4. Following Aristotle, Aquinas expresses the point succinctly, "Now the rule and measure of human acts is the reason, which is the first principle of human acts... since

can form part of a larger goal which in turn might belong to a sequence of goals forming a more long-term, overarching goal. My interest here is with the goal-seeking processes which lie at the very bottom of these goals or goal-sequences. What are the most fundamental purposes that we humans seek after? As I will explain later, the deepest motives are mostly unknown—or only partly known—to us, and it often comes as a sobering surprise to discover the fundamental goals we pursue throughout our lives.

Focus on Social Motives

Now, in saying I am interested in the most basic motives, I must immediately add that I am also limiting myself to what we might call *social* motives. In giving an idea of what these are, let us first think about non-social purposeful behavior. Consider what happens when you breathe in some foreign body and your cough reflex is triggered. This is goal-seeking or motivated behavior triggered by our body, since it has a distinct purpose of clearing our airways. Similarly, our body pushes us to act so as to make ourselves comfortable when our limbs tell us that such an adjustment is necessary or helpful, and we breathe more deeply when our oxygen levels are lowered. At a more developed level of motive, we make efforts to nourish our bodies when parts of our brain sense that we need more food and drink. Unlike coughing and deeper breathing, the behavior prompted by the hunger and thirst can be very complex, taking up much of our time and energy, and is often part of our social life.

In contrast to these bodily actions and motives, here I am interested in those motives which have goals achieved through interacting with other people. For each of the types of goal-seeking behavior I have mentioned so far, this is not necessary.[5] For social motives, contact and

---

it belongs to the reason to direct to the end, which is the first principle in all matters of action, according to the Philosopher (Phys. ii)." (Aquinas, *Summa Theologica*, I–II, q.90, a.1)

5. There is another very important system of goal-seeking behaviors that have to do with self-preservation from harm or death. These operate in many circumstances of daily life, from when we are driving a car, to chewing our food properly, to exercising at the gym, to avoiding breathing in car exhaust. I would categorize this motive of harm avoidance as basically non-social, although it has social elements to it. It will be mentioned from time to time in this book.

engagement with other people is at their very core. Without that they cannot be satisfied.

Five Basic Social Motives

Still the best summary of human social motivation explained from an evolutionary viewpoint is that published in 2000 by the psychologist Daphne Bugental.[6] In it she identifies five basic social motives (although she does not use the terminology of motive or motivation): attachment, dominance, coalitional grouping, reciprocity, and mating. It is this scheme which I will be following at least for the most part. As the reader will discover, I treat coalitional grouping not as a separate motive, but as forming part of both attachment and dominance. Also, I add another motive, that of conscience, which I view as the motive which holds the others together.

So, we will explore five social motives. In doing so, we will have covered the most important inner forces that shape our thoughts and actions.

What Does This Approach Add to Traditional Ways of Addressing the Same Questions?

The reader might be wondering what advantage there is in the approach taken here over the ways used in the past to describe the human mind. I hope that the answer to that question might become clear to the reader as he or she proceeds through the book. But as a pointer to an answer, I would say that earlier ways of understanding the human mind from the point of view of faith have tended to rely heavily upon abstract concepts, have focused strongly on the influence of human reason and on our ability to learn new ideas and skills. To say that such-and-such behavior is the result of our desire for happiness, or because we rationally weigh up the pros and cons in our minds, or because that's how we learned to act, all these explanations are often at least partly the truth, but they are not especially illuminating and do not take account of all that we have

---

6. Bugental, "Acquisition," 187–219. Literature offering related theories of social domain structure include: MacCrimmon and Messick, "A Framework for Social Motives," 86–100; Fiske, "The Four Elementary Forms," 689–723; Foa and Foa, "Resource Theory of Social Exchange," 15–32.

discovered in recent times about the human mind and its similarities with the minds of non-rational animals.

Much of our new knowledge, developed as it has during the past 160 years or so, is based on evolutionary understandings of nature. We believers have had to take this into account, and the task has been quite painful for many. But it has also raised questions about the faith that, as we have worked through them, have allowed us to see God's revelation in a new and fuller light. As the reader will observe, this development in our understanding of ourselves has played a key role in the explanations I provide for the various aspects of human action as it relates to the Christian faith.

So, with these general comments about motives and how important they are in gaining a grasp of how we humans think and act, let us turn now to an account of the five key social motives and consider them one by one.

2

Dominance

Dominance in Nature

STUDENTS OF ANIMAL BEHAVIOR have long observed that a vast range of species across much of the animal kingdom order their interactions by ranking individual animals in dominance hierarchies. At its simplest, a dominance hierarchy within a social group of animals is created by the differences in some valued quality related to reproductive potential, for example fighting prowess or physical appearance. These qualities signal suitability for bearing offspring, such that those with greater levels of the valued quality are placed higher up the ordering and those with less are relegated to the lower places. Position is often established through conflict between two members of a group, but commonly this is achieved merely by the display of indicators of fighting ability. There is no use picking a fight if it is clear that you are not going to win!

There are, of course, a wide range of ways that dominance hierarchies have evolved across species. Male deer have acquired antlers which signal to others in a herd the relative dominance of an individual animal. Male peacocks vary in the quality of their feather displays but the establishment of a dominance hierarchy is the same underlying effect. Among females, physical indicators of health and readiness for bearing offspring are typically prized, and variations in these qualities lead to differing ranks.

In species where the male mates indiscriminately with multiple females, we typically find that there is less evolutionary pressure for the females to rank themselves hierarchically, so it is the males who develop more complex systems of dominance.

The evolutionary value of this way of arranging members of species within a group is not difficult to discern if we keep in mind that those animals higher in a hierarchy have preferential access to females of the group, in particular those possessing higher reproductive value. This means that the quality of the offspring within the group is gradually enhanced and thus the species' chances of survival are strengthened. In short, dominance hierarchies serve the end result of improving species survival through a process of selective breeding.

All this applies to non-human primates, such as chimpanzees, gorillas, orangutans, monkeys, and the like, although in quite varied forms. The better specimens in a species, such as the alpha male in a troupe of monkeys or gorillas, has control over sexual access to the females within the group, but much can complicate this simple process. Thus, kin relationships, for example, between mother and son, can affect orderings through the power of protection of otherwise weaker members. Also, females of some species show greater hierarchical ordering than others, and in that case there will be two sex-specific hierarchies often with slightly differing goals. In this instance, the high-ranking males might attempt to mate with as many females as possible, whereas the more dominant females would make themselves available to only the most impressive males.

Interestingly, in the primate genus *Pan*, that which is closest to humans, we find two species, *pan troglodytes* or the common chimpanzee, and *pan paniscus* or bonobo, which feature distinctive forms of social ordering derived in large part from the differing ecologies in which they evolved. The chimpanzees display more aggression overall, greater male influence within social groups, the formation of male groups, or gangs, which complicate dominance sorting, and generally the male hierarchies are relatively unstable. The bonobos, by contrast, have evolved to operate with a less aggressive mode of relating involving heightened sexual interaction, more frequent positive social interactions, mother-only (rather than female-group) infant rearing, and greater influence of females in determining dominance hierarchies. So, we can see that even among closely related species, there can be markedly different ways of working out the processes of dominance.

Similarities in Human Dominance

Similar variation appears across human societies; there is great complexity in the way dominance behavior shows itself. Yet, the same basic processes are still in play. Humans order their societies and smaller communities into dominance hierarchies whose "purpose" is to maximize the quality of offspring through the pairing of "good quality" males with "good quality" females. Yet something has changed during our specifically human evolution which has led to the redefinition of what "good quality" means. The change I am referring to is the dramatic increase in how long it takes for young humans to reach full maturity. Even today, with our longer average span of life, well over a quarter of that span is taken up with the process of working towards full adulthood. Among our shorter-lived human ancestors, the fraction was much greater. Compared with other primates, the change is even more dramatic. But how does that affect our view of "good quality"?

Because infant humans are vulnerable for a much longer period of time than the infants of other primates, human offspring will be more likely to survive and thrive on their path to maturity if there are two available parents involved in the task of family rearing rather than the mother alone. Thus, the human female has evolved to prefer not simply a male partner who is strong and able to protect her during the vulnerable times of later pregnancy, birth, and lactation, but someone who also possesses such qualities as being able to provide for her and to be dependable. The human male for his part seeks a reproductively healthy partner to bear his offspring, and this is signaled by such attributes as curvaceous body form, clear complexion, healthy hair, facial symmetry, and the like. But, in addition, because he can never be absolutely certain that his pregnant partner is carrying his rather than another male's child, he is also looking for a trustworthy and respectful character in his partner so that the risk is minimized of him investing his time and energies in helping to raise the child of another male. So, we see that, more so than in our primate ancestors, not only physical but also psychological qualities are valued by both sexes, yet in a way that does not overlap entirely.

With this background in mind, let us consider the specifics of human dominance.

Human Dominance Behavior

Humans have their own systems of dominance behavior made more complex by the variety of cultures and by the extraordinary complexity of some of those cultures.[1]

And yet it would be strange indeed if human societies did not display closely related kinds of social ordering to those which we find among non-human animals. The fact is that there are remarkable similarities both in the way the ranking is organized and in the ultimate effect of species survival that dominance hierarchies serve. The more we explore this area, the more we find the same processes in play. This can be a little disconcerting at first, since it demonstrates that a core purpose of human behavior is the seemingly selfish aim of climbing a ladder or pecking order in such a manner that any individual's gain is always at the expense of someone else. Yet, there is no use putting our head in the sand if this is the truth about ourselves. Better to face up to it and address it from the point of view of our faith, knowing that we are not defined simply by this one—though core—feature of our human nature.

How Do Human Dominance Hierarchies Develop?

From the first few days after birth a human infant will be able to distinguish between someone touching his body and his own touching of himself. The sense of agency that this points to is in-built, as it were, in the way infants develop, and in time it becomes apparent that when a four-month-old child repeatedly hits a toy hanging over his head and listens to the noise it makes, he is gaining some kind of "reward" for his actions. The mere power of "having an effect" on the external world is reinforcing. Over time, with increasing skill, actions which impact the external world become more and more sophisticated, from babbling to articulating words and word combinations, from pushing a ball to throwing it and then to catching it. This is the foundation of dominance in human life, and it is sometimes termed *competence*.

By about eighteen months, we find another sphere emerging powerfully, that is, the social domain. A sense of oneself as a social being whom others can observe and interact with as a self comes into play, and

---

1. The literature on social dominance among humans is extensive. For an example of work in the area by one of its leading researchers, see: Hawley, "Ontogeny and Social Dominance," 318–42.

this opens up the possibility of a child comparing him/herself with other individuals. Thereafter, dominance behavior, competing for attention, attempting to control others, managing access to toys, physical aggression, and the like become key parts of interaction among young children. As language develops, the ways of communicating dominance increase dramatically, as do the possibilities of developing working alliances with others in the interests of maintaining or improving one's position in some peer hierarchical ordering. Note that with increasing age comes a much greater range of hierarchies available to the individual: sporting abilities, scholastic performance, social influence, physical attractiveness, musical accomplishment, family status, and much more can all serve as bases for dominance ordering. By the stage of late childhood, we find in basic form the shape that dominance will take in the adult world.

To further illustrate the intricacies of the operation of the dominance motive, consider two men who meet each other for the first time. Within a few seconds, both have performed—subconsciously—a multidimensional assessment of indicators of dominance status: height, body size, facial appearance (e.g., jaw shape), subtle pointers to level of intelligence, signs of wealth, any signs of defects, etc. All of this will be rapidly processed in order to arrive at a way of relating to the other based upon a provisional assessment of dominance on some key status hierarchies. "Surface" thoughts will, naturally, focus on what to say, and where the interaction is heading, but all this will be powerfully shaped by underlying dominance considerations. Is this person worth getting to know? Do we share important commonalities? Perceiving low status in the other will prompt an earlier closure of the contact; high status might lead one to display more "pleasing" behavior towards the other in the hope of cultivating the relationship.

What Are the Goals and Rewards that Dominance Seeks?

In the above example, the man who turns out to be dominant in the interaction, call him A, would be satisfied if the other man, B, initially and provisionally accepts A's evaluation of himself as dominant. Yet the level of satisfaction would not be such as to provide a powerful reward to A since, very early in the conversation, he will have assessed his position vis-à-vis B, and his efforts to put that into effect would have been mainly driven by concern that he not fail in his efforts, that is, fail to establish dominance in the relation. With success, all that is achieved is *confirmation* of A's view of himself in relation to someone of B's status.

The real energy behind the dominance motive, however, comes from the prospect that we might *increase* our status, in other words, improve our position or ranking on a significant social hierarchy. This can be achieved by gaining a promotion or being appointed to a senior position in an organization, graduating from a prestigious university, winning at a major sporting competition, earning great wealth, and many other lesser accomplishments. All that is required for our status to grow in these circumstances is that others recognize and acknowledge what we have achieved and that we act according to our new status.

Another pathway to status improvement is through having others pay attention to us. Of course, we can gain attention for the wrong reasons, such as when we act so as bring shame on ourselves. But here I want to highlight the profound, subconscious effect on our sense of self of others looking at us and listening to us. For example, many women complain of becoming "invisible" after they reach a certain age. When they were younger, they were attended to, especially by men, but as they have lost their earlier external attractiveness, they notice that others tend to ignore them or not take seriously what they have to say. Within gatherings of friends or colleagues, the amount of group attention an individual receives is closely correlated with their status. Dominant people tend to gain the lion's share of the gaze of others and more note is taken of their words; what they say creates momentum and shapes the discussion of a particular topic, whereas what a less dominant person contributes might be acknowledged by others but is more likely to be contradicted or at least dropped in favor of another line of discussion.

The higher the overall status of participants in a conversational gathering we are part of, the more rewarding is any attention and acknowledgment the group gives to us. The pleasurable experience can be from gaining recognition for what we believe should be our true status ("Now they see how good I am in regard to..."), having to revise upwards our view of our status in the light of the kind and level of attention others have given us ("Wow! I'm even better than I thought I was!") or having high-status individuals (or groups) including us in their circle of associates so that we attain a higher level of social acceptance.

Finally, another goal we can pursue when driven by the dominance motive is that of being able to exert an influence or power over others. The saying "drunk with power" reflects the strong motivating force that power over others, be it authority, control, or influence, can have on an individual.[2] These three forms of power generate different experiences for those who possess them, but common to them all is the sense that our own personal competence is multiplied through the effects on the world of all those over whom we have influence. The CEO of a company can only be in one place at a time, but he can issue a directive to hundreds or thousands of employees and the effect on the whole corporation can be profound. A social justice group that is struggling to have its voice heard and feels impotent as a result can get people to stand up and listen if it is able to persuade a famous celebrity to promote its message. Both group and celebrity can therefore be strongly rewarded in their dominance behavior if they are able to generate action among community leaders or the wider public.

The other side of this is that people can also experience a great sense of "power" reward—and here I am still referring specifically to rewards achieved through the operation of the dominance motive—when they are able to thwart what they consider is the unjust or otherwise inappropriate exercise of power by those who possess it. The members of a local environmental protection group who are able to stop the construction of a freeway through an ecologically sensitive area by means of a protracted pursuit of the matter through the courts not only feel relief at their victory but much more strongly a sense of influence over those who normally exert control, that is, governments and large corporations. On a more general level, we all value and take pleasure in a sense of autonomy in relation to those who would exercise power over us. We prefer to be given freedom to make decisions and have an impact on our own portion of the world rather than having our boss or the government issuing us with orders or too closely monitoring our actions.

So, the three major pathways to dominance satisfaction are those of (1) recognized increase in status through achievement, (2) eliciting of positive attention from others, especially those who themselves are of higher status, and (3) growing in one's impact on the world through gaining power over others, whether that be through authority, influence, or (non-sanctioned) control, or, alternatively, through the thwarting of those who possess power. How these pathways show themselves depends on many culturally specific factors.

---

2. Schultheiss, "Implicit Motives," 603–633; Schultheiss and Brunstein, "Inhibited Power Motivation," 553–82.

How Does Culture Influence Dominance?

Western societies themselves are quite diverse in the way they handle the dominance motive. And our experience of dominance is made broader from the increased exposure we have had in more recent times to people of non-Western backgrounds. More often today we interact with or see interactions with individuals from societies, sometimes wealthier than our own, whose dominance behavior is initially quite mysterious to us. Here, however, my focus will be chiefly upon Western culture.

In most Western nations, the consciousness of dominance as a fundamental motive for behavior is typically masked. Social norms, especially among some groups, discourage *overt* ladder-climbing or competitive behavior more generally. In line with this, individuals acquire skill at both the pursuit of dominance *and* at concealing the public display of this pursuit. The senior secondary student who is striving for a place at medical school is more than likely fully conscious of the status that success in this endeavour will bring him in an important social dominance hierarchy. Yet, he does not seek to communicate to his friends that he is in fact very competitive and believes himself worthy of such a high social ranking. Rather, he explains his career choice as being driven by a desire to help people or some similar reason. The woman who has been able to climb the ladder in the business world is no doubt driven by a belief in herself as better than those whom she has bested along the way up, and at times she might have to have been somewhat ruthless in her pursuit of dominance in her chosen field. However, she is unlikely to articulate this reality as that which is driving her actions. Rather she might explain her behavior as a conviction that she can "make a difference" or, perhaps more philosophically, that her life goal is to "leave the world a better place."

It is not difficult to recognize significant cultural differences, even within Western culture, in the way dominance is expressed in social settings. The examples I have just given illustrate behavior which is common in the English-speaking world and among Northern Europeans. Status is determined mostly by the achievements one has under one's belt, one's wealth, professional position, particular skills, and the like. So, one's status does not have to be trumpeted about because it is always there and ready to be communicated to others—subtly, of course—if needed. Most of those with whom a high-status person comes in contact will already know of their achievements and will show the appropriate deference (if they themselves are of lower status). Steve Jobs could dress in jeans and Bill Gates can wear pullovers; there was no necessity for them to "power dress" in order to project status because knowledge of their power and wealth has gone before them. Reputation, then, is the key to dominance within these cultural settings.

In Southern European, and even more so in Middle Eastern cultures, status is typically claimed in the here-and-now, often in the following ways: by confident and commanding demeanor and expensive dress; by taking the initiative in speaking within a conversation and controlling its flow; by acting as the arbiter of truth and falsehood, value and disvalue, on every matter being addressed; by expressing graciousness and generosity at whim; and by expecting and eliciting expressions of deference from one's conversation partner.

Of course, in these cultures, not every such dominant individual is able to preserve their position because life circumstances change, and any consequent loss of status routinely leads to the experience of shame which is powerfully disturbing to the sufferer. Societies where this style of interaction is the norm are labelled by sociologists as honor-shame societies. The expressions of dominance or of one's honor are communicated in an up-front manner unlike the earlier described achievement mode; there is, therefore, much less attempt to conceal or play down one's dominance beliefs, intentions, and behaviors.

However different the two types of society might appear on the surface—and at the surface level there are a vast array of differences—underlying both modes is the same biological/psychological motive: dominance. The behavior in both is "designed" to construct and maintain hierarchies within settled communities and societies, with high status or position serving as an indicator of reproductive suitability. This leads to mating behavior that is optimized for quality of offspring and ultimately to the preservation and improvement of the species *homo sapiens*.

The Relation of Dominance to Everyday Consciousness

So far, I have described dominance behavior from the outside, considering individuals as they would be observed in their public actions and utterances. But what about the inner experience of the operation of the motive? How does it reveal itself?

Within Western culture—or at least that part of it which is primarily achievement-driven and my focus here—most individuals who have some measure of self-awareness possess a limited consciousness of the dominance motive. Social norms about its overt expression—perhaps an effect of the influence of the Christian religion on the culture—tend to obscure or weaken such consciousness. Yet there usually exists some vague sense of its existence. Stronger and more prominent to awareness, however, are those attitudes we hold which serve to *conceal* the self-centered purposes which our dominance motive dictates. Among these are attitudes such as that which holds that "I want to be the best that I can be" or "I have been given talents that I want to develop; I don't want to waste them." Attitudes of this kind give us socially acceptable reasons for engaging in dominance behavior. Note, however, that they work to extract the competitive element from status pursuit so that one presents oneself as simply pursuing the goal of *competence*, the precursor to competitive dominance that we described in the development of the motive. All this is what we offer for public consumption; comparison with others, however, usually continues under the surface to drive our behavior.

The dominance motive has a very close connection with how our self operates in everyday life. Simply put, we can say that the typical consciousness that you and I experience of ourselves is normally the outworking of the dominance motive. The self that we have constructed, and which society has helped us to shape, has the function of maintaining or enhancing our position on various dominance hierarchies. The self and self-esteem are primarily products of the dominance motive.

Most of the thoughts we have in our waking hours are the result of the expression of our self as a dominance-controlled system of mental processes. Here are a few concrete examples: our thinking about what clothes we will wear each morning; our routines of cleaning our house or apartment; whether or not to answer a phone call from someone; thinking about (getting annoyed about) a political issue or a matter related to our work; our thoughts when we are shopping or accessing social media; interacting with work colleagues; the experience of watching a movie or reading; learning a new skill; driving a car; daydreaming, etc. If we reflect on these for a moment in light of what I have written above, I think it will be clear that in each of them we can detect the presence of one of the three forms of dominance motive I listed above (achievement, social acceptance, control). In short, any inner experience which involves the social self—and that is something which occurs in all these examples—at the very least, is influenced by the drive for dominance but more commonly is controlled by it.[3]

There are, of course, other motives which contribute to our inner life—we will consider the attachment, social reciprocity, mating, and conscience systems later—but the reality is that, while each of these can at times take over from dominance as the controlling motive, we never set aside our sense of self, and thus our dominance system never goes to sleep, as it were. It is always there, often as the primary driver of our thoughts and actions, but at times it takes on the role of a backseat driver. Fear of physical danger, barracking for our football team, lovemaking between a husband and wife, and thinking about how we are to be true to our conscience in a particular situation—these relate to non-dominance motives, but even when we are in full flight, in any of these actions, dominance is not far away. In sum, then, I want to affirm for our selves *the dominance of dominance.*

When we are first exposed to what I have described here, it can be somewhat unsettling to us. In fact, when we are first confronted with this close link between the self and dominance, many of us employ psychological defenses to avoid letting it into our full consciousness. Intellectually, we hear it or read it, and then something stops us from seeing it for what it really is, a truth that is perceived to be so jarring to the self that it cannot be permitted to find a place in our self-image. Again, the way through this difficulty is to face up to the truth and to open our eyes to the way dominance shows itself in our lives. Later we will find that, fortunately, there are other motives which we can use to help us mitigate some of the worst effects of dominance.

Dominance and Conscious Reasoning

I hope that it will be clear to the reader from the examples I have provided above that we are not generally aware of the dominance motive driving our everyday behavior. But can we say more about the mechanisms which connect that motive with our up-front, conscious thoughts

---

3. I refer to the "social self" here to distinguish it from those aspects of the self which are not normally social. The core of our self-awareness is also touched by experiences such as physical pain and pleasure, itching and other experiences of bodily discomfort such as breathlessness and tiredness. These kinds of experiences are those we share with many other animals, including those which do not possess an awareness of themselves as social beings.

and actions? This is a complex area, but perhaps it is helpful, in responding to this question, to highlight one key aspect of our selves which has emerged within Western culture over a period of centuries and that is our sense of ourselves as reasonable or reason-guided selves. This is a pervasive dimension of (at least) the Western self. When called to explain our actions, we give reasons which demonstrate that we link what we do to a range of principles, to a body of knowledge about the world, and a careful, coherent linkage between the two. "Why did you purchase that brand of yogurt?" "Because it's cheaper than the other brands (and I want to save money)" or "because it contains the sort of bacteria that suits my digestive system (and I want to look after my health)" or "because the manufacturer is more environmentally conscious (and I want to help preserve the natural world)." Our cultural ideal is the person who acts reasonably rather than being controlled simply by passion. Certainly, reason does not stand by itself, for it has to make use of values, as is clear in the yogurt explanations. But as long as it employs values which are universally shared and not particular to any religious or philosophical worldview, it stays within the bounds of rationality. Such is how our culture and especially those who have received an extensive education in it think about the self.

What is more, this view of reason and its importance for right (and successful) human conduct, according to our cultural understanding, is generally seen to stand in contrast to any view which places motives at the core of human action. So, we either act on the basis of reasons which make sense to others (reason) or we are driven to act on the basis of the dominance motive (passion). It is a matter of either reason or non-reason impulses or motives, and the former, reason, in this telling, represents the ideal mode of acting.

However, my claims about the centrality of dominance in the operation of the self suggest that something different is happening here. In this account, what we Westerners think of as the true foundation of our actions, that is, reason, is only the surface or instrumental level of a more extensive, deeper system which is normally driven by the dominance motive. Reasons for acting are closer to our awareness most of the time; the drive of dominance is, in contrast, mostly hidden from our view. So, the way I would describe the matter is that reason is the *instrument* of dominance, not an alternative and preferred guide of our behavior.

This alternative—and I would say truer—approach contains the following difficult-to-digest implication: your thinking about what I have just described here is itself driven by a motive, and that motive is not that of reason. (Just as my thinking in writing about this is!) Reason is a capacity, not a motive. This means that one cannot stand outside—in a neutral, unmotivated sense—the account I have given and evaluate it on a purely rational basis. Our thoughts about this matter belong to and are driven by a motive, most likely that of dominance (but not necessarily!—as we will see in later chapters).

Consider the following example of how this phenomenon shows itself in practice. A paper published in the British medical journal *Lancet* offered evidence that the world's population will soon begin to decline, and quite dramatically so, because we are approaching a situation in which almost all nations will have below-replacement-level fertility rates (the average number of children per woman). A BBC journalist, in reporting on the research, announced the story thus: "Fertility rate: 'Jaw-dropping' global crash in children being born," and in interviewing one of the authors of the paper, noted that the fertility rate decline "has nothing to do with sperm counts or the usual things that come to mind when discussing fertility. Instead, it is being driven by more women in education and work, as well as greater access to contraception, leading to women choosing to have fewer children."[4] Now, education, employment, and the use of contraception look like rational choices that people make in response to their particular life circumstances and goals. But the researcher, in identifying some of the truly dramatic consequences of population decline, remarked to the journalist that "I find people laugh it off; they can't imagine it could be true, they think women will just decide to have more kids. [But] If you can't [find a solution] then eventually the species disappears." As a demographer, he knows that these global changes are driven by more than simply rational choice, and that other deeper forces, much less amenable to manipulation by humans, are at work. If you consider the factors the researcher mentioned—education, employment, and access to contraception—it is not difficult to see in them aspects of life which are strongly driven by dominance: education and employment to improve one's status, and contraception to remove hindrances to a woman's pursuit of these goals. The conscious reasons, then, are more likely to be the surface of a deeper dynamic which is dominance driven. We think that we "do our own thing," but the reality is that in many respects "things are doing us."

4. Gallagher, "Fertility Rate."

To say this, however, raises the question of how it is possible for our (rational) self to take control of our thoughts and direct them in the way we reasonably think they should go. How can we think of ourselves as free? These questions, in turn, raise in our minds the quandary of where our true self lies and what is its manner of operation. To deal with these questions we will need to wait until we consider our final motive, that of conscience. But simply mentioning that one will already give a clue to the reader.

Everyday Thinking: Taking Account of Dominance

To understand and to take into account the suggested relationship between dominance and reason is a difficult and long-drawn-out process, but I believe pursuing it is nonetheless most helpful for us. The first task is to test its truth in one's own experience: when I test it as a way of understanding my actions and thoughts, does it make sense of my experience?

If we follow through with this testing process, we might discover things about ourselves of which we had a vague awareness, but which now become much clearer to us. For example, the extent to which we over-value our own qualities, especially positive qualities; the way we think the status ladders we are working at climbing are more important than others in which we are less interested, these habits of mind show themselves with greater lucidity. We tend to think of our self as being smarter in general, more astute, more knowledgeable in particular areas, more moral, more considerate of others, happier, and better at solving problems than an objective valuation would show us to be. We are so invested in our self for the purpose of defending, maintaining, or advancing our status in the eyes of others that it is very difficult for us to be truly honest with ourselves.

Along the same lines, we usually think of ourselves as distinctive or different from others. So, when we read that last paragraph about our inability to be honest with ourselves, instinctively most of us will think: "Yes, that's true of most people, but it's not the case with me." We are almost incorrigible in over-valuing and setting ourselves apart from others. This is the effect of the dominance system on our thoughts and attitudes.

The other side of this over-valuation of our selves is, of course, the undervaluing of others. In conversations, we frequently hear utterances such as, for example: "Although most people pay lip service to the need to care for the environment, really they do not care much about it." Implication: "But I do." Or, "Most people vote from their hip pocket," which comes with the implicit, "But I don't." This bias distorts our view of the world quite seriously since it does not take into account the great number of similarities we share with others, and indeed it is rather sobering to realize and to acknowledge just how similar we are to many other people. The truth, however, is that we cannot afford to think this way because that would undermine our determination to pursue status and achievement goals.

There are several other reality-distorting psychological mechanisms that our dominance motive employs (unwittingly) to assist it in the pursuit of its goals, but those I have described give a flavor of how they work. Taken together, they point towards the idea that there is no independent truth-seeking rational motive guiding our thinking, but rather our every thought is prompted and shaped by the motives I have identified, motives which have quite other, non-rational goals.

In the material I have already covered, I have described in broad outline the dominance motive as it works mainly in relation to Western people. Apart from describing its basic operations, I have emphasized two points: its pervasiveness in human affairs, and its truly foundational role in the construction of the social self. There is more that I need to add to fill out this picture, but at this point, it is worth reflecting, from the perspective of faith, on what I have described so far. Where do we find the Scriptures taking account of dominance behavior? What do they have to say about it?

The Scriptural Witness[5]

Old Testament

The view of mankind which underlies the broad sweep of the Old Testament assumes the good of that part of the dominance motive which I

---

5. These discussions of the biblical witness on various topics begin with a consideration of Old Testament teaching followed by that of the New Testament. Partly, they aim to draw attention to trajectories of development in revelation through the period of salvation history. It must be born in mind that Jewish reflection on the faith, as with its Christian equivalent, has continued to be extended, purified, and enriched in the centuries following the time when the final Old Testament texts were penned. Thus, we cannot identify Old Testament teaching as viewed through the lens of the Christian faith with the Jewish teaching in our own times.

have called "competence." The first chapter of Genesis describes the Lord God working through the stages of creation, and at the conclusion of each day—and more emphatically at the conclusion of the six days of creative activity—he stands back, as it were, proclaiming in satisfaction, the goodness of his work: *"And God saw that it was good."* Following the creation of mankind, God charges our first parents thus: *"Be fruitful and multiply and fill the earth and subdue it and have dominion over the fish of the sea and over the birds of the heavens and over every living thing that moves on the earth"* (Gen 1:28). Competence in interacting with the world in which God placed them, including power over the other creatures, is divinely sanctioned and valued. The Psalmist assumes this when he prays to the Lord, *"Establish the work of our hands upon us; yes, establish the work of our hands!"* (Ps 89[90]:17).

This approval of competence—on the assumption that the competence is expressed in good actions—is further confirmed by the many instances where the Lord strengthens or enhances human action through the working of his Spirit in man. Thus, during the time of the people of Israel's wandering in the wilderness, Bezalel and his coworkers are gifted with competencies for crafting all manner of furnishings for the Tent of Meeting. *"See, the Lord has called by name Bezalel . . . and he has filled him with the Spirit of God, with skill, with intelligence, with knowledge, and with all craftsmanship, to devise artistic designs . . . for work in every skilled craft"* (Exod 35:30, 32a, 33b).

At times, however, God works against the pride that can corrupt the human pleasure which generally accompanies the expression of competence. In preparing Gideon's army for war with the Midianite oppressors, the original gathering of over 30,000 Israelite men had to be whittled down to three hundred. *"The Lord said to Gideon, 'The people with you are too many for me to give the Midianites into their hand, lest Israel boast over me, saying, 'My own hand has saved me'"* (Judg 7:2). Still, at root here is the cooperative work of God and man and the usefulness and indeed the goodness of human competence.

In the Old Testament, competence easily and with little hesitation moves into dominance. In fact, throughout the Psalms we find strong expressions of joy in accomplishment when the writer is exalting in finding himself "above the head of his foes" or in being able to crush and destroy his enemy. But the ideal of dominance as honor within one's own (stable) society is better expressed by Job when, in his defense, he recalls his status prior to being struck down by calamity: *"When I went out to* the gate of the city, when I prepared my seat in the square, the young men saw me and withdrew, and the aged rose and stood; the princes refrained from talking and laid their hand on their mouth; the voice of the nobles was hushed, and their tongue stuck to the roof of their mouth" (Job 29:7–10). Here we can sense Job's barely restrained pride, his sheer joy at seeing others acknowledge his dominant status.

Yet, at times we read that, for various reasons, the Lord undermines or calls into question the human hierarchies that society constructs. When God commands Samuel to go to Bethlehem to anoint one of Jesse's sons as king, he is presented with the eldest son, Eliab, who displays all the qualities of dominance suitable for a leader of the people. *"But the Lord said to Samuel, 'Do not look on his appearance or on the height of his stature, because I have rejected him. For the Lord sees not as man sees; man looks on the outward appearance, but the Lord looks on the heart'"* (1 Sam 16:7). It is the youngest son, consigned to looking after the sheep, the one whom no one could imagine that Saul would choose, who finds himself being anointed. Again, lurking beneath the surface here is the idea that God's people need to rely upon him rather than their own capabilities to achieve their safety and welfare. In Psalm 49(50) we observe a similar challenge to human dominance, but something different is happening here. The writer affirms: *"Be not afraid when a man becomes rich, when the glory of his house increases. For when he dies, he will carry nothing away; his glory will not go down after him"* (Ps 49[50]:16–17). Here we find—and also in other late texts of the Old Testament—the emergence of a broader sense of God's time and of eternal life, and this has the effect of transforming the perception of dominance so that it no longer possesses the absolute value with which humans tend to invest it.

New Testament

In the New Testament, this last notion I mentioned is developed further, and we find a radical rethinking of the cultural understanding of the dominance motive. Certainly, competence continues to be valued; when the seventy-two disciples returned from their mission, they were ecstatic: *"Lord, even the demons are subject to us in your name!"* And Jesus said to them, *"I saw Satan fall like lightning from heaven. Behold, I have given you authority to tread on serpents and scorpions, and over all the power of the enemy, and nothing shall hurt you"* (Luke 10:17b–19). The Lord rejoices with the disciples at their experience of Spirit-enhanced competence (which, however, is immediately qualified by a reminder of the greater value of salvation in the age to come!).

Yet, what strikes us about Jesus' instruction on dominance is, first, its significance within the overall body of his teaching and, secondly, just how critical he is of its power over humans and of the serious efforts required of his disciples in working against that power. Here, I can give only a couple of examples of that teaching. James and John ask of Jesus, "*Grant us to sit, one at your right hand and one at your left, in your glory.*" The other disciples hear of this request and are indignant. After things settle down, Jesus offers the following teaching: "*You know that those who are considered rulers of the Gentiles lord it over them, and their great ones exercise authority over them. But it shall not be so among you. But whoever would be great among you must be your servant, and whoever would be first among you must be slave of all. For even the Son of Man came not to be served but to serve, and to give his life as a ransom for many*" (Mark 10:42–45). There will be varying levels of glory in the kingdom of God, but on earth our greatest joy is to be a servant who seeks not status in a human hierarchy but rather that which gives glory to God.

In another illustration of Jesus' teaching on dominance, in Mark 9:35–37 we read of Jesus discovering that his disciples were discussing among themselves who was the greatest. So, he gathered them together and spoke to them: "'*If anyone would be first,*' He said, '*he must be last of all and servant of all.*' *And he took a child and put him in the midst of them, and taking him in his arms, he said to them, 'Whoever receives one such child in my name receives me, and whoever receives me, receives not me but him who sent me.*'"

While it might seem from these two passages that Jesus is urging his disciples to deliberately seek the lower positions on human status hierarchies, in fact, his actual message is somewhat different and more radical than that. In fact, he wants his disciples to refrain from participating in the whole system of status seeking and rather to focus on being obedient to God's will. This will almost necessarily lead us to being treated as lowly in status, but the follower of Christ is not to accept that attribution since he has put behind him that whole system of dominance-seeking (i.e., dominance behavior as well as submissive behavior!) and aims to treat all alike as people whom one must serve with the truth and with love. He acts, in relation to others, neither in a dominant nor a submissive manner but seeks instead to serve their needs. (Later, in chapter 10, we will consider how authority relates to this whole question.)

In Paul's letters, we find echoes of Christ's teaching on dominance. One should not be surprised by this, but so radical is that teaching and so counter to human instincts that it is remarkable that it even saw the light of day in later apostolic instruction. Consider the early chapters of Paul's first Corinthian letter: In chapter 1, the theme is introduced: *"I appeal to you, brethren . . . that there be no division among you"* (1 Cor 1:10). But we soon discover that Paul puts this problem of division down to the claims of status which individuals and groups make. Pursuit of dominance is the fundamental cause of division within the community. As a remedy, Paul points the Corinthians to Christ and his death on the cross: *"But God chose what is foolish in the world to shame the wise; God chose what is weak in the world to shame the strong; God chose what is low and despised in the world, even things that are not, to bring to nothing things that are, so that no human being might boast in the presence of God"* (1 Cor 1:27–29). This is to be the framework within which Christian believers are to conduct their relationships with one another. In concluding his discussion of community divisions in chapter 4, the apostle reminds his readers that claiming for oneself and as one's own possession a superior status or value over others simply does not accord with reality: *"For who sees anything different in you? What do you have that you did not receive? If then you received it, why do you boast as if you did not receive it?"* (1 Cor 4:7).

It is the case that Paul himself finds it difficult to relate his own apostolic authority to this teaching on dominance, and at times, especially in his second Corinthian letter, the tension between the two becomes acute. Yet always he ends up on the side of service rather than status. For him, the seeking after dominance in all its forms runs counter to the way and example of Christ. This message is dotted throughout his writings, whether it is the exhortation, *"Do not be haughty, but associate with the lowly"* (Rom 12:16) or that to the Philippians, *"In humility count each other more significant that yourselves"* (Phil 2:3). Note that humility does not mean passivity in the face of the dominant behavior of the other, but an *active* serving, a *proactive* seeking after ways of serving even the insufferable self-promoter.

One of the seeming contradictions we observe in the New Testament teaching on the dangers of dominance and the need to counter it with humility is that it also holds up to us the glory and honor that will be ours at the end of the age! It seems that then dominance will be okay after all, and that we only avoid its entrapments in this life for the sake of indulging it in the next! We can think of Jesus' exhortation to choose the lower place at a banquet so that the host might honor us with a higher place, or his warning that *"if anyone would be first, he must be last of all and servant of all"* (Mark 9:35) and many other passages. Seemingly the urge to be able to gloat over one's own honor at the expense of others is incorrigible! Yet, I do not think we need to think in those terms. At the very core of the competence/dominance drive is the desire to be valued, firstly for what we have done, but by extension for who we are. In the age to come, we will be fully in Christ, but we will not shed that individuality which God gave us and foreknew from the foundation of the world. One aspect of dominance is the desire to be valued by high-status others. We value the expert's opinion about ourselves much more than that of the ordinary person. In the age to come, it will be God's valuing of us much more than anyone else's which will thrill us. As the writer to the Hebrews tell us, at that time we—so we hope—will be part of *"the whole Church of first-born sons"* (Heb 12:23). In other words, we will be valued in the way that the firstborn son was in former days, but without the gloating pleasure of being the *only* firstborn!

To conclude this brief review, we might say that dominance behavior, which is ubiquitous among humans, has had acknowledged benefits in the human struggle for survival. Yet, in the light of the kingdom of God, we can see that it no longer serves all the purposes it did in former times and indeed now results in great harm to the cause of equal human dignity. Over the course of the history of revelation, we have found that there was, in the Old Testament, a move towards a constricting of its power, but such a movement gained a special impetus in the teaching and example of Jesus Christ, thus shaping the apostolic ministry of the early church.

Reflections of Faith

Dominance—Part of the Good Creation?

The Christian believer might well be challenged by what he or she has read here. How is it that creation, which we affirm is good, can throw up a mechanism so powerfully influential within human existence which is at the same time so opposed to the moral values not only of Christians but also of non-Christian religions? To answer this question, we need first to recall that creation is good, but it is not perfect; rather in its imperfect goodness, it has perfection as its goal. It was not created complete and fulfilled and then allowed to run its course; instead, it has always been in a condition of moving forward, from simpler to more complex, from less perfect to more perfect.[6] Theologians describe creation as being *in statu viae*, in a condition of journeying towards fulfilment. Because dominance is such an ancient, prehuman biological mechanism, we can be sure that it primarily serves bodily and species survival rather than the purposes of social morality. That is, it helps to improve the gene quality of a species and thus its survival. The moral rules we humans draw on for our societies also evolved to assist cooperation and thus survival, but they came much later. Beyond that, we believe that they have a further and more important purpose which is to prepare us for life with God. So we, being in the "between times," that is, in the transition from biological species to fully complete in Christ, have to negotiate the difficulties of the dominance motive in a kind of "between times" manner.

Dominance in its full form operates as a selfish drive: me against you, or me and you against others. The believer, of course, cannot abide this way of living and so must set it aside—which is no easy task. Here we need to recall that in its development, dominance builds on the foundation of competence, and it is this—competence—which we can accept and incorporate into our lives. We are to feel joy in our accomplishments; we are to work towards the development of the talents with which God has graced us. (We will have more to say on this when we consider conscience in chapter 9.) The essential thing, though, is to shun comparisons (competition, seeking preferential attention, control of others)—for this is the step that transforms competence into full-blown dominance—and to learn how not to be offended when others seek to dominate us or to treat us as lower on some pecking order. That this is not simply one aspect among many of the Christian moral life but is its foundation stone was recognized by St. Gregory the Great who wrote that "humility [is] the mistress and mother of all virtues."[7]

---

6. See the *Catechism of the Catholic Church*, sec. 310.

7. Gregory, *Morals*, bk. 23, 24.

Dominance, the Fall, and the Human Intellect

We have seen that there are moral difficulties associated with the dominance motive. Following on from that, I want now to reflect on some of the important implications that arise from the idea that dominance, in its broad sense, is truly fundamental to the operation of the self. For example, we can say that if it, rather than our rationality, is the main driver of our thought and actions, then efforts to grow our rational abilities, increase our knowledge of the world and of ourselves, and develop ever-more-sophisticated technologies, all these things will change the *manner* in which the dominance motive expresses itself, but they will not have any effect on the *centrality* of the motive itself on our existence as humans. We can see here why the idea of progress, which has been so integral to Western thought in recent centuries, is difficult to defend in its usual form. Growth in knowledge and technical capabilities cannot alter the very motive that actually drives that growth. Given the moral ambiguity associated with the dominance motive, we would expect to see continued defects in the moral judgments and actions among all human societies, and, if we look at the matter with a dispassionate frame of mind, we will acknowledge that the West is no exception here. Improvements in our capacity to create wealth, care for society's vulnerable people, systems of justice, and many other social goods which mark the best Western societies are counterbalanced by growth in anxiety and depression, the wholesale killing of millions of unborn humans, the emergence of depressing worldviews which sap meaning from people's lives, and the erosion of familial and local community bonds. There is no *overall* progress, since our purpose of accessing and managing the very source of our failings (all of which are rooted in division and preferencing of the self), in other words, to somehow deal with the dominance motive itself, cannot be fulfilled *from within the operation of the selfsame motive*. Only by stepping outside of it can we accomplish that purpose, yet the capacity to do so has, it seems, been lost to Western societies. That will be a topic which we will address later in discussing conscience.

Following on from these considerations is the idea that in the outworking of the dominance motive we can see a particularly clear expression of what we know of as the effects of the fall. In whatever way we understand the biblical account of its occurrence, we know from our faith that the effects of the fall include the infection of all human beings with this propensity to sin, and furthermore that we cannot eradicate this infection from our being through the use of our own capacities and knowledge. Our very thoughts are caught up in the weakness. We also know that this impediment has an impact not only on individuals but also on human societies and we can see how dominance, with its essentially self-centered operation, if left to its own devices, can become the agent or carrier of this spiritual disease.[8]

Since the eighteenth century, within Western culture, most of its educated classes have resoundingly rejected the doctrine of the fall, and we can see now why this has been the case. If rationality is untouched by the effects of the fall, if we are able therefore to make not just scientific and technological progress but also moral progress by exercising our thinking abilities, then the idea of a limit on such a capacity as is taught by the doctrine of the fall cannot be affirmed; it simply does not accord with reality. From this understanding, those who affirm the doctrine of progress, that is, the conviction that progress is possible in *all* domains of human endeavour, are quite assured in their position. When challenged to take into account the incredible catastrophes, with their human slaughter and misery, which occurred during the twentieth century, and even more, the depressing manifestation of sheer inhumanity which they demonstrated, those committed to progress commonly respond that these facts of history do not undermine their belief but rather must be viewed as problems to be solved, as signals that we must try to do a better job in the future.

If, however, we see ourselves as in fact being led by our indulgence of a poorly directed dominance motive to always move towards sin, no matter what the state of our rationality, knowledge, and skill, then we are in a position to make much better sense of the horrors of the human condition which continue to occur even in the face of non-moral forms of progress. We can never, solely through the use of rationality, reach the core of the problem evinced by human evil because rationality itself—that is, in its "normal" operation—is the agent of a dominance motive increasingly run wild whose core dynamic is self-centered in the sense of working for the interests of the self often at the expense of that of others. With this awareness, the Christian teaching of the fall is seen to make

---

8. It is important to note at this point that the dominance motive in itself is not immoral or sinful. As part of a creation which is good but still "on the way" to perfection, its workings often require of us the effort not to indulge those of its promptings that would lead us into sin. As we will see in later chapters, dominance plays a useful part in the growth of human achievement, in the process of male-female pairing, and in the exercise of authority in society. However, our fallen human nature is prone to giving in to some of the harmful directions it can take us.

much better sense than the optimistic but unrealistic alternative of the doctrine of reason-driven progress.

Dominance and Mortality

At a certain age during childhood, individuals become aware of their own mortality and realize that, at some time in the future, they will die. Some find this more difficult to deal with throughout their life than others, but all of us are affected by it. It is true that very occasionally we experience moments in life when the thought of our mortality does not disturb us. Here I am thinking of those usually rare times when we achieve a difficult and long-pursued goal and think to ourselves at the time, "I can now die happy at having accomplished my goal!" Something like that awareness can also occur following lovemaking with one's spouse. However, the reality of our mortality is, throughout life, a conscious thought, or else it lurks beneath the surface. Signs of death such as funeral parlors and cemeteries are unwelcome intrusions into our consciousness because they remind us that we too will share the fate of those who have died, while on the other hand the murder mystery we watch on TV tends not to unsettle us too much because murder is not something we expect to happen to us. Through the perspective of those seeking to solve the murder case, we are helped to treat the victims in these stories as "other" than ourselves.

The connection between the dominance motive and awareness of our mortality is an interesting and complex one. The most obvious tension here is that most of us pursue goals in life which we consider very important at the time, but when we take a step back and evaluate them in view of the fact of our death, we cannot help but sense that many of our efforts are a waste of time or at least of very little consequence. Virtually any paid employment we engage in can be viewed in this light. The person working in, say, the bathroom fittings industry who enthusiastically and with great effort advances to the highest levels of his company will simultaneously feel pride at his achievement and, in moments of sober reflection, wonder what it was all for. Most of the time the challenge presented by the possibility of enhancing one's dominance status will help suppress awareness of the ultimate futility of one's efforts, but sometimes events such as the death of a loved one or close friend, or a serious health scare, can push the latter thought into our awareness.

How we respond to this tension can make a significant impact on the way we conduct our life. Not facing up to it can push us in the direction of redoubling our efforts to achieve something with our lives in the hope of leaving our mark on the world. Yet, if we think about this for a moment, we will realize that no matter how profound our impact on the lives of others might be, at some point in the future, we will be forgotten. The world will know us no longer. Another response which fails to deal with the tension is to lessen one's efforts in the interests of dominance, and to invest more of our energies in discovering the experiences that this life has to offer, be it enjoying the pleasures of gastronomy, seeking out new experiences, or simply being entertained by TV, social media, the internet, or computer games.

The Christian understanding of reality offers another way—I believe a better way—to deal with the dominance-mortality tension. It is convinced that existence is, at its deepest level, *personal*, or something like personal (rather than impersonal) and that, given the clear signs of the interest of this personal Reality in us human beings, signs that are revealed in the remarkable history of the Jewish people and which culminate in the life death and resurrection of Jesus Christ, we have good reasons to trust in a reality for ourselves which extends beyond the life we know at present. The Christian faith tells us that what we do here, how we relate to other human beings (whom God loves as much as he does ourselves!), will have effects which extend beyond the span of our own lives. A life truly well lived, a life of service to God and to others, can therefore carry a meaning which surpasses the limits of our mortality. The contributions to the lives of others that the bathroom fittings industry can make might not have eternal significance, but those who participate in that area of life can be assured that the way they treat other people during their career is part of the much wider process of building a civilization of love which will one day serve as a foundation for an eternal kingdom of heaven. Life, therefore, can have a deep meaning, one which inspires and energizes us, and in doing so helps us to respond positively to the mortality-dominance tension.

Our treatment of dominance has required a consideration of several dimensions of human thought and action. However, it does not end at this point, for there is another aspect of the motive that we must now address—that of the phenomenon of group dominance.

3

Dominance: Extending the Picture

IN WRITING ABOUT THIS motive so far, I have kept attention on the self as an individual, and so I have described how a person, driven by dominance, perceives his or her self as a single person in relation to other individuals. We all know, however, that the boundaries of our self extend well beyond that of our skin, and psychologically we include within our self our memberships of various groups. It is these aspects that dominance works on as well.[1]

Extended Self-Identity

We observe group identification in operation, for example, when someone criticizes our mother or brother or child. Our identity includes membership of our family, and so we are hurt when someone criticizes others in our family circle in a way similar to how we would feel when we ourselves are disparaged. Similarly, we know how much energy many parents invest in their children so as to given them the best chance at life, which, in the context of our present discussion, usually means the highest status that their child can achieve. Clearly a strong identification with the success of their children drives this process; their success is in large measure also the parents' success.

However, our self-boundaries extend well beyond our families to include many other groupings, both social and non-social. We identify

---

1. For an introduction to group dominance, see Sidanius and Pratto, *Social Dominance*.

with our professional or industry group, our religious denomination (or our lack of one), our culture, our nation, our language group, our social class, the area or locality where we live, the company or organization that employs us, the group of people linked to a common interest or hobby we share, the political views we hold along with others, sports teams we support, and many other groupings. For each of them, we recognize that the group is ranked on a dominance hierarchy; we take an interest in the advancement of its position up the ladder and are disturbed when it loses status.

The ease with which we enter into these identifications is quite remarkable. Imagine attending a sporting match in a sport which has had little interest for you up to that moment. The teams are closely matched, and you are there with a friend who is vigorously barracking for one side. Before long you find yourself engrossed in the competition and powerfully identified with one team, most likely that of your friend. At that moment, the fortunes of "your" team are included in your self-boundaries, and the struggle for dominance between the sides is truly your struggle. This common experience demonstrates just how fluid such boundaries can be.

Some group identifications are not so obvious to us, and we only notice them in particular situations. Under normal circumstances our national identity, e.g., Australian, American, British, does not figure much in our everyday awareness. However, being away from our home country for an extended period typically leads to feelings of nostalgia for our culture and people. In that situation, meeting up with fellow-countrymen brings home powerfully the importance played by a shared homeland.

By contrast, other group identifications, such as those relating to our worldview or to political allegiances seem to exercise a strong influence on our hour-by-hour consciousness, shaping our attitudes to matters presented to us in the various media. Viewpoints expressed in public or social media, in conversation, through a movie or novel, are all interpreted through the values framework with which we identify, and this creates in-groups (those on our side) and out-groups (those on the other side) in our minds. Here we can think of progressive, liberal, conservative, green, socialist, and other political commitments. The ballot-box success or failure of our party or persuasion can affect us almost as keenly as if we ourselves were running for political office.

What I have described here I will refer to as group dominance, dominance in which the units of competition are not individuals but groups with which we identify. Such groups are like proxies for our own self.[2] Although we are not describing here a different motive, it is true nevertheless that dominance as it affects group identities has some of its own qualities as well as sharing much with its individual form. We will now consider some of its features.

Group Dominance: Its Processes

Group dominance bears the stamp of the key process associated with individual dominance, which is the sharp distinction from the other and preferencing of the self at the expense of the other. The unit of comparison in the former is, of course, the group. Football league tables serve for teams (groups) what chess rankings do for individual players. This plays out in everyday life in many unnoticed ways. Imagine a group of company representatives gathering for an industry-wide meeting. In small group discussions, participants are wearing badges identifying themselves and their company. Immediately there is a kind of default group dominance ordering in the group, with greater attention, interest, and respect given to those belonging to the largest and most successful companies. At a different level, for example, in international gatherings such as the United Nations, we observe that more attention is paid to the views of a major nation, and those of, for example, a poor African nation are treated as of little consequence. This is the case even though, as an individual, the representative of the poor country might be someone of much higher achievement or finer character than the one from the more influential nation. So, as with individuals, groups also form hierarchies when people evaluate them *as groups*.

Now, we know that groups are successful when their members stick together. To maintain this cohesion, the individual members are typically required to conform to group discipline, whether that occurs through demands for an adequate level of commitment from each member, adherence to group beliefs and attitudes, support for other members, or holding negative views of other groups and their members. In strongly cohesive groups, we notice that norms and rules are well expressed,

2. Daphne Bugental (see chapter 1) refers to something like what I have described as "coalitional grouping" and classes it among the basic social motives along with dominance, attachment, and others. What she has in mind, however, is identity-based cooperating coalitions (as opposed to the simple presence of shared identity features). See Bugental, "Acquisition," 187.

widely accepted and applied, that punishment is effectively implemented against backsliders, freeloaders, and defectors, and there is contempt for out-groups. In fact, it seems to be the case that the more contempt for out-groups, the more cohesive a group is, whereas less cohesive groups show less such contempt.

This mechanism operates in a great many situations in every society (and nation), and unfortunately throughout history it has been the source of great human suffering since it involves the de-personalization of the other ("You who belong to the out-group are less than a person"), opening the way to treating members of out-groups as "non-persons." Against this, various religious traditions since at least the middle of the first millennium BC have proposed rules of action along the lines of "Don't do others what you would not want them to do to you." This kind of rule requires that we treat people, whoever they are, as like ourselves. And yet it has been difficult if not impossible for nations, social groups, or individuals to apply consistently such norms when it comes to the members of out-groups. The mechanisms of group dominance are simply too powerful to be controlled, it seems.

The Scriptural Witness

Old Testament

In surveying the general theme of dominance in the Old Testament, we notice the greater role played by groups than by individuals. There we find that group affiliation is at the core of self-identity, whereas individual characteristics are much less prominent, except for kings and other leaders of the people. At times, this can be somewhat disconcerting for us Western readers, especially when we observe the failure in the Scriptures to recognize individuality amongst groups. Thus, we are particularly affronted by how group dominance works when we see it in accounts such as that of the conquest of Canaan. Having entered the city of Jericho, the Lord God commanded the Israelites to destroy all within it. And this is what they did: *"Then they devoted all in the city to destruction, both men and women, young and old, oxen, sheep, and donkeys, with the edge of the sword"* (Josh 6:21). God's people were to view each person—and even each animal—purely as a member of the group belonging to the city of Jericho. The individual did not matter. This is but an extreme example of a process that generally applies in group dominance.

In the Old Testament, group dominance shows itself in the differential status that various groups receive. We see this in the early accounts of how different nations originated. For example, Isaac, son from Abraham's wife, Sarah, was viewed as a forefather of Israel, a favored group, whereas Ishmael, son of Abraham's slave-woman, Hagar, was considered the father of a disfavored nation, the Ishmaelites or Arabs. Such ranking is repeated throughout the Old Testament and appears, for example, in the distinction between Jew and Samaritan in Jesus' time. Typically, there is little or no reflection on the matter, it being simply part of the reality of social life. We see this, too, in attitudes towards the sexes. The society of the time treated men and women primarily as members of their gender, and in both the private sphere of family life and in public life, men and women were strongly socialized to relate to each other according to their gender and much less so as individuals.

New Testament

The good news of Christ focuses upon the responsibility of the individual to accept or reject that message. And because we Westerners have been brought up in a culture that has been profoundly influenced by its focus, when we read the New Testament, we instinctively assume that on matters of dominance it is its individual form that is being talked about. But, as Robert Jewett, in his commentary on Romans, has shown, when the apostle Paul addresses his readers, his interest is not primarily in how they live out their separate individual lives, but rather the manner in which they relate to each other as members of a group, usually that of the numerous house churches that made up the church in Rome.[3] When Paul uses the word "you" in giving his advice or teaching, he had in mind the group and its interactions. For example, he writes, *"I appeal to you therefore, brothers, by the mercies of God, to present your bodies as a living sacrifice, holy and acceptable to God, which is your spiritual worship. Do not be conformed to this world, but be transformed by the renewal of your mind, that by testing you may discern what is the will of God, what is good and acceptable and perfect"* (Rom 12:1–2). Here the apostle is talking to individual believers in Rome, but he is addressing them as *group members,* and his aim is to help them relate *to each other* rather than to provide guidance on how to live out their own separate lives. We tend not

---

3. Jewett, *Romans,* 59–69.

the see this, but when we are made aware of it, we can see how it fits with the rest of chapter 12 with its teaching on interrelations between believers. In fact, group identity is much more important in the New Testament than we might imagine.

When we considered the Old and New Testaments on the matter of individual dominance, we observed quite radical changes moving from one Testament to the other. We find similar though less profound contrasts with dominance in its group form. On the one hand, the focus of Jesus' public ministry upon his own people, the Jews, contrasts—at least by implication—with the outgroup of the gentiles. And yet, something deeply unsettling to these arrangements occurs in many Gospel stories. Certainly, we see numerous instances of Jesus interacting with people in his own Jewish circles, such as Mary, Martha, and Lazarus, or other Jews such as the widow of Nain, the rich young man, and various sick or disabled individuals. But there are so many exceptions among the characters we come across in the Gospels that it very much looks like Jesus is intentionally seeking to subvert or undermine the received group dominance attitudes of the society of his time. But if that is the case, in what way, precisely, is he doing this?

One common view today is that his ministry sought to engage with those who were poor, oppressed, or marginalized. Thus, his purpose would have been to break down the *social* barriers that existed at the time. Certainly, this is true, for example, of the blind man in John's Gospel, the Samaritan leper (Luke 17:11–19), adulterers and other sinful women, as well as in his teaching on the good Samaritan. However, two difficulties come to mind in attempting to understand Jesus' obviously subversive intents in this way. First, there are instances which do not easily fit. The faithful centurion whose servant Jesus healed (Matt 8:5–13) belonged to a Roman occupying force, and was certainly not among the poor, oppressed, or otherwise marginalized. And as we see elsewhere in the New Testament, the relations between Romans and Jews could be mutually respectful and even friendly (as we observe in the story of Cornelius the centurion [Acts 10:2, 22] and elsewhere in Acts). So, the centurion episode does not fit the picture. And neither does that of Jairus, whose daughter Jesus cured, and who was a "ruler of the synagogue." As such he could hardly be counted as oppressed, and while Zacchaeus, being a tax collector, was seen by his fellow Jews as immoral for the way he earned his income, neither was he to be included among the downtrodden social classes. Adding to these exceptions, we find among Jesus' contacts Simon the Pharisee, with whom he shared a meal, and Nicodemus, the member of the Sanhedrin.

I believe a better way of understanding the distinctive, subversive elements of Jesus' ministry is to see them as further evidence of his rejection of the pursuit of status in whatever form this takes, whether of the individual or of the group. In the Gospels we come across numerous variations on this theme: the good Samaritan is not poor and oppressed but rather an enemy to Jesus' listeners, and here we find the Lord honoring a member of the hated outgroup. It is similarly the case with Zacchaeus, the woman caught in adultery (John 8), the sinful woman who anointed Jesus' feet, the centurion who showed profound faith, and the Samaritan leper. In each case, Jesus is reaching over the boundaries which separated his own Jewish people from various despised or separated outgroups.

We can view Jesus' teaching on love of one's enemies in the same light of group dominance. This is clear in a passage like Luke 6:32–33: *"If you love those who love you, what benefit is that to you? For even sinners love those who love them. And if you do good to those who do good to you, what benefit is that to you? For even sinners do the same."* In place of such an attitude, Jesus teaches that all, regardless of the status of their group identifications, must become as little children, that is, outside the group dominance mentality, since no group can claim superiority over another before God. Love is the rule despite the existence of outgroups!

This, too, is the teaching that informed Paul's ministry among gentile believers. In the church communities with which he was associated, he taught that Jewish identity among believers carried no implications of greater spiritual worthiness. Nor did being male afford any advantage in God's eyes. *"There is neither Jew nor Greek, there is neither slave nor free, there is no male and female, for you are all one in Christ Jesus"* (Gal 3:28).

We can also recognize the influence of Jesus' opposition to the harmful outworking of group dominance in other parts of the New Testament. Perhaps the most overt is that found in the letter of James (James 2:1–2): *"My brothers, show no partiality as you hold the faith in our Lord Jesus Christ, the Lord of glory."* Thus, the principle is first enunciated, and then the letter proceeds to contrast treatment of *"a man wearing a gold ring and fine clothing"* and *"a poor man in shabby clothing."* Treatment favoring the wealthy over the poor is condemned while impartiality is encouraged.

Again, as with dominance between persons as individuals, so in its group form, we observe a path through the Scriptures that leads towards the view that dominance can be both socially and spiritually destructive. Vigilance is required of believers.

Reflections of Faith

A Confession

It is a sobering fact of history that the harmful outworking of the group dominance process I have described has featured prominently in the story of the Catholic Church. I say this to my great shame as a Catholic believer. For example, the vehemence with which church councils anathematized heretical positions and their supporters during the age of the fathers is quite confronting to us moderns. Arians, Monophysites, Apollinarians, Origenists, and many other groups suffered strong hostility from orthodox Christian leaders and people. The justification for this contempt was thought to be soundly based, since at stake was the eternal salvation of those who were seduced by error. However, lurking in the background was the corrupting power of political support for the Church. If one could persuade the emperor of the heinous belief-crimes of one's opponents, then they could be sanctioned not only spiritually but also with the full power of the state.

Later evidence of hostile group dominance processes—often defended from the Scriptures—is seen, for example, in the mutual excommunication of Western and Eastern Churches, the antagonism of Dominicans and Franciscans during the Middle Ages, the Albigensian Wars, the "pope versus emperor" conflicts, Catholic-Protestant wars, the treatment of Jewish people, the "othering" of colonized peoples by Catholic nations, and much more. Certainly, we can see in most if not all of these and other examples the influence of the Catholic Church's enmeshments with political power through the centuries, a problem that continues to dog her life even into our own times.

Yet, as we noted, in both the teaching and example of Jesus and the apostle Paul—the two fullest scriptural exemplars for us in the matter of dominance—we do not find such contemptuous attitudes to out-groups. It is true, both spoke harsh words to those who led unsophisticated believers away from God, and at times, too, we hear of groups, for example the Pharisees, or, in Paul's case, the Judaizers, who are condemned. But this does not lead Jesus to "other" the Pharisees, since we know that he continued to associate with them throughout his ministry, and even enjoyed table fellowship with some of them. And Paul, rather than despising those who had defected from the faith he taught, weeps over their condition. He expresses his approach to all groups as follows: *"I have become all things to all people so that by all possible means I might save some"* (1 Cor 9:22). The Christian attitude toward the other, and to groups external to that of the faithful, is grounded in Christ's practice of reaching beyond group boundaries so as to touch with surprising compassion those who were outsiders. This reach extended not only to what we would call nowadays the "vulnerable" but also to those with power and influence, indeed to *any* outside group, since all fall within the scope of God's love.

With this teaching of the Scriptures, one might imagine that the Catholic Church throughout her history would have more carefully guarded against the dangers of contempt for those outside her bounds. That she has succumbed so often demonstrates the power of the dominance motive working through group allegiances in shaping human behavior and society. Sometimes the Church thought that her survival depended on the protection offered her by political leaders; at other times she gave in to the temptation to take hold of political power herself. But whatever the reasons, the Catholic Church has had an awkward relationship with the state for much of the past two millennia, and for that reason—and no doubt for other reasons—she has compromised Christ's teaching and practice which so insistently warned against the denigration of the other by his disciples.

The former Anglican Archbishop of Canterbury, William Temple, encapsulated Christian teaching on this matter in his comment that "the Church is the only society that exists for the benefit of those who are not its members."[4] To have as its fundamental purpose that of existing primarily for the sake of others should serve to prevent the negative effects that so easily attend the working of group dominance. All those outside the visible bounds of Christ's body are potentially members of that body. Yet, by claiming for the church a special, even unique calling and capacity to counteract the harmful effects of group dominance, Temple is alluding to something very important: that it is only in virtue of the grace of God in Christ that these effects can be overcome, and in fact, at times have

---

4. The German theologian Dietrich Bonhoeffer expressed the same idea in his *Letters and Papers*, 382: "The Church is the Church only when it exists for others . . . not dominating but helping and serving. It must tell men of every calling what it means to live for Christ, to exist for others."

been overcome, even if the church's failure to avail itself of this "resource" is what most commonly comes to mind.

It is one thing to affirm this distinctive capacity of believers to deal with group dominance. It is another thing altogether to know how she might effectively access it. The New Testament consistently teaches the existence of a clear boundary that separates believer from nonbeliever, even if around the edges there are a few uncertainties.[5] This clarity is for the sake of the inner cohesion of the church, but also—ultimately—just as much for the benefit of those who are outside its bounds. For, as we have observed in our own times, when as believers we begin to adopt the attitude that nonbelievers do not really need the salvation of Jesus Christ which he charged us to announce to them, we very quickly lose the motivation to do so. This is no doubt disastrous for nonbelievers, who no longer hear the good news, while also having a knock-on, dispiriting impact on the church's life itself. So, carefully managed boundaries between the church and "the world" are therefore essential. We cannot do away with groups and group boundaries!

Yet, just as necessary is the acknowledgement that every single person who is not yet a member of the church is also someone for whom Christ died. There can be no limits to the scope of Christian love, and this is especially the case in the face of antagonism and hostility. However significant is a shared faith in Christ, even more important is what we have in common with all men: that Christ loved us and gave himself for us.

Minimizing Group Identification: A Solution?

As we have seen, group dominance, like the individual form, causes problems for us humans mainly by pushing us to treat those outside our groups negatively—sometimes very negatively! We might imagine that we could reduce the difficulties that group dominance presents for us by minimizing both the number and the strength of our various group identifications; this is what efforts to eradicate racist and anti-immigrant attitudes aim to do. If we could accomplish this, then we could avoid the harms associated with group identity and we would be left with only having to deal with dominance between individuals, something which, it seems, is much less destructive. After all, there might be ill effects from

---

5. This boundary is not the same as the one created by the judgment of Christ at the end of the age.

competition for promotion and advancement in the office, and people who have little to boast about usually do not feel good about themselves, but at least we would be ridding ourselves of such scourges as anti-Semitism and antagonism towards same-sex-attracted people.

Yet, I do not think the matter is as straightforward as it might first appear. To begin with, our group identifications do not always or necessarily lead to efforts to dominate those outside our group. As an Australian, I do not feel negatively towards people of neighboring countries such as New Zealand, Indonesia, or Singapore. Similarly, like most males, I view females as different but rejoice in that difference. In fact, we have several group identifications which are quite harmless because they do not bring with them the competition and conflict that often come with group dominance. Even such group identities like supporting a particular sports team and experiencing the joy of our team's victory and the pain of its defeat is relatively harmless since it does not usually translate into antagonism towards the members of the other teams in the competition. So, many of the group identifications we have cause little harm to others and provide life with a richness that we value. But more than that, it seems that ridding ourselves of our identifications with groups can lead to poor outcomes for people who have lower status in society. Let us see how this can happen.

Generally, we can say that those people whom society as a whole considers lower in status cannot readily gain a sense of value from their individual accomplishments (for they have few), so, in order to acquire a positive self-identity, they are more likely to put store on those group memberships which can be a source of pride to them.[6] "I may not be very educated and I have no permanent work, but I support (insert here a successful sports team) and I live in such-and-such locality which is better than . . ." Valued sources of group identity for those in lower social classes include nationality ("I'm from Australia, the best country in the world!"), ethnic background ("We Anglo-Australians made our country what it is!"), and gender ("We men are good at [such-and-such] and we are proud to be able to support our families!").

---

6. Harry Triandis's distinction between individualism and collectivism maps the difference between individual and group dominance quite well. See Triandis, "Individualism-collectivism," 907–24. For an example of work drawing attention to the importance of social class on individual versus group identity, see Marshall, "Variances," 490–95.

By contrast, the highly educated, successful, and financially well-established person typically possesses a self-identity which is marked mainly by personal rather than group distinctions. "I graduated from (high-status university), I am a (high-status profession), I have been appointed to (various senior positions) and I am good friends with (well-known persons)." The accomplishments of such a person's children also figure prominently in their sense of self, since what their children achieve reflects upon their own status.[7]

So, what happens when a developed nation moves in the direction of dismantling some of those group identities which are relied on by lower-status groups? From what I have described so far, it seems clear that higher-status individuals will be little affected by such changes, since their identity is not bound up, to any great extent, with membership of groups. Lower-status social groups, however, will be significantly impacted because the sense of self of members of those groups depends much more on group identifications and they can be harmed psychologically by the dissolving of those identities. Let us consider a real-life example.

For many decades now in Western societies there has been a widespread movement to change how we feel about ourselves as males and females. One part of this has been a commitment to ensure equality between the sexes in the workforce, even if it means overriding the sexual differences which nature and culture have created for us. Consider the historically normal element of womanhood which is the practice of looking after young children. This has been the object of a multi-pronged push in Western societies to dismantle it. Several means, both direct and indirect, have been employed: efforts to increase the workforce participation of women, rejection of the idea of a single living wage sufficient to support a family, indoctrination of women into ideals such as that the care of one's own children is less valued than paid employment, that families should be small, that women are "strong" (rather than vulnerable), and that the pursuit of so-called gender equality stands as an unassailable cultural goal worthy of investing oneself and one's life. A complementary effort has worked to reshape the male identity. Thus, for example, the honor of being a family's breadwinner is now typically scorned; society rejects the idea of a division of labor in operating a household; governments are increasingly incentivizing men to share with their partner the

---

7. Among the examples I give, "high-status university" and "high-status profession" are partly group identities, but membership is achieved by individual abilities and effort. This is much less the case for low-status group identification.

burden of taking time off work to care for young children; and men are encouraged to display emotional characteristics which have traditionally been associated with femininity.[8] In short, the aim has been to reduce both the perceived and the actual differences between men and women in the interests of the value of gender equality.

Here we can see that for individuals of higher status with their distinctive personal qualities, gender identity ("I am a man/masculine" or "I am a woman/feminine") need not figure prominently in their sense of self since gender is a group identification and as such is of relatively less importance to them. On the other hand, those who are of lower social status rely heavily on any group identities they possess, gender being one of them. When society seeks to minimize the distinctiveness of the sexes, it is the lower-status groups that suffer most as a result of the inevitable increases in marital conflict, domestic violence, divorce rate, and all the emotional and mood conditions that flow from these social ills, not to mention the effects of all this on children. High-status individuals, for their part, will often view themselves as winners, seeing this change as an opportunity for new experiences of novelty and change, and wonder why it is that lower-status people cannot get their lives together.

Other examples of this kind of process would be the de-valuing of the institution of marriage, the casualization of the workforce, and the demonization of "Anglo" or white culture. I hope the point I have made is clear: in developed nations, those who belong to lower social classes, that is, those at the bottom levels of major dominance hierarchies, have been seriously harmed by some of the seismic shifts in social attitudes and behavior which have disrupted key group identities. Seeing how group identity and dominance work, we believers will better understand the underlying processes and realize that reducing the importance of *some* group identifications in society can paradoxically lead to the detriment of vulnerable segments of society.

As I have described it, the dominance motive is an extraordinarily pervasive and powerful force in the initiation and guidance of human behavior. I have argued that it is virtually always present at some level, and most commonly is the motive which controls the operation of our conscious

---

8. To add to the mix is the whole question of the notion of gender as a social reality or construction that has arisen through liberation movements of same-sex-attracted, transgender and other groups.

self. This is so even though we do not see it for what it really is and possess only a vague awareness of its workings. And yet, in terms of the power to affect our *emotional* life, we must consider dominance as less important than another motive to which we will now turn our attention: attachment.

4

Attachment

As I OBSERVED IN chapter 1, most human motives have their roots in our non-human animal past. This is the case with our next motive: attachment. We see attachment behavior in many species, especially mammals, but also birds and indeed any species in which there is parental protective behavior towards the young, and a corresponding drive on the part of the immature offspring to seek out that protection when necessary.[1]

Attachment among Non-Human Animals

The famous student of animal behavior Konrad Lorenz demonstrated these phenomena with birds such as the greylag geese he studied, whose young leave the nest early. He described the mechanism by which they instinctively attach themselves to the first moving object they encounter upon leaving the nest. This, of course, is typically their mother, but as Lorenz showed, under the right conditions, it can even be a human being. He removed newborn goslings from their mother during the first day or two after birth, and then, after they had been exposed to his own moving physical form for a time, reunited them with their mother. In this situation, they did not follow after her but rather Lorenz himself as the first moving object they saw at the critical time in their early development.

---

1. Rather than reference every mention of research in this chapter, I would point the interested reader to an excellent collection of articles relating to the principles and research basis of attachment theory: Cassidy and Shaver, *Handbook of Attachment*.

In many species, we observe parents' protective behavior and proximity-seeking behavior on the part of the young. A female animal protects her offspring from attack from a predator; the offspring move close to the mother when they observe a threat in their environment. It is not difficult to see the evolutionary value in a motive that drives and sustains such a relationship between parent and offspring. During the period of vulnerability, protecting a young animal from being preyed upon increases the likelihood of its survival, but the complementary system that sensitizes the young to strange or dangerous situations and pushes them to seek the protection of parents further reduces the risks to survival. When we talk about attachment it is usually this latter aspect of the process that we refer to even though the former is also a key part of the motive.

To illustrate further the basic notion of attachment with an example from the study of primates we might consider the classic experiments carried out on infant monkeys from 1950s to the 1970s by the US psychologist Harry Harlow and colleagues.[2] In his first reported experiment, he placed two metal mesh surrogate "mothers" in the cage of a young rhesus monkey which had been separated from its mother. One surrogate had a nipple from which the monkey could drink milk, while the other "mother" had no nipple but was covered with a soft, furry material. Typically, the monkey subjects would access both surrogates according to their needs, but when they were frightened with a loud noise, they instinctively clung to the furry surrogate. That this was not simply a matter of the monkeys wanting the comfort of the furry material was shown by the fact that only when that surrogate was present did the animals explore their environment. Those without it would lie down on the floor, rocking rhythmically and sucking their thumb. Later experiments in which monkeys separated from their mothers were raised with only the nipple-attached metal surrogate led to them displaying what the experimenters viewed as profound psychological disturbances. What we see in Harlow's work is a deep psychological need that must be sufficiently satisfied in the early years of development if normal emotional maturity is to result. Let us now consider how this need shows itself in humans.

---

2. Harlow, "The Nature of Love," 673–85; Suomi et al., "Social Rehabilitation," 1279–85.

The Human Attachment Motive

Humans have known of the central importance of the parent-child bond since time immemorial, and the phrase "women and children" has entered our language not just to indicate vulnerability and innocence but also to signal the significant role that mothers play in the early life of their children. The basis for this bond, explained in scientific terms, was first described by the British psychiatrist John Bowlby.

During World War II, Bowlby developed an interest in the characteristics he observed in young children who had been separated from their parents for extended periods of time due to their evacuation for reasons of safety. Further study, this time of delinquent children, confirmed him in his growing belief that when the attachment relationship of a young child to its mother (or other key parent figure)[3] is disrupted for extended periods of time, profound psychological impairments are often the consequence.

From Bowlby's initial work, and through its refinement and extension by many other researchers, the theory of attachment has matured into a broadly accepted theory within the area of developmental psychology. During the second half-year of life, infants display "stranger danger," a fear of unfamiliar persons, a fear which comes to be generalized to novel situations. Given "good-enough" parenting during the first few years of a child's life, this fearfulness is quelled by the proximity of the mother figure. That is, if the mother proves to be a reliable responder to the child's fears, she comes to be relied upon to provide comfort and security to her child in fearful situations. On the other hand, parenting that is unresponsive or inconsistently responsive leads to insecure or even avoidant (detached) attachment relationships.

The kind of relief or succor provided by a mother is not limited to situations where the child is fearful or anxious but includes circumstances of stress more generally. The young boy who falls and hurts himself, becomes ill, or gets frustrated can experience an easing of the distress through physical holding and soothing from his mother.

---

3. For convenience, I will refer to the mother as the key attachment figure, fully aware that there are circumstances where it is some other person, e.g., a father or a foster carer, who fulfills that role. In the vast majority of cases, however, it is the mother with whom a child develops their most powerful attachment bond. I suspect that, with the frequently noted avoidance of the use of "mother" as the typical attachment figure, we are to discern ideological considerations at work.

The early years represent a kind of "sensitive period" in that it is during this period that a child develops an inner working model or set of expectations about how others will respond to his or her inner states of fear and anxiety. These working models show themselves in the subconscious ways we relate to others, even in adulthood. "I get nervous in many social situations because I assume that others will reject me." Or "I present a mask of my true self to others because I cannot risk being emotionally vulnerable and suffering rejection." Or "I tend not to worry too much about how I am viewed by others because most people are supportive." Such expectations are established in the first three or so years of life and are resistant to substantial change in later life.

Long-term romantic relationships are those which most reflect the qualities of early childhood attachment experiences. We can see attachment bonds developing in a couple after about twelve months of close and intimate contact. After that period, we observe deep distress at disturbances, disruptions, and severance of the relationship. In these adult attachment bonds, we are both parent and child, providing and receiving both emotional support to and from our partner. Unlike the early childhood version of attachment, where physical safety is a priority, in adulthood, the emphasis is more often on psychological or emotional security in the face of external threats to the self-identity.

Attachment Processes Are Mostly Hidden from Us

The strength of the attachment relationships we have is not apparent to us under normal circumstances. In our day-to-day awareness, we are not conscious of being in need of our spouse, for example. Unlike dominance, for which we could point to everyday experiences that linked to the motive, attachment does not often show itself. The "complaints" it makes when it is not being fed properly are typically indirect, a vague feeling of unease, a lowered mood, a loss of vigor, or a sense of being under stress. Sometimes, when we are listening to certain types of music, usually of a calming kind, we might experience a wave of relaxation sweep over us which is a sign that it is triggering the attachment motive.

The main signs, however, arise when there are disruptions to our significant relationships. When, for example, there is marriage conflict of a level which raises the possibility of a split, attachment emotions relating to the separation or the fear of separation come to the fore, and we are consumed with anxiety, fear, anger, depressed mood, a sense of despair, inability to concentrate, and general impairment to our social and work functioning.

Divorce among couples is an experience which generally reveals the depth of attachment in married relationships. I remarked above that attachment between married spouses is well established a year after the beginning of a close relationship, but breaking that bond can take years, and one might doubt whether it is ever truly dissolved. As one reviewer of the literature on divorce and attachment has noted: "[The research] suggests that attachment bonds may be established fairly quickly but are broken slowly, and that the loss of an attachment bond is as difficult for those married a few years as for those married many years."[4] New relationships do not necessarily take the place emotionally of a former attachment bond. Even after the initial pain of divorce has subsided and the parties have formed new romantic bonds, it is quite common for feelings about the first relationship to retain their strength. On the basis of research in this area, it has been noted that "only a few years after their divorce, a majority of remarried men say that they regret having divorced their former wives."[5]

As we will see later, attachment figures centrally in the Christian faith. For that reason, the reader will need a sound grasp of the motive before moving on to its theological implications. What I have noted about attachment so far is only a skeleton account. In order to flesh out the picture, I will describe several elements of the working of the motive in ordinary life.

Attachment: Some Further Elements

The following twelve points cover the main attachment processes through the lifespan:

1. In the first weeks after birth, human infants show no obvious signs that they distinguish between familiar and unfamiliar persons. Yet, there is evidence that, within hours of birth, they respond differentially to their mother's voice and body odor. And parents often note that their baby is unsettled at night if he or she has been handled among unfamiliar persons during the day. By six months, infants

---

4. Feeney and Monin, "An Attachment-Theoretical Perspective," 940.
5. Feeney and Morin, "An Attachment-Theoretical Perspective," 940.

are more socially engaged, and for the next six months they begin to display avoidance responses to strangers which are eased when held and soothed by the mother.

It is also during that six-to-twelve-month period that babies become mobile, and from then on we observe proximity-seeking behavior, that is, seeking close contact with the mother when a stranger appears on the scene, the child is faced with a novel and confronting situation, or is hurt or stressed in some way. This is the classic example of how the attachment motive works and for the rest of our lives, at least for most of us, this same basic model applies.

2. At about the age of eighteen months, a child develops a sense of self as an "I" in relation to other people. By then, they are able to look at themselves in a mirror and recognize the image as being that of themselves. With this emergence of the social self, attachment behavior begins to display another dimension such that a child becomes aware of *psychological* threat or stress in addition to physical danger or hurt. He or she seeks proximity to an attachment figure in the face of psychological hurt inflicted by others even without any physical danger or harm. When two toddlers claim ownership of a toy and one removes it from the hands of the other, its loss is perceived as a psychological assault that warrants not merely adult intervention to repair the "injustice," but also parental support to soften the emotional pain.

3. Cortisol is a chemical produced in our body (adrenal gland) so that we can respond to stress of various kinds. An hour or so before we normally wake in the morning, our bodies begin to pump out cortisol in readiness for the activities of the day, which, though not always stressful, require a certain level of cortisol for their normal performance. As the day progresses, cortisol levels begin to subside until, in the hours before bedtime, our body winds down production to quite low levels. So, we see a twenty-four-hour cycle in the production, release, and diminution of cortisol. Apart from that cycle, when significant stressors confront us, our body produces larger amounts of the substance to face the immediate demands.

Young children (under three years of age), when they remain at home with their mother, show this cycle of higher cortisol in the morning and reduction in the afternoon. However, when they attend daycare, it has been found that their cortisol levels remain at a higher level throughout the day, and this occurs even though their demeanor, their activity levels, their social interactions, and their willingness to attend childcare all appear normal. Furthermore, children do not really "get used to" childcare, since their cortisol levels do not return to normal (low stress) patterns even with continuing exposure to out-of-home care over a period of weeks or months.[6]

4. After the age of three years, a child will typically cope quite well in situations where their mother is not available. Experiences such as kindergarten attendance does not usually cause them stress. One explanation for this is that by that age, a child is able to conceive of their mother as continuing to exist even though not present, something they cannot appreciate prior to that age. We need, however, to be mindful that only about 40–50 percent of children have what is known as a secure attachment, that is, a relationship with the mother which is trustful and reliable. Other children manifest, to varying degrees, either an insecure-anxious attachment (the child is overly anxious about the availability of the mother either physically or psychologically and shows clingy behavior) or an avoidant anxious attachment (unreliable and/or rejecting parenting that leads to emotional "shutting down" on the part of the child who displays few signs of fear of strangers or strange situations). The descriptions of typical behavior I have given here apply to the first category of children.

5. When there is more than one child in a family, it is common for there to be jealousy between the siblings—at least at some times. This is an outworking of the attachment relationship since it shows that a child perceives the threat her brother or sister poses to her own immediate access to her parents and often also the challenge to her view of herself as the preferred child, the one with whom the parents have the deepest relationship. Here we see an important attachment principle at work: it is not only the absolute strength of attachment that shapes children's behavior but its strength relative to that of other siblings. Perceiving oneself as being disfavored compared to a sibling can be powerfully disturbing to a child.

---

6. Drugli et al., "Elevated Cortisol Levels," 1684–95; Groeneveld et al., "Children's Well-being," 502–14.

6. By middle childhood, much of life for children in Western societies centers on the dominance motive rather than that of attachment since, in usual circumstances, attachment needs are more or less sufficiently catered for. A child who is securely attached to his parents also acquires the expectation that the other significant adults in his life will reliably support and care for him when he needs it. When that support fails him and, for example, he experiences persistent conflict with his teacher at school, this can cause proximity-seeking behavior by which he seeks out the psychological soothing of a parent. With that support, his secure attachment allows him to display before his parents the emotional vulnerability of tears, which he might be reluctant to allow otherwise.

7. Commonly, a pair of teenage girls will develop a bond of friendship in which there is frequent and extensive contact, and deep sharing of inner thoughts and feelings. They become inseparable, taking joy in each other's company and pining when contact is prevented. Here again, physical safety is not an issue but rather that which is psychological. In their interactions, they not only share their inmost experiences, but this sharing is received and accepted by the other. What we observe in this kind of bond, then, is a subsidiary or lesser form of attachment. Each child is a safe haven for the other from the psychological difficulties than can mark female adolescent group relationships.

8. As I have emphasized, the attachment motive does not manifest itself in an obvious manner in the way that, for example, hunger or sexual desires do. All the same, even though it is unrecognized, it does profoundly color our everyday consciousness. Although a feeling of contentment or peace can be upset by many factors in our life, and some of these are purely biological, it is also the case that problems with attachment will typically present in the form of a loss of inner peace. In its place will be a restless and persistent seeking after various imagined solutions, whether they be the achievement of personal goals or the pursuit of experiences, but people commonly report that these do not provide the expected satisfaction. And only when they enter into or recover close, long-term relationships do such people chance upon the "solution" to their unease. They find that a sense of serenity does not come through any kind of accomplishment or achievement, but rather it "finds" a person

when he or she deeply entrusts themselves to another (whether that be another human being or God).

9. "Falling in love" is not something that is found in every culture, but in ours it describes the fairly sudden onset of feelings of delirious infatuation that couples experience prior to the more emotionally settled time after they marry. In many other cultures, love grows gradually, *following* marriage, and there is little of the fireworks of "falling in love" in their experience. However, regardless of this, we can say that attachment relationships between spouses, though they vary in strength, are universal. In Western culture, once a man and a woman meet a set of "non-negotiable" conditions that each applies to any future partner, the attachment process usually develops through the sharing of the inner world of each to the other and the simultaneous acceptance by each party of what they have heard. When, for example, the woman shares *with an attitude of vulnerability* increasingly personal elements of her self, and the man accepts this and communicates that by it he is growing in regard and love for her, attachment grows. The potential threat that each might have posed for the other dissipates and, over time, trust is strengthened. The whole process, as long as it goes relatively smoothly, is powerfully self-affirming and enjoyable.

10. We have already discussed the attachment bond in relation to divorce, but how does it show itself in normal married life? Something like what I described in the previous paragraph continues in the early years of a healthy marriage, although the frequency and depth of inner sharing tends to reduce over time. This is because, with the day-to-day experience of living together, there is not much new material, that is, new and significant aspects of the self, which emerge and call for sharing with one's spouse. Still, the security and the nurturing power of the relationship are sustained with occasional sharing of inner lives; couples can relax in the physical presence of each other and not feel the need to conform to the expectations that they experience in other social contexts, such as having to maintain the flow of conversation.

A major element of marriage not present in other attachment relationships is that which occurs in the bedroom. A satisfying sexual relationship calls for the "guard to be let down" and aspects of oneself to be on display which, if revealed to any other person, would produce feelings of shame. Acceptance from the other means that they can be on display freely and without embarrassment. Within this context, sexual activity can flourish. At the time of orgasm, the body releases a powerful hormone, oxytocin, which produces the experience of peace, trust, and openness to the other that lovers know about. It is this experience which is the signature of a fulfilled attachment relationship.[7] (See chapter 8 for further discussion.)

Finally, there is the aspect of physical safety that a woman often feels in the presence of her husband, and for her this harkens back unconsciously to the time of early childhood when she felt the security of her parents. In a complementary way, in the husband we usually find a kind of protective quasi-parenting response which is likely modelled on what he observed and experienced of the protection provided by his parents. All these aspects of attachment come together in a marital relationship at its best.

11. As couples age, the various components of an attachment relationship change in their relative importance. Sexual intimacy becomes of lesser significance to the marriage in most cases. Attachment as physical security follows a similar path. And even earlier habits of close sharing of the inner worlds with each other routinely diminish in later years. On the other hand, the willingness to "be oneself" in the presence of one's partner typically remains strong, and there is also the assurance that, when one spouse suffers physical impairments or limitations, the other will provide the care that is necessary. Finally, elderly spouses possess between themselves a large body of shared knowledge and experiences which can serve as a reminder of

---

7. Oxytocin is a hormone which is closely linked to expressions of attachment in humans. Its primary *physical* work is twofold: to shrink the uterus back to normal size in a woman who has just given birth. This helps the placenta to be discharged. The substance also helps the release of milk from milk ducts and down to the nipple in mothers who breastfeed. Many women report feelings of peace and closeness to their baby at this time, and this, too, is an effect of oxytocin. But the hormone is also closely connected with particular social/emotional experiences which are part of the attachment drive. When doses of oxytocin are given to people via nasal spray, subjects feel less socially anxious and more trusting of others, even strangers. In individuals who "fall in love," levels are also elevated. And as noted above, oxytocin is released at the time of orgasm during lovemaking, and it is possible that such a mechanism evolved so as to help bind together those who engaged in sexual intercourse, since such a bonding would assist in the circumstance that the woman should fall pregnant and bear a child.

the unparalleled unity that exists between them in comparison with every other relationship.

12. Death of a spouse is, in most cases, one of the most psychologically painful experiences which humans have to face. As Bowlby observed: "There are few blows to the human spirit so great as the loss of someone near and dear."[8] Usually, the experience of bereavement does not involve as many complications as that of divorce. Unlike the case of the latter, when a spouse dies, there is not normally a feeling that the deceased intended to reject the surviving party. Also, with the death of a spouse, there is no longer any possibility of restoration of the relationship, and the numerous other complicating factors in divorce are not present. Yet, surviving spouses generally report continuing feelings of loss and loneliness even many years after their life-partner's death. Here, as with divorce, we observe the power of the attachment motive. In view of this, we can affirm with some confidence that, more than any other large-scale feature of the human psyche, it is the dynamics of attachment relationships which best represent what we mean by the term "the unconscious." Under everyday circumstances, it is not normally available to our awareness, and even when we have an intellectual understanding of it, we cannot directly manage it. Yet, when it is triggered by some event, it reacts strongly, and we are often surprised and bewildered by the feelings it provokes, and their source is a mystery to us. It truly is a "subterranean" reality in our psychological makeup.

From these elements of the operation of the attachment motive, we can see its great power to influence the thought, emotion, and actions of individuals. Yet, it also operates with groups.

Attachment and Groups

Recall that the dominance motive operates not only on the self as individual but also as member of various groups. With attachment, we also need to extend the picture we have painted thus far so as to include the ways in which it relates to our group identifications. We experience feelings of exuberance when our favorite sports team wins an important match (group dominance), but we also might feel safe when our nation

---

8. Bowlby, *The Making*, 67.

easily defends its borders against an aggressor, or, in the case of a more recent example, when our government is able to diminish the harm inflicted on our community by a disease pandemic. In that latter case, fear and anxiety were widespread across the community, yet there was also extensive acceptance and compliance with government directives aimed at reducing the spread of infections. It is not difficult to recognize here underlying processes at play which are similar to those we saw in relation to a young child who feels fear and anxiety in the presence of a stranger.

Further reflection will show that we typically belong to many groups which provide us with a sense of security, especially in times of threat and anxiety. Workers trust their union to support them in a conflict with their employer, and health insurance companies provide financial compensation for medical costs which might otherwise be far beyond the means of a person needing extensive treatment. However, belonging to a union or to that group of people who are insured with a specific health insurance company requires little more from us than paying fees or insurance premiums. Normally these memberships are only peripheral to our identity, and with them we are not required to participate in group activities or conform our behavior to an extensive set of norms.

Matters are different for membership of, say, a church. The Catholic Church, to take one example, provides assurances of salvation from sin and from the separation that sin creates in our relationship with God, but it also calls its members to obedience to God's law, as well as to various ecclesiastical laws, such as attending Mass each Sunday. Furthermore, there are in place various expectations as to how one is to behave as a member of the Church. Included among these are the way we are to relate to those in positions of authority as well as to other believers. Participation in the life of the Church is for many a source of psychological security, since it exposes them to the example of other believers who display confidence and trust in the faith they affirm. Especially for believers who live in a multicultural or multi-religious society where there are many people who do not share their faith, their participation in the life of the Church can become a core element of their identity.

Religious identification is not the only form of group membership which is able to figure prominently in an individual's sense of security. In some societies, ethnic and tribal groups can confer security on their members such that if an outsider threatens an individual group member, his or her fellows can provide the needed protection. Street gangs serve the same function is some Western urban settings.

A final example of group attachment is that which we form with our culture. Particularly in societies without one dominant culture, where interaction with those of different cultural backgrounds is a common occurrence in everyday life, at a subconscious level, anxiety is generated because of uncertainties about how to relate to people who are different from us. Questions arise about what we might expect of someone from a different culture or language group, about what can be assumed as shared knowledge, about whether or not there are broadly overlapping worldviews, and about what behaviors are appropriate in the circumstances. It is not difficult to recognize how different it is when we engage with someone of our own cultural background (and age group) and how there is a greater ease of interaction. There anxieties created by engaging with someone from another culture do not arise and we feel more secure in that situation. The process underlying this phenomenon is of such importance that it warrants its own label of cultural attachment.

One further comment about group attachment is in order here. As we have seen with group dominance, so too in group attachments, outgroups—and this includes not only those which are hostile but also neutral outgroups—are typically devalued in significant ways. This occurs simply because it is more difficult for a group member to identify with someone who does not share their key beliefs, attitudes, and experiences which are associated with their own group. We have considered the role of oxytocin in the attachment motive above, and here too we can point to research linking it to how it affects the way we relate to outsiders. When it is given as a nasal spray to subjects, within a few minutes they start to experience feelings of warmth and openness to other people, similar to those we have when we meet up again with an attachment figure after an absence. But researchers have also found that not only does oxytocin enhance feelings of warmth in someone who is interacting within a group, but it also has the effect of making that person act in a more negative manner towards those outside that group. So, it is not a chemical that makes us "love humanity," since it seems to work only in connection with our in-groups.[9]

---

9. See, for example, De Dreu et al., "The Neuropeptide Oxytocin," 1408–11.

The Scriptural Witness

Old Testament

To identify the presence of the attachment motive in the Scriptures, we need only to look for instances where individuals experience the emotions of fear or anxiety. A stand-out example of this is found in the book of Exodus, when the people of Israel were faced with their slaughter at the hands of the Egyptian army, and as they stood before the seemingly unbridgeable barrier of the Red Sea, they saw this destruction as a certainty. By this point in time, the Israelites had had some experience of the Lord's power to save them through the pressure brought to bear on the Egyptian pharaoh in allowing them to leave his land. As the narrator of the story is at pains to demonstrate here and elsewhere, the people were slow to acquire a sense of reliance upon God, and so, at this critical juncture in their escape from slavery, they do not trust in the Lord God but rather give in to despair. The mighty hand of God which brings them to safety is a powerful demonstration of the trustworthiness of the Lord, and thus of his status—at least psychologically—as an attachment figure for those who would seek his protection. As he says to his people: *"You yourselves have seen what I did to the Egyptians, and how I bore you on eagles' wings and brought you to myself"* (Exod 19:4). Further episodes during the wilderness wanderings reiterate, in similar ways, the same dynamic of fear or anxiety on the part of the Israelites, and the intervention of God to help them in their need. However, we can observe an important difference here compared with the way attachment emerges in the life of a young child. For children, at least under ideal circumstances, attachment grows *without* the intentional and conscious effort on the part of the parents to demonstrate their trustworthiness. From well before the child has any awareness of fear, the parents have provided him with the safe environment he needs for optimum development. We might say that in this case, attachment develops naturally. In the case of God's people, though, during the time of the Exodus until the crossing of the Jordan, they struggled to reach a point of genuine reliance upon the Lord for their protection and safekeeping. Only in some descriptions of Moses himself do we find hints of a deeper, more familiar trust in God: *"And there has not arisen a prophet since in Israel like Moses, whom the Lord knew face-to-face"* (Deut 34:10).

Of all the scriptural texts that we might consider from the point of view of the attachment motive—and the prophetic books provide many examples—it is the Psalms which most insistently speak of the Lord God in terms of attachment. Psalm 17(18) begins with the words: *"I love you, O Lord, my strength. The Lord is my rock and my fortress and my deliverer, my God, my rock, in whom I take refuge, my shield, and the horn of my salvation, my stronghold."* It then continues in the same vein, praising the support the writer has received when faced with difficult circumstances. Many other psalms draw upon these and similar images. We find the metaphor of God as rock, for example, twenty times throughout the Psalms and other expressions of security and protection would add many more instances to that number. But for an expression of the believer's attachment to God, perhaps clearest of all is that of Psalm 62(63), for example, *"My soul clings to you; your right hand upholds me"* (Ps 62[63]:8).

Sometimes the psalmist applies the image of "king" as attachment figure to God. He is a ruler who works to preserve his people from enemies without and oppressors within. *"Give attention to the sound of my cry, my King and my God, for to you do I pray"* (Ps 5:2). Here the emphasis is upon the vulnerability of the petitioner and the gracious assistance of God. But here we need to distinguish between different uses of the "king" image. When a young child is confronted by a strange and fear-inducing situation, for example, in coming face-to-face with an unfamiliar adult, retreating to the physical closeness of its mother relieves the anxiety, since the assumption is that the parent, to the extent that she is a reliable attachment figure, is a safe haven. There is, in the child, simply no thought of the mother's own vulnerability. However, in the case of Israel's king as attachment figure, there was frequently some doubt as to whether the king could, in fact, serve as a safe haven in view of an uncertainty as to whether he could resist and defeat the aggressing enemy. For this reason, when attachment themes surface in relation to a king, they are often joined by imagery of the king as leader of a group for which dominance over the enemy is the goal. The same idea appears in relation to the Lord. *"For the Lord, the Most High, is to be feared, a great king over all the earth. He subdued peoples under us, and nations under our feet"* (Ps 46[47]:2–3).

In the Old Testament, when questions of security arise, we find that, by and large, the "unit of preservation," as it were, is the people as a whole rather than the individual. Throughout the story of the Exodus, on the way to the promised land, many individual Israelites died as a result of various tragedies, and even Moses was not permitted to cross the Jordan

River into that land. Yet God preserved the people *as a people* through many threats and hardships, and so the promise of the Lord, that he would give his people a land, was fulfilled. Certainly, we find that King David, as an individual, was provided with divine protection, but here again, the primary "unit of preservation" was David's house; the promise to him was that the line of David would be preserved. On the other hand, we find only rarely the use of parental imagery for God, since that implies not so much the safety of the people as a whole or of one's descendants but of individuals themselves (e.g., Ps 88[89]:26; Jer 3:19). When we turn to the New Testament, we find a dramatic development in this respect.

New Testament

Jesus' use of the epithet "Abba," that is, "Father," (but more intimate that that word sounds to English-speaking ears) appears in the Gospels as a striking change in the way God as attachment figure is to be viewed among the first disciples. People of the time must have perceived that label as lacking in reverence for God (whose name was more commonly spoken of only in oblique terms) but also as making claims about the importance of the *individual* Jewish believer beyond what could be sustained by appeal to the Old Testament writings. Yes, God looks after his people as a people and can be relied upon to do so in the future, and yes, he is more supportive to those individual believers who follow his law than those who reject it. And we notice that in the latter parts of the Old Testament, the image of God as Father appears, though rarely. But the claims of Christ, that his followers could, as individuals, rely upon the heavenly Father as children can rely upon their own fathers (assumed here, of course, is the perspective of the kingdom of heaven!) was often just too difficult for many of the scribes and the Pharisees to accept, whereas many, especially those lowest in the society, *heard him gladly* (Mark 12:37).

This kind of security, the kind that provides a sense of protection given by the heavenly Father in this life, regardless of how it may turn out, and an eternal security and blessedness in which all earthly vulnerabilities are removed and all the pain of traumas is healed, this security that Jesus offered, had significant consequences for the lives of those responding to the call to discipleship. First among these consequences is the fact that family was no longer to hold the central place in a believer's system of attachments. *"If anyone comes to me and does not hate his own father and mother and wife and children and brothers and sisters, yes, and even his own life, he cannot be my disciple"* (Luke 14:26). At least as *ultimate* attachment figures, God and his community of the kingdom were to take its place.

But also, the authority of the Jewish religious leadership—and the security that accompanied that authority—was qualified by the word of Christ and the authority with which he taught. He did not merely speak the word of God but *was* the Word of God. And in time, and in the light of the gospel, the security of belonging to God's old covenant people was exchanged for something greater and more reliable than simply Jewish identity. As John the Baptist expressed it to his Jewish hearers, *"And do not presume to say to yourselves, 'We have Abraham as our father,' for I tell you, God is able from these stones to raise up children for Abraham"* (Matt 3:9). Security in the kingdom comes from a relationship of faith and trust in the paternal King rather than solely from membership of the chosen people.

To the reader of the New Testament with eyes open to the processes of the attachment motive it is truly remarkable to see how prominently these processes appear throughout the sacred text. In Jesus' public ministry, the miracles he performed gave people trust in his power to save them. Judging from the response of the disciples, his resurrection both strengthened that trust and gave it a particular shape, that is, the resurrected body which the risen Christ possessed was what believers could look forward to for themselves. The confidence with which the apostles carried out their mission and their willingness to suffer death for the sake of that mission are further pointers to what we might call the existential security that the early church experienced in the light of Christ. One could scan through the Pauline and other New Testament texts and find repeated examples of this newfound trust, sourced from a fundamental change in attachments of those who wrote them. In some, for example Paul, we mostly see the individual form of attachment expressed; for others who were members of the various church communities, we might imagine that group attachment played a somewhat larger role in their inner experience. Still, within the Christian faith, the two forms are not to be clearly distinguished, since ultimately it is Christ himself, whether it be the One whom we worship or the One who nourishes his church through his Spirit, who exists as the believer's attachment figure.

Reflections of Faith

Understanding Attachment in the Light of Faith

From our brief review of attachment themes in the Scriptures, we can see that they are so pervasive because of the fact that the sacred text deals with salvation history, the story of God's saving work among his people. Salvation and security are closely linked. It might appear, then, that our discussion of the matter is laboring a fairly obvious point: security is important to faith. And from this perspective, growth in the faith is to be conceived of as primarily a matter of deepening our *understanding* of God's saving work and allowing that truth more fully to shape our daily lives. Individual believers might vary between themselves in how much their emotions enter into the matter, but they can be assured that the more profoundly they grasp the *truth* of God's saving actions, the more secure will they find themselves in their relationship with him.

Something like this has been the dominant view within Western Christian culture for many centuries. As others have observed, it is based upon an understanding of human nature that emerged within Greco-Roman culture and which, in many respects, has served theology well. Yet, like much of the knowledge about the world that we find in ancient times, it requires adjustments and even correction in the light of the knowledge we continue to gain through our own careful study. In relation to the way the Scriptures speak about our security in God and how this connects with our understanding of the human attachment motive, I would like to suggest some ideas based upon that deeper knowledge.

First, we need to reread the biblical text to see just how large a role emotion plays when security is the issue. Fear, anxiety, longing, clinging—all these and more appear when safety is under threat; relief, joy, and exultation take over when a threat is averted and safety is assured. This shows us that the processes involved are primitive ones. As attachment theory affirms, the way that attachment works in us humans builds upon the foundations that evolved many millions of years ago in our mammalian ancestors. As a legitimate part of our human nature, we must accommodate ourselves to it rather than "think" it.

Secondly, we are to view questions of security as ones which virtually every human being has to face since attachment is at the core of our being. We know that some people are more anxious than others—often they are born that way—but speaking generally, every one of us has to address seriously our sense of security in relation to God at the level of emotion as well as thought. Biblical knowledge or training in theology by themselves will not help us; the question of existential security has to be faced at a deeper level.

Thirdly, attachment theory tells us that, in our relationship with God, we build upon our prior attachment history, especially upon the way our parents related to us. From that history, each of us has a set of expectations about how worthy we are to be cared for and how responsive others will be in our need, and we bring these expectations with us as we enter into times of prayer to God. A rather unsettling reality for many Western believers is that, however mature we might think ourselves to be, we will always carry around with us the effects of our experience during the early years of our life.

Fourthly, and following on from that last point, we need to acknowledge that this set of expectations is quite difficult to improve on, and indeed we cannot *directly* alter them. What do I mean by that? I will be able to explain this more fully in a later section, but for now I can say that direct attempts to deepen our attachment to God fail because, if we have to get God to demonstrate his reliability and trustworthiness to us, psychologically we will not be convinced by such evidence. Generally, our attachment relationships to both humans and to God are much more elusive and out-of-reach than we imagine. We make most progress through indirect means, that is, by deepening our relationships with other believers, by more fully immersing ourselves in the life of our church and by opening ourselves up to God in prayer. However, as soon as this becomes programmatic, something we manage, it will fail. Attachment is essentially about engaging with persons *as individual persons*, and that means engaging with the Lord God in a non-manipulative, non-problem-solving manner. We Western believers find this terribly difficult to do.

The Scriptures paint a picture of the profoundly existential character of our relationship with God and of the bond of trust that is to characterize that relationship. It is about terror and peace. Intellectual understanding has a place in the formation of that relationship, but as the example of many ordinary believers through the centuries has shown, it is not essential to the experience of a profound trust in God. Through divine accommodation, in the Scriptures we read that God shows himself and connects with us humans in ways which take full account of how we have been made, and one of the truly core dimensions of our nature is our powerful motive to form attachments with others. According to the mechanisms of this motive, we can enter into a trusting relationship with God.

Christ and Attachment: Some Thoughts on Its Practice

For most of us, it is our parents who serve as our primary attachment figures. Others, such a grandparents, older siblings, and close friends adopt subsidiary roles as sources of attachment. As we mature, we find that we ourselves take on the function of an attachment figure in relation to others, such as friends, spouses, and our own children. For those of us with faith in Jesus Christ, as we have noted already, he, too, becomes another source of attachment, another haven of safety and source of succor to whom we can find support in our vulnerability and stress. How strongly he serves in that role, however, depends, to a significant degree, upon what model of attachment we have developed during our growing years. Especially important are our early relations with our parents, but other bonds we formed since that time can also shape those early foundational expectations of trust or distrust we acquired. And so it is that we bring our unconsciously formed attachment expectations to bear on our relationship with Christ. We need, then, to consider how this works out in practice.

Before dealing with this, however, we must clarify what kind of attachment we might be able to have to Christ. To begin with, we have to take account of the fact that we cannot routinely expect that the Lord will protect us from the various vicissitudes that affect human life. Faithful believers are not immune to sickness, to random accidents, to loss of loved ones, financial ruin, emotional disorders, or most other causes of suffering, even if some of them occur less commonly as a result of the believer's way of life. If we look at the lives of believers of past times, we find this is the case. Furthermore, we do not yet see Christ face-to-face, and this limits the kind of bond we can have with him. We must therefore keep in mind what the Scriptures tell us, that *"we walk by faith, not by sight"* (2 Cor 5:7). So, we need to be clear as to what it means for us to *rely* on Christ if he is truly to be a key attachment figure in our lives.

Most important is the salvation he offers us: *"Though you do not now see [Jesus Christ], you believe in him and rejoice with joy that is inexpressible and filled with glory, obtaining the outcome of your faith, the salvation of your souls"* (1 Pet 1:8–9). We who believe have heard the good news and have responded in faith. The word of God gives us hope of eternal life with Christ, even though we cannot imagine what it will be like.

Also, we are encouraged in our faith by observing that of other believers, and also the faith of those who have gone before us. For us Catholics, the saints, among whom Mary is the preeminent example, are a key part of that encouragement. And as we immerse ourselves in the life of the worshipping Church, with its incredibly rich and inexhaustible culture, we grow in our attachment to Christ through a kind of subordinate attachment to his Church on earth. The weekly rhythm of worship, the annual cycles associated with Lent, Easter, and Pentecost, the preparations of Advent, the joy of Christmas, the celebration of the saints and other feast days, and all the ways these touch our lives through various traditions; this totality works in an unconscious way to shape within us a group or cultural attachment (i.e., us as members relating to the Church) which can support and supplement that which we have with Christ himself. Other Christian traditions have elements that function in a similar manner.

The life of the church—at least at its best—is also *koinonia* or fellowship, the intimate friendship of a stable group of believers who share each other's lives and who can be utterly relied upon to render assistance in those times of vulnerability that a member might face. Paul puts it pithily: *"Bear one another's burdens, and so fulfil the law of Christ"* (Gal 6:2). This level of support and security does not take away from responsibilities to and for one's family (see 1 Tim 5:3–4, 8) but it does provide a setting for a believer *as an individual* (not simply as a member of the church) to become attached to a particular fellowship group.

Crucial for many of the faithful is the life of private prayer they have developed. There, going into their room, they are alone with Christ, they give themselves time to quieten their heart, they set aside their public mask and seek an authentic sense of themselves before their Lord. The Scriptures are their companion as they converse in their hearts with Christ. Although they do not feel him physically, often they know a kind of intimacy that recognizes his loving presence with them. Their concerns and anxieties are eased, and they find something of that safety and peace with characterizes attachment bonds. Subordinate to this relationship with Christ, but significant for Catholics, all the same, is the attachment we have to Christ's mother. Her maternal features as described by tradition draw us into a prayerful closeness to her which nurtures our spirits and points us to the way of her Son.

Finally, there is the expectation that a believer can have of Christ, that he or she will be given guidance in daily life as to how to live it out. What is the good thing to do in this situation? What can I discern of Christ's will for me in this matter? The believer, too, can offer frequent prayers to God for blessings and for miracles, great and small, some of which are granted for our good and for the glory of God. All of this deepens our trust in Christ.

Thus, we can see that attachment to Christ is a rather complex matter in practice involving many aspects of the life of faith, but in its main outlines it has to do with a personal relationship with Christ, a subordinate attachment to the church as Christ's body both through the security of immersion in its life and culture, and via the more particular attachment that the experience of stable *koinonia* or brotherhood can provide.

Now, returning to the question of how our attachment to Christ plays out in the light of our own attachment history, we can say first that, unless we take advantage of all the above-described resources provided by our faith to grow our relationship with Christ, we will likely conform our attachment to him so that it mimics that of our own family and relationship history. And that can very often be limiting to our growth in the faith. If our inner, unconscious model or set of expectations shows itself as insecure-anxious attachment, then we will tend to cling excessively to aspects of our faith and may indeed become very "religious," but underneath we will continue to be quite anxious about many everyday matters, death anxiety will dog us, and we will be unable to find a sustained peace in our faith. Or our fundamental attachment might be of the "avoidant insecure" type, that is, we have had early experiences of seeking support only to be frequently disappointed in the response we have received, and this has led us to become emotionally withdrawn and lacking trust in others. This same set of expectations will then operate in our faith, and so, however much we might confess the truths of the faith and live devoutly our life in the church, our inner life will be little touched by it all, for we will not be able to experience Christ as an existential safe haven. The occasional consolations that even the insecure-anxious person might experience from time to time will be unknown to us. Unlike them, our life of faith will not necessarily be marked by persistent anxiety, since we will avoid situations that are associated with much uncertainty, but when our faith is put to the test, such as in life-threatening events, it will quickly express itself as withdrawal, despair, and hopelessness.

On the other hand, if we have grown up within secure attachment relationships, we will at least have *the potential* to enter into a similarly secure relationship with Christ and his church. All those aspects of the faith that I mentioned earlier can be developed so that as believers we live trustingly in Christ, are nourished by our life in the church, and look forward with confidence to the age to come.

In writing this, however, I do not want to give the impression that we can do nothing about a less-than-satisfactory upbringing. We are not condemned to impoverished lives of faith because of how our parents treated us! Other relationships in our lives can have ameliorating or softening effects on earlier distorted attachments, and this is especially the case for marriage bonds. Relationships with other believers, life in the church, trustworthy friendships, and psychological counselling can change, to some extent, our fundamental expectations. So, while our childhood experiences lay the groundwork for the kind of faith we develop, they are not the end of the story. There is, however, another complication we must consider which affects the attachment of faith that we have as believers.

Other Sources of Existential Security

In Western cultures, there exist other, "alternative," non-faith-based sources of attachment, particularly in its group form. Earlier, when I wrote about group attachment, or the security that comes from being a member of a group that serves as a source of protection and safety, I noted that this could include things like medical insurance, trade unions, governments, street gangs, and ethnic groups. Each of these in its own way can provide individuals with a sense of security. For those of us who have grown up in a developed Western culture, if we look within ourselves, we will discover that there is much about that culture which gives us a sense of safety. Here are some examples: the rule of law that means that everyone, no matter who they are, is bound by the law of the land and thus we can (usually) be free of the anxiety that someone might oppress us; an educational system that provides citizens, and especially those with tertiary qualifications, with a broad body of knowledge that is shared by a large proportion of our society and which works to grease the wheels of its operation; a medical and hospital system that everyone can access and which is skilled at assisting us in emergencies; finally, there is a system of philosophy, generally referred to as "liberalism," central to which is a belief in continual progress whether that be in knowledge, in technology, in moral sensitivity and conviction, and more generally in civilization. According to this philosophy, things will get better.

Just how attached we citizens of Western nations are to these sources of security is not normally made clear to us. Perhaps when we travel to less developed countries, we sense it, or when we study other periods of history and imagine what would have been the experience of life in those times, we become aware of a feeling of relief that we live in our own times and society. That is, we, momentarily and in a slight way, grasp our connection or attachment to our culture. But under normal circumstances, the reality of that connection exists as an unconscious process.

Seen in this way, it becomes clear that such a source of group attachment can easily interfere with the believer's experience of attachment to Christ, and also make it difficult for nonbelievers to relinquish what is really an attachment to our culture for the sake of the salvation which the Lord offers them. I would even suggest that the stronger and more influential that cultural attachment is in a society, the weaker is the commitment of faith. Such an idea has been proposed by sociologists Pippa Norris and Ronald Inglehart, who have provided extensive evidence for what they call "existential security" or all those things I have mentioned above which work together to provide people with a sense of safety in the world.[10] They show that religious faith becomes less significant in people's lives as a society moves in the direction of a deepening of its members' sense of "cultural" security. Scandinavian and Northern European nations have shown most progress in this direction. There we find extensive social and health services, high levels of education, excellent rule of law and administrative effectiveness, and all this is carried out by an overtly non-religious state. In line with the Inglehart-Norris thesis, we also observe very low levels of church attendance, belief in God, belief in life after death, and other indicators of faith.

Some have argued that such an association linking levels of culturally-created existential security and loss of religious faith is at least partly spurious since some highly developed nations—and the chief example offered is that of the USA with its strong religiosity—do not show such

---

10. Norris and Inglehart, *Sacred and Secular*.

a pattern. However, as Norris and Inglehart demonstrate, though the US is a wealthy, highly developed nation, its level of existential security is in fact relatively low, especially for those of its citizens who are poorer. They cite the absence of a universal healthcare system, limited unemployment benefits, somewhat haphazard welfare provisions, and high levels of crime in large urban areas as signs of this deficiency.

It seems, then, that existential security, or, as I have called it, "cultural attachment,"[11] is a powerful force which undermines faith in Christ and obstructs the work of the gospel. So, while an individual living in a Western society who has a history of secure attachments might in principle be open to substantial growth in Christian maturity and a deep sense of trust in Christ, the reality is that this is less common than we might imagine because opposing cultural forces are generally too powerful. They push us to find security in what our society offers us rather than in Christ. Considering ways in which we might address this problem would take us well beyond attachment theory, but elements of a response will be found in chapters 14 and 18. At this point, my hope is that the reader will have gained an idea of how powerful yet hidden are attachment relationships with both individuals and with groups, and that our relationship with Christ can be deeply compromised by attachments we have to society as a source of security. Thinking of this in terms of idolatry is not wide of the mark, since we are talking here about fundamental commitments. As Jesus said, "no one can serve two masters," and, we might add, neither can anyone place their ultimate dependence in two sources.

Having considered the motive of attachment and its place in our lives, we now need to think briefly about how it connects with the dominance motive. We have seen that both are very powerful and that both operate mostly under the radar of our consciousness, although attachment more so. The next chapter will address the question of their interrelationship.

---

11. In fact, these two are not the same. Existential security, as it is described by Norris and Inglehart, does not really provide a full sense of peace and security in one's existence; it only goes part of the way, since culture cannot fully take the place of faith in Christ.

5

Attachment and Dominance

SO FAR, WE HAVE separately considered two of our most powerful motives, dominance and attachment. Each operates in different ways to influence profoundly our thoughts and actions. The question we must address now is: How do they relate to each other? Are they normally well-coordinated, or do they frequently come into conflict? Which is more important or has priority, and in what circumstances? Is their typical interrelationship well aligned with what our Christian faith requires, or does our faith call for us to work towards a different way of coordinating them? I think the reader will have recognized from what I have described so far that the matter of the interrelationship between dominance and attachment is fundamental to how we live as believers.

Linking the Two Motives

Attachment and Dominance: Parallel Development?

To gain an idea of how dominance and attachment relate to each other, let us remind ourselves of how they each emerge in the first few years of life. In describing these motives, we observed that both show themselves, at least in embryonic form, during the first year of life. Then an infant's bond with parents grows, as does fear of strangers, and this sets the scene for the typical attachment behavior we observe towards the end of the first year: clinging to the mother or father when faced with frightening situations or unfamiliar people as well as in stressful situations more generally.

With the appearance of the "I," the self, at about eighteen months, the scope of attachment is ready to include not only matters physical but also psychological safety and support. Within the same timeframe we find infants gradually extending their repertoire of skills and activities, and this provides its own reward apart from any other positive reinforcement their actions might receive from others. The development of the self, and of a sense of oneself in relation to other selves, gives the child a basis upon which comparisons with others can be made, and thereafter we see emerging in children's interactions behaviors expressing competition, attention-seeking, conflict, alliances, and self-promotion, all of which characterize the dominance motive. Thus, it appears that, under normal circumstances, the two motives, attachment and dominance, develop in parallel and, at first glance, seem to be barely related to each other.

Yet, there is a deeper, less obvious link between them. We can see this connection most clearly when we observe young children playing. When a securely attached child is playing in the presence of her mother, even when there is a stranger also present in the room, the child is usually well engaged in her play and willing to explore her immediate environment because she has no anxiety about her safety; her mother is there and the joy of competence in play is in full swing. If the mother leaves temporarily, the child soon sets aside her play activity and her attention turns to the absence of her mother and to the threat posed by the presence of the stranger; that is, the attachment motive kicks in. We can generalize from this situation by saying that competence (as a core part of dominance) is given free rein only when the child's attachment needs are being met. Attachment figures thus provide not only a safe haven for a child, but also a *secure base* from which to explore the world. Further evidence of this ordering is found among young children who are anxious-insecure in their attachment and find themselves in a similar situation of play in the presence of both their mother and a stranger. Here their play is much less involving, and in fact the child might not play at all since she is preoccupied with the stranger and generally prefers to cling to her mother. If the mother departs the situation, the child's fearfulness is compounded. Again, we note that when attachment needs are not well met, as is the case of the insecure-anxious child, the competence motive is subordinated to that of attachment and therefore cannot be given full expression.

Based on research in this area,[1] we can reasonably conclude that secure attachment serves as the foundation upon which a child can fully develop his/her competence/dominance goals. Secure children, compared with those who possess less secure attachments, acquire more effective social skills, engage in less fighting and aggression with their peers, and perform better academically, all other things being equal.

How the Two Motives Interact in Adulthood

Seeing how this might apply to adulthood, we find similar patterns. Securely attached adults have more energy to pursue the development of their skills and talents and are better able to experience the pleasure of doing something well. For the well-attached individual, pursuit of status typically figures in all of this, but it is achieved with less conflict and overt competition than for a person who is less securely attached. The latter can easily become more preoccupied with attachment issues, either in their close relationships or in being accepted among their friends or work colleagues. This means that they are more prone to defensiveness, direct competition, overt attention-seeking, attempts at controlling others, and generally experience more difficult social relations. In terms of the pursuit of status, it is commonly found that they drive themselves very hard to achieve their personal goals as a way of compensating, as it were, for the deficiencies in basic security. It is as if they say to themselves: "If I cannot find full acceptance and nurture of myself in my close relationships, then I will strive with extra effort to gain acceptance and recognition of my achievements in the eyes of the world."

There are two things to note about this dynamic: first, the acceptance and nurture of the self in the attachment system is of the inner self, that which is the deepest part of one's being, whereas acceptance in relation to the dominance motive, that is, the recognition of one's self and one's achievements, relates to less core aspects of the self and therefore can never really make up for impaired or limited attachment bonds. Secondly, in the case of acceptance through attachment, those who provide it do so as individuals, typically only one or two persons, who, at any given time, are irreplaceable. Apart from a deep relationship with Christ, they and they only can give a fuller security to the self. In contrast to this, for

---

1. Again, the best gathering of research for this and other attachment-related matters is Cassidy and Shaver, *Handbook of Attachment*.

acceptance through competence/dominance, it is not the particularity of those providing the recognition and acceptance that is important, but rather their number and their status. Having many adulators is powerfully rewarding, as also is the attention and affirmation of high-status individuals. However, such positive experiences of recognition, if they are to continue, demand that one sustain one's achievements, and also, typically, require persisting efforts to stay in the public eye. Unlike attachment acceptance, this form is, in the long run, less satisfying, even though at times it can be quite exhilarating and even addictive.

As a final comment on this comparison of forms of acceptance, we should recall that an individual cannot stand back from the situation and ask himself, "Now, which form of acceptance will I pursue?" He has subconsciously already "chosen" in accord with his attachment history and success in the pursuit of achievement and status. Once the pathways have been set, it is quite a difficult task to redirect them, though it can be done, often most successfully with outside help rather than by oneself.

Summing up this discussion, we can say that it is not difficult to grasp the different dynamics operating in securely and insecurely attached individuals. The former have a powerful source of affirmation and security in their familial and intimate relationships, and together these serve as a secure base for the pursuit of a form of dominance behavior which is chiefly directed towards competence and *relatively* less so to preferential comparison with others. The insecurely attached person, by contrast, in many situations in life, has to worry about whether or not her family and intimate relationships are going to provide the support she needs, and so to achieve affirmation of herself she must work very hard to prove herself to others. She also has fewer emotional reserves to be able to manage failures and disappointments, personal slights, and the stresses that occur in interpersonal conflict. While she may accomplish many things, her success never fully and in a sustained manner satisfies her, and she does not achieve that sense of personal acceptance and peace that only a secure attachment can provide. In short, the pursuit of dominance in such a person serves as a substitute, though a fairly poor one, for secure attachment.

The Scriptural Witness

The scriptural material relating to our theme is rather limited, especially in the Old Testament. What we are looking for are texts that show an awareness of the link between the security of faith and the freedom and energy of living fully the life of faithful obedience. Certainly, it is present, but mostly in the background. Recall the account of the giving of the law on Mount Sinai. In the nineteenth chapter of Exodus, which recounts the people's purifying preparations before the event, we read that the Lord commanded Moses to say to the people, *"You yourselves have seen what I did to the Egyptians, and how I bore you on eagles' wings and brought you to myself. Now therefore, if you will indeed obey my voice and keep my covenant, you shall be my treasured possession among all peoples, for all the earth is mine"* (Exod 19:4–5). Then in introducing the Ten Commandments, we read: *"And God spoke all these words, saying, 'I am the Lord your God, who brought you out of the land of Egypt, out of the house of slavery. You shall have no other gods before me'"* (Exod 20:2–3). In both texts we can recognize the sequence: demonstration of the Lord's care for his people, the proof of his power to give them security, followed by an expectation that they will have the capacity or the competence to follow his laws.

Yet such a juxtaposition of these two themes is rare elsewhere in the Old Testament. Certainly, we find texts which link a more general help sought or provided by God as a condition of his people's obedience, for example: *"In your steadfast love give me life, that I may keep the testimonies of your mouth"* (Ps 118[119]:88). Yet this and similar passages are still a long way from directly articulating the connection between secure attachment and competence in action. For a clearer expression, we need to turn to the New Testament.

In Jesus' public ministry we do not come across explicit teaching linking attachment and dominance/competence, but we do find some examples of the relationship as it has been described above. To the woman caught in adultery, at the conclusion of the episode, Jesus addresses her: *"'Woman, where are they? Has no one condemned you?' She said, 'No one, Lord.' And Jesus said, 'Neither do I condemn you; go, and from now on sin no more'"* (John 8:10–11). Here we sense that Jesus is linking the forgiveness and acceptance he gives to her with her renewed freedom to be able to avoid the sin of adultery. A more obvious example is that of the woman of ill repute who anoints Jesus' feet while he is dining with Simon the

Pharisee. Addressing his host, Jesus says, *"Therefore I tell you, her sins, which are many, are forgiven—for she loved much. But he who is forgiven little, loves little"* (Luke 7:47). The woman, who experienced forgiveness from Christ, entered dramatically into a reassuring, secure relationship with him and is now empowered to love in a manner unknown to those who have not welcomed the good news. A similar kind of dynamic appears in the story of the woman at the well (John 4:1–41), the Zacchaeus episode (Luke 19:1–10), and also in Jesus' teaching on trust in him and the disciples' power to do greater works after his return to the Father (cf. John 14:12). In the early chapters of the Acts of the Apostles, we find that, following the assurance which Jesus' resurrection provided to his followers, their timidity and fear turned to boldness in proclaiming the good news. Here the same attachment/dominance link is exemplified.

In Paul's writings we notice that the matter comes more plainly into the foreground because, as the apostle viewed things, those legalists who opposed him, especially those of the circumcision party, were so directly challenging the priority of God's grace in the work of salvation. We observe his deep understanding of the issue in the following passage from 1 Corinthians 15, after he has enumerated the appearances of the risen Lord: *"Last of all, as to one untimely born, he appeared also to me. For I am the least of the apostles, unworthy to be called an apostle, because I persecuted the church of God. But by the grace of God I am what I am, and his grace towards me was not in vain. On the contrary, I worked harder than any of them, though it was not I, but the grace of God that is with me"* (1 Cor 15:8–10). First there is the bestowal of the grace of forgiveness and the security of salvation, which then opens the way for Paul to work harder than any of the other apostles in preaching the gospel, yet all the time with an awareness that his striving is made possible because of his new relationship with the Lord. The same way of thinking is repeated in the letter to the Philippians, where Paul contrasts that righteousness that comes from the law, in other words, acceptance by God *in response to* the keeping of the law, with a righteousness and a capacity to strive for perfection which is *the result of* God's acceptance of us through faith in Christ (see Phil 3:2–16).

In sum, then, we can conclude that, in the Scriptures, it is primarily through the teaching on grace with its twofold emphasis upon the priority of divine salvation and inner security and the *consequent* freeing up for the works of love that something of the interrelationship between attachment and dominance/competence is set forth and affirmed.

A Reflection of Faith

Holding to the Priority of Grace

The precedence of attachment, which is generally true as a psychological principle, also manifests itself in the way that God relates to us in the sphere of salvation history. Yet, it must be said that, for believers, it has been an extraordinarily difficult idea to hold on to and to apply over the long term. We only have to look at the history of theological reflection in the centuries after Paul to see the gradual eating away of the scriptural truth. Part of this was the enmeshment of the church with political authorities beginning in the early fourth century, and we might add to that the demands on the church to accommodate the wave of new conversions that following the Peace of Constantine at that time. A kind of depersonalized process developed by which the path to Christian salvation became one of requirements and rules, of order and discipline, and even faith itself became more a hurdle that one surmounted and less a mysterious gift of grace. The pinnacle of this watering-down of the primacy of grace and the exaltation of sheer obedience was reached with the idea that the church in its hierarchy was a *societas perfecta*, a society complete in itself, possessing both spiritual and political power: God has given authority to the church, its leaders set the rules, the people are to obey, and those who do not comply can be punished with secular punishments, even death. Fortunately, this way of seeing things has never squelched the deeper truth that at the very center of the church is to be found the sacred, compassionate, and gracious heart of Jesus. But certainly, in the sixteenth century, there was enough evidence of distortions of this truth to provoke Luther's rebellion in the interests of his (admittedly also distorted) "grace alone" and "faith alone" principles. His intuition was that the fundamental Christian conviction of the priority of grace must show itself throughout the life of the church. Even his third principle, Scripture alone, was aimed at this goal in that it sought to give oxygen especially to the teaching of Paul, which had by Luther's time largely been suffocated into powerlessness.

The Catholic student of church history should no longer be defensive about these matters. It is a reality that prompts shame in our hearts but not despair. For the Lord of history is the One who calls us to repentance and to a renewed openness to his grace and empowerment. The path set by the reforming Council of Trent in the sixteenth century, which has led to that of Vatican II in our own time, has been one of a retrieval of the biblical truth of grace before obedience, of the joy of knowing oneself redeemed that is the ground and precondition for the task of *"pressing on towards the goal for the prize of the upward call of God in Christ Jesus"* (Phil 3:14).

Concluding Comments

In concluding these two chapters on attachment, I trust that my emphasis on the centrality of this motive for how we experience the world and our relationships has come through to the reader. By now you should have a sound grasp of its main features and especially the fact that it operates mostly beneath our awareness. But I do not believe that a merely intellectual understanding is sufficient if we want to make use of the material that has been covered. What is needed is for us to "feel into" the way attachment has worked in our lives. If we have suffered a bereavement of someone close to us, do we remember how our thoughts through the day were taken over by that experience, and not just for a short while but for months? Do we recall the arguments we have had with people we are close to and how they triggered feelings of hurt and distress which, again, seemed to prevent us from thinking rationally or clearly? Or have we lived through a rupture in a romantic relationship and remember just how powerfully distressing it was? On the positive side, perhaps we have experienced that wonderful sense of joy that washed over us when we discovered that we were deeply loved and accepted by the person who would one day become our spouse. To know experiences of this sort but more importantly to "sense" their connections with the attachment motive is to enter a new world, as it were. It is to see our lives in quite a different light and to have gained a truly fundamental insight into the way our minds operate. If this has been your first exposure to the concept of the attachment motive, I hope that, drawing upon the material found in these two chapters, you will be able to incorporate an experiential knowledge of the motive's workings into the way you view your life and how you live it.

Having looked at dominance and attachment as central motives in human life, we now turn our attention to another motive, social reciprocity, that displays a notably different character in that it does not *drive* behavior so much as *shape* it. Relatively few people are consumed by reciprocity compared with those who place dominance front and center in their lives. And we can get by without paying too much attention to reciprocity in a way that we cannot in relation to attachment. And yet it is pervasive across human cultures and plays a pivotal role in the way a society runs. It will become the third key element in the sketch we are forming of the processes of the human heart.

6

Social Reciprocity

Social Reciprocity: A Description

SOCIAL RECIPROCITY REFERS TO our tendency to "pay back"—to pay back good for good and harm for harm. Bugental includes it among her key social "domains" or motives, and in doing so she is indicating that it is not just something that cultures develop, like reading and writing or the institution of marriage, but is as much a *biological* motive as are attachment and dominance, though a more recent one. Well, how can we describe social reciprocity more precisely? Bugental tells us that the effect of the motive is not so much that things should work out fairly for each individual but that human groups might work better. Through reciprocity, a group, and therefore also its members, will be more likely to join together to ward off external threats, for example, from other humans, or even internal challenges such as disease. This occurs because the motive encourages group members to see themselves as being "in the same boat," as it were, and therefore more willing to provide support to each other and the group as a whole. In sum, humans who are driven by the motive will have a better chance of surviving if they coordinate their activities rather than if individuals are left simply to "do their own thing."[1] She adds that coordination grows when all members of a social group (kinship

---

1. Bugental, "Acquisition," 199: "Reciprocity-based interactions serve the function of facilitating coordinated, and matched, mutually beneficial action processes between related or unrelated individuals. Reciprocity is defined here in terms of the provision of equivalent benefits (including affective benefits) over a period of time between functional equals."

group, tribe, community) act so that what one person gives to another is closely matched by what they in turn receive from the other; *quid pro quo* is the rule. This rule of "repayment" does not necessarily have to be applied immediately, but over a period of time that is recognized by both parties.[2]

As with attachment and dominance, so with social reciprocity, we can trace its origins to prehuman species and observe its continuing existing in present-day non-human animals. The Dutch ethologist Frans de Waal has carried out work in this area, identifying forms of social reciprocity among primates and some other species.[3] This research suggests that, although it takes quite complicated forms in many human societies, and this might lead us to think of it as something purely cultural or rational, in reality it was around long before we humans developed culture or reason. That puts it in the same camp as the other biologically based motives.

Cultural Variations

Some cultures have developed elaborate expectations about how social reciprocity should operate so that, as a motive, it drives and shapes a substantial proportion of the total social interaction. For example, in some African cultures, the negotiations between the families of a bride and groom can be so complex as to last for days. Also, in some cultures, reciprocity has developed into an "art form" whereby an individual works to gain personal advancement through a series of calculated *quid pro quo* moves. "If I do this for (person B), then he will be obliged to do this for me; I will then use this to obligate (person C) to do this for me . . ."

Other cultures have not developed it as much and it tends less to serve the purpose of individual advancement. Western cultures are mostly like this. If you are a work colleague of mine and invite me to your home for a meal, you might not have any ulterior purpose in doing so—it might be simply to get to know me outside of a work context—but I will likely feel a sense of obligation to do the same or similar to you at some time in the future. Or if I take the trouble of sending someone birthday

---

2. For an account of human social reciprocity primarily from the cultural evolutionary point of view, see Fehr et al., "Strong Reciprocity," 1–25.

3. De Waal and Luttrell, "Mechanisms of Social Reciprocity," 101–18; de Waal, "The Chimpanzee's Sense," 241–55; see also Wilkinson, "Reciprocal Altruism," 85–100; Taborsky, "Social Evolution," R486–R488.

greetings, I might take note if I fail to receive a similar acknowledgement from that person when my birthday comes around. These are not usually openly expressed expectations in our culture; our schoolteachers do not directly teach positive reciprocity rules to their students, nor do governments make it the focus of community education campaigns. Yet it is still part of our consciousness, and it shapes our social interactions in thousands of little ways.

In Western culture, also, where we have a strong awareness of the "equality" of all people, the expectations arising from reciprocity are fairly straightforward: if I do a favor for you that requires me to put myself out in some way, I can expect that you will reciprocate in a similar way within a reasonable length of time, or alternatively I will be able to call on you for a favor at some point, again, within an undefined but finite period of time. In many traditional cultures, where status and honor are openly acknowledged dimensions of social life, the rules linked to reciprocity can be quite complex, and the forms of repayment can vary greatly depending on the relative status of the parties. If a high-status individual provides a benefit to someone of low status, any repayment in kind from the low-status person might be impossible due to his limited means, and so something different, perhaps multiple small gifts or a portion of his time, might be required to fulfil the debt.

According to Bugental, one thing that is common to cultures is the requirement that the "load" of a benefit given to another, that is, the effort involved, the financial cost, the time it requires, is taken as the measure of how the other is to reciprocate. A significantly lesser "repayment" benefit would be interpreted by its recipient as "breaking the rules" and would typically lead to a souring of relations between the two parties.

Another point that Bugental makes in her definition is that the provision of equivalent benefits can include *affective* or emotional benefits. What she means here is that if I do something for you, you might respond not with a single, concrete "repayment" but with a number of signs of your goodwill towards me which can take the form of being more friendly, speaking positively about me to others, or voting for me when I am running for some elected position. What is given in exchange can be more emotional or attitudinal than a tangible gift.

Reciprocity and Social Groups

So far, we have looked at the works of the social reciprocity motive when it guides interactions between two individuals. But it is also the case that it can have a powerful impact on the operation of social groups. In previous chapters we saw how we can become attached to groups of people as well as to individuals just as we can gain dominance and status not only by ourselves but also through our participation in groups. Social reciprocity comes into play in groups since typically there are expectations of mutual responsibility which are placed on members of a group who might be advised in the following terms: "If you are going to receive the benefits that come from being a member of our group, then you will be expected to fulfill the obligations that such membership places upon you." One of the major problems which groups face in surviving over the long term is the existence of "freeloaders," those who gain benefits without contributing to the life and maintenance of a group. There are ways of dealing with the problem such as making entry to the group more difficult so as to discourage those who would be freeloaders from applying, giving individual members the specific responsibility of "weeding out" freeloaders in a group, strengthening group cohesion (that is, a sense of commitment to the group among members, so that individuals are less tempted to become freeloaders), and ensuring that the rules and norms of the group are communicated frequently and effectively. Returning to the idea that social reciprocity evolved as a way of improving cooperation in groups, we can now see that it is not only the open breaking of the group rules but also the more hidden and insidious phenomenon of freeloading that the motive of reciprocity serves to counteract.

Reciprocity as Justice

In what I have said about dealing with freeloaders, it is clear that reciprocity does not deal only with the giving and receiving of mutual *benefits*; it also applies to situations where harms are reciprocated with harms. Failure to fulfill the obligations of reciprocity usually leads to some kind of sanction against the offender, whether it be something as limited as not spending as much time with him/her to a heavier punishment such as group shunning. In many traditional cultures, such a punishment can have serious effects on the psychological well-being of an alienated member, whereas in individualistic cultures like ours, where individuals might belong to a range of social groups and can easily change groups and commitments, social exclusion might not seem an especially serious penalty. Yet, there is solid evidence that, even in our own culture, when shunning occurs in large groups or in a group which has major significance for a member, it can have quite dramatic effects, e.g., loss of life meaning, depression, and loneliness, on the well-being of persons who suffer it.[4] It seems that we really do not like being viewed in a negative light by others, especially by those with whom we have been closely involved.

This brings us to the institutionalized form of social reciprocity which is justice.[5] Being such a broad and complex area of human social life, all I can do here is to highlight just a few of its connections to the concept of reciprocity. Aristotle's definition of justice as "giving to each that which is his due" has served as a reminder of what, at root, the concept is about, and one could be forgiven for thinking that it is all that we need to explain how justice works in a society. It seems to be the case that giving each person their due is simply the reasonable thing to do, given that we all alike are human beings, each of whom wants to be treated in a fair manner. Yet, things look different in light of the idea of reciprocity as a *biologically* evolved motive which serves to improve group survival through the cooperation of the group members. In this view, we can see more clearly that Aristotle's definition cannot *by itself* work as a genuine rational foundation for how society operates because it is merely an abstract concept that appears to make good sense.[6] Put another way, we can say that our sense of justice (as an abstract rule) is not the reason why social reciprocity works, but rather the motive is the reason why we have a sense of justice. We exercise justice *firstly* because we are *motivated* to do so, not because it is the rational thing to do.[7] Here again, we meet the notion that human reason is at the service of non-rational motives rather

---

4. Twenge et al., "Social Exclusion," 409–23; Stillman et al., "Alone and without Purpose," 686–94; Lambert et al, "To Belong Is to Matter," 1418–27.

5. De Waal, "The Chimpanzee's Sense."

6. It does, of course, relate to God, but it is not easy to explain how. It seems to us that God is bound by the rule of justice just as much as we are, in which case, justice is still an absolute principle sitting there all by itself. But if God is not bound by the principle of justice, that suggests that he is able to do things that we would consider unjust or unfair, something most believers would find problematic. For those who are interested, chapter 9 on conscience in my book *Chalcedonian Personalism* offers one way of approaching this dilemma.

7. For a discussion of the claim that human morality is founded upon the evolved processes of social reciprocity, see Gintis et al., "Strong Reciprocity," 241–53.

than being their supervising manager, as it were. As we will see later, we need to take full account of divine revelation if we are (a) to make sense of the ideas about justice that our culture has passed down to us and (b) to avoid the pitfalls that can arise from the reciprocity motive.

Before moving on, we need to take note of another psychological mechanism (though not a motive), also with very ancient origins, which feeds into the working of justice. I refer to the human capacity for empathy which is commonly—though not always—provoked in the face of suffering in another person, or indeed of any sentient being. Dog owners are typically aware of this capacity in their pets, and many other species also display empathic behavior. In a sense, empathy constitutes the other half of the biological basis for how justice works in society. If reciprocity tells us that there must be negative consequences, authorized and carried out by the government, for a citizen who has harmed another, we gain a sense of *how serious* those consequences ought to be by tapping into our sense of empathy to determine how much suffering was inflicted. Defrauding a wealthy person and an impoverished widow both offend the norms of reciprocity, but the latter case typically attracts greater empathy and also often a heavier punishment.

Reciprocity and Dominance

It is not difficult to see that reciprocity and dominance can easily work against each other. Dominance pushes us to make distinctions between individuals on any given power or status hierarchy. You, being higher up the pecking order than me, can claim benefits and privileges that are unavailable to me. Higher status means winning in life; lower status is viewed, in a sense, as losing in life. Reciprocity, on the other hand, tends towards balance in the relationships between any two individuals (or families or groups). When I do something for you, then I can expect that you will reciprocate with an equivalent benefit to me. Given this, we may ask, how are these two motives coordinated in practice?

Often, they do not conflict in a significant way because one or other of the motives predominates in any given relationship. Friendships often show little signs of dominance and thus reciprocity is free to serve as the primary driver of the relationship. And even then, between close friends, reciprocity might not be applied in a rigid way. A kindness shown to one party might not create the expectation that it be reciprocated by the other, at least in the short- or medium-term. Similarly, in a dominance relation, for example that of a boss and an employee, the stark status differences will generally shape the interactions between the two, and there might be little interest in exchanging benefits, as occurs when social reciprocity applies. Reciprocity in this kind of relationship would mainly express itself in a negative sense through an expectation that both boss and employee would not act unfairly towards the other.

There are many circumstances, however—more so in some cultures than in others—when the two motives come into conflict and the most common outcome is that dominance takes precedence. Much depends, of course, on the systems of law and order that a society has in place, but generally speaking dominance is given much leeway in working out its ranked and unequal relationships before its excesses are brought under control. Staying with the employer-employee relationship in modern societies, we note that it is so structured by law as to preserve at least the appearance of a fair relationship. There are many rules applicable to employers which prevent them from abusing their workers, underpaying them, not providing a safe and healthy work environment, and so on. Likewise, the employee is bound by rules to provide service to his employer in ways that are fair. Yet, right from the beginning of the relationship, we can see that there are signs that dominance trumps reciprocity.

Consider the initial job interview: the careful applicant will have studied up on his future employer primarily with the aim of being able to communicate during the interview that he is familiar with its operations. He will have spent hours in preparing a job application which meets all the requirements demanded of him. At the interview, he will be quizzed extensively and tested carefully, and towards the end of the time available, he will be asked if he has any questions, as if this part of the proceedings is of little importance. And how often does a job applicant contact the interview panel afterwards to say that he is not interested in being considered for the position? Much more commonly, he waits around anxiously hoping for a phone call telling him he is successful. The relationship between company and applicant is strongly driven by the dominance motive.

We might object to that description and note that a company needs to be certain that it is selecting the right person for a position, so clearly much care should be taken in any appointment process. But this overlooks the non-rational foundations of the whole interaction and sees only the reasoning and the rationalization which are the *means* of achieving the ends determined by the dominance motive. The reality is that the vast majority of employer-employee relationships are unbalanced in favor of the former. This is because generally for an employee to lose her job is a much greater burden on herself than on her employer, and this difference is the basis of their essentially dominance-driven relationship.

In Western nations, there is a common way of thinking which says that fairness is an essential and controlling force in the way citizens relate to each other. We talk about the "rule of law" that applies to everyone no matter who they are. From the prime minister or president down to the lowliest individual, all are equal before the law, and no one is above the law. Such a principle has been of great assistance in reining in many of the excesses to which the dominance motive is prone. And yet, as the employer-employee illustration shows, beyond a certain point reciprocity as justice is relatively ineffectual against the power of dominance. To see that this is the case, consider how our society uses monetary fines as punishment for many infractions of the law. The relative "painfulness" of a fine depends on an offender's financial resources. A wealthy individual, and thus someone higher in status, will suffer little from a $1,000 fine, whereas someone on unemployment benefits will find it deeply distressing. What looks fair on the surface, equal fines for the same offence, is biased in favor of the higher-ranked people in society. Some nations have begun to recognize the problem here; Finland, for example, has a system which calibrates fines for traffic offences according to the annual income of the offender.[8] Yet, how blind most Western societies are to the limits of reciprocity in relation to the power of dominance is shown by how controversial and radical such an arrangement is seen to be.

What I hope is apparent in this discussion is the frailty of the social reciprocity motive when it comes up against pressure from that of dominance. It appears that a large, complex society will move in the direction of inequality unless there exist powerful ideological or religious commitments towards equality which are able to work to correct such a process. Perhaps, too, in the smaller groups we participate in, a similar process might be observed over time.

---

8. A helpful discussion of this idea, from the point of view of the US Constitution, can be found in Schierenbeck, "The Constitutionality," 1869–1926. See also Fiske, "The Four Elementary Forms." Fiske's four forms of sociality include three which broadly match the attachment, dominance, and reciprocity motives which I have discussed. His fourth, which he terms "market pricing," is a development of reciprocity such that it takes account of ratio rather than absolute values.

These, then, are some of the ways that the reciprocity motive operates in our lives as individuals and also in the wider society. Having been part of human social life for millions of years, it obviously has some important advantages for us as social animals. And yet, we can see, too, some of its limitations. To find a perspective on it that is informed by our faith, let us now turn to the Scriptures.

The Biblical Witness

Reciprocity Shapes Social Expectations and Behavior

As a purely social phenomenon, we frequently find reciprocity at work in the Scriptures. For example, when an angel visits Manoah and his wife to announce to them that she will bear a son who will be called Samson, Manoah is quick to offer a meal in reciprocation for the blessing he and his wife will receive (Judg 13:8–20). On the other hand, we find Nabal failing not only in his duty of hospitality to a group of David's men but also in neglecting to reciprocate for the "protection" provided by them, and in David's eyes this was to be accounted a grievous affront. Only due to the efforts of Abigail, Nabal's wife, to compensate for his failing did Nabal not suffer immediate death at David's hands (1 Sam 25:2–38).

We see reciprocity at work in a powerful way in the story of Naaman, the commander of the Syrian army. When he learned that there was a prophet in Israel who could cure him of his leprosy, he visited the king of Israel with a letter from his own king requesting that he be healed. Knowing himself subordinate to his Syrian counterpart, the king of Israel felt strongly compelled to comply with the request, but knowing its impossibility, he saw it as a maneuver to provoke conflict. Only the prophet Elisha's intervention saved the king from a serious failure in social reciprocity (2 Kgs 5:1–14).

One of the common contexts of reciprocity in the Scriptures is hospitality. This obligation to open one's home to a visitor, even to a stranger, it seems, was part of a broad Middle Eastern cultural norm. In the New Testament, however, we see the occasional challenge to social expectations surrounding the outworking of this expression of the motive. In the Gospels, some religious leaders chide Jesus for his habit of receiving hospitality from those for who are outside the system, as it were, people whom one should avoid in order not to be obliged to return a favor. Thus, tax collectors, prostitutes, and others whose work marked them either as immoral or ritually unclean ate with the Lord. In doing so, Jesus stretched the rules of reciprocity beyond their assumed limits.

Expectations of reciprocity are clear in the case of Zacchaeus. To him, Christ's willingness to honor him with a visit, despite his employment as a tax collector, was a surprising and unexpected sign of God's generosity and prompted his "return favor" of repairing the harm from fraudulent actions he engaged in as part of his work (Luke 19:1–10). This illustrates a central theme in Jesus' teaching: God shows to us an entirely unmerited graciousness, a graciousness that knows that the recipient cannot repay, and asks only that we follow suit in our relations with others. Reciprocity does not strictly apply. *"If you love those who love you, what benefit is that to you? For even sinners love those who love them. And if you do good to those who do good to you, what benefit is that to you? For even sinners do the same. And if you lend to those from whom you expect to receive, what credit is that to you? Even sinners lend to sinners, to get back the same amount. But love your enemies, and do good, and lend, expecting nothing in return, and your reward will be great, and you will be sons of the Most High, for he is kind to the ungrateful and the evil. Be merciful, even as your Father is merciful"* (Luke 6:32–36). From this we can see that for Jesus' followers, reciprocity is seriously qualified in light of the norm-breaking generosity of the heavenly Father.

Reciprocity as Justice in the Scriptures

A Consistent Message . . .

The idea of social reciprocity as justice runs right throughout the Scriptures from the first pages of Genesis—where Adam and Eve, having been gifted with an abundantly fruitful garden to live in, are bound by a simple dietary rule—right till the last chapter of the book of Revelation in which we are reminded that there can be no full justice in this world but only in the age to come. As the Lord Jesus says, *"I am coming soon, bringing my recompense with me, to repay everyone for what he has done"* (Rev 22:12).

In reading the Scriptures, we find that they do not always align with our own cultural expectations. Mostly, it is true, what we observe makes sense to us, and we pass over its many instances without much thought. So, at least in principle, we can see the justice of the situation in which Noah, being *"a righteous man, blameless in his generation"* (Gen 6:9) is saved along with his family, while the rest of humanity are destroyed, since *"all flesh had corrupted their way on earth"* (Gen 6:12). We might wonder whether, in fact, Noah and family really were the only good people in those days, and all the rest of humanity was utterly corrupt, but we know where the writer of the story is coming from in his idea of justice. On the other hand, as we saw when we looked at group dominance, we find ourselves wondering how it was that the Lord could order Joshua and his army to destroy every living creature in Jericho. Here, the "social unit" on which the motive operates is not, as is ours of the West, the individual, but rather the family, the tribe, the community, the city, or the nation. When this is the case, if an individual commits an offence against someone belonging to another social group, that group views the offender not as a single person with their own identity and responsibility but as simply a representative of his own group and "pay back" is therefore achieved when *any* member of the offender's group suffers punishment for the crime. To our Western way of thinking, this is completely unfair, for surely the one responsible must pay. And we are supported in our understanding by a passage such as that found in the book of Ezekiel, where the Lord, through the prophet, declares that the proverb, "The fathers have eaten sour grapes, and the children's teeth are set on edge" no longer applies, and that *"this proverb shall no more be used by you in Israel. Behold, all souls are mine; the soul of the father as well as the soul of the son is mine: the soul who sins shall die"* (Ezek 18:3–4; see also Jer 31:29–30).

And yet, the Joshua passage does carry a message of special importance for us in our cultural situation—something we *need* to hear—that we as individuals cannot isolate ourselves morally from others but must bear *some* responsibility for others' actions; our community bears—certainly in a weakened sense—the character of a family. In the church, this is even more the case. Paul captures the psychology of this matter when he writes of the believing community: *"If one member suffers, all suffer together; if one member is honored, all rejoice together"* (1 Cor 12:26).[9] We can think, too, of the case of incest in the Corinthian church; there the apostle shames the whole community: *"And you are arrogant! Ought you not rather to mourn?"* (1 Cor 5:2). From this, we might conclude that we

---

9. Though pursuing this matter further would take us beyond my purposes here, it is worth noting in passing that, in notions of corporate responsibility that we come across in the Old Testament, we are being prepared for the New Testament teaching about the spread of the effects of the first sin to all people, and even more importantly how Christ is able to present his sacrifice on the cross to the Father on our behalf.

need to take care in making value judgments based on our own Western culture about how other cultures express the reciprocity motive. It is better to be guided by the word of God, which judges all "principalities and powers" and all cultures. In relying upon the Scriptures for our appreciation of how reciprocity is to shape our lives as believers, however, we need to take account of both its constant teaching *and* the ways in which it changes across the history of salvation.

Although it is easily overlooked, at the very foundation of biblical justice is that intimate connection between the people's worship of the one true God and the justice which is to mark their community life. For Israel, loving the Lord God involves acting justly towards one's neighbor and caring for the poor, the widow and the orphan, a linkage that other cultures and religions do not universally recognize. We might wonder, though, why the principle of justice figures so prominently—to an almost obsessive degree—throughout the Old Testament.

Yet when we come to the new covenant, we begin to see the wisdom of that earlier emphasis. In both Jesus' teaching and in that of the apostles, we find an understanding of sin as profoundly impacting the human heart, and of the grace of God as its necessary antidote. Yet with this message—of God's "excessive" generosity that seems to flout all the rules about justice—the basic principle of justice could easily have been overwhelmed if it had not firstly been well established. Only in the light of the cross do we see that divine grace is truly costly grace, and the cost was the Son's fulfilment of all righteousness or justice through his suffering.

Forgetting the bedrock principle of justice in God's plan has sometimes led followers of Jesus to serious distortions of the faith. For example, the apostle Paul's teaching about the power of sin and of grace working in the human heart has at times in Christian history been interpreted as undermining God's law, or at least as masking the truth that God will judge each person on what they have done. Paul complained of those who asked, concerning his own teaching, "wouldn't it be better, according to your view, if we were to continue to live sinfully, because then God's grace would abound all the more?" (Rom 6:1) "By no means!" was his response. Through identification with Christ's cross, he explained, we are given a new life which enables us to live according to that essential law of justice which so tightly binds together our worship of God and our care for others.

St. Augustine's explanations of the apostle Paul's teaching, in the late fourth and early fifth centuries, sought to oppose the view of Pelagius, who overvalued the human capacity to resist sin and minimized the work of the Holy Spirit in strengthening that capacity. However, famous theologian though he was, Augustine's teaching had to be somewhat qualified by later church councils in the light of the fundamental law of justice found in the Old Testament.[10] When nuances in the connection between law and grace were lost, as happened in some of the Reformers' use of Augustine, and also among the later Catholic Jansenists, again we find a failure to take account of the Old Testament insistence on the absolutely foundational notions of the justice of God and human moral responsibility. The basic rule that guides the motive of reciprocity undergirds all of this, and it shows itself consistently throughout the biblical witness.

. . . And a Developing Message

We have looked at the consistency of the biblical idea of justice; now let us consider changes over time that have arisen as a result of the emergence of the idea of an age to come beyond this life. First, we can say, as many others have noted, that in the Old Testament, earlier texts were written with the assumption of a shadowy and limited notion of existence after death, and this meant that the demands of justice required that punishment and reward be accomplished in this life. Such is the persistent affirmation found in the Deuteronomistic history (the books of Deuteronomy to 2 Kings): keeping God's law will lead to blessings in this life; neglecting it will result in punishment and afflictions similarly in the here and now. The view is repeatedly emphasized in many of the Psalms, in Proverbs, and elsewhere in the Old Testament. The difficulties in arguing its truth in the light of lived experience, however, were great. Writings which wrestled with the problem also found their way into the sacred Scriptures, and the matter was considered in works such as Job and Ecclesiastes and in some of the Psalms. Ecclesiastes, for example, without a theology of the age to come, oscillated, on the one hand, between wanting to argue for the value of keeping the moral law in achieving the good life, and, on the other hand, reaching the rather more sceptical conclusion: *"Behold, what I have seen to be good and fitting is to eat and drink*

---

10. See, for example, the decrees of the second Council of Orange (529). The council was not uncritically supportive of Augustine's doctrine of grace. For a discussion of the controversy over grace and human responsibility, see Weaver, *Divine Grace and Human Agency*.

and find enjoyment in all the toil with which one toils under the sun the few days of his life that God has given him, for this is his lot" (Eccl 5:18).

In the Old Testament, only in writings dating from a little before the time of Christ do we find explicit expressions of hope in the age to come, that is, in the book of Maccabees, Wisdom, Daniel, and in some late Psalms. But with that development, the problem of how God was going to vindicate the righteous and punish the unrighteous was solved, as it were. Though the evildoer might thrive in this life, divine retribution in the age to come will have the last word. As one of the seven Maccabee brothers uttered to his torturer as death drew near for him: *"One cannot but choose to die at the hands of mortals and to cherish the hope God gives of being raised again by him. But for you there will be no resurrection to life!"* (2 Macc 7:14).

Jesus' public ministry represents the continuation of this changed perspective linking God's final justice to the age to come. Thus, we find the Lord chastising the Sadducees for not accepting the truth, mostly hidden in the Old Testament, of life after death. Entering here, as well, is the idea of Jesus' death as in some way *pro nobis*, or for our sake, that is, as offered to the Father and to his justice, for the eternal salvation of mankind. Being saved in all its fullness is explicitly tied to the return of Christ as Redeemer at the end of the age. We will consider this further in the reflection below, but here it is worth emphasizing that Jesus' teaching about *rewards* to be received in the age to come is consistent with this. But this is not simply a matter of pure justice, since, as Paul's letters make clear (e.g., 1 Cor 4:7; Phil 2:13), there is at work in the believer the hidden activity of the Holy Spirit, the Spirit of divine graciousness, that undergirds any of our actions that might "merit" such rewards (cf. Jude 1:24). In the end, all is justice, yet all is grace.

Reflections of Faith

The Cross and Social Reciprocity

This conclusion—all is justice, yet all is grace—leaves a big unanswered question: if God adheres carefully to the principle of justice, and at the same time appears to contradict it through the graciousness that issues from the cross of his Son, how can we possibly understand how it all works? One of the things that we note in pondering the New Testament treatments of the significance of Christ's death is that there is no single answer to the question of its meaning. Links to the suffering servant passages in Isaiah are prominent in earlier New Testament writings, while imagery that speaks more explicitly of sacrifice predominates in later texts. Passover, redemption, reconciliation, atonement—these are the main concepts used to describe the meaning of the cross, yet none of them by itself seems to capture the full picture. What we do notice, however, is that behind each of them lies the more fundamental workings of the reciprocity motive, that is, there is a *quid pro quo*. But at the same time, as noted above, there is also present the idea of Christ's death *for us*, Christ as representing us in this reciprocal action.

Through the centuries, various attempts have been made to find a way of understanding the cross which would provide it with a convincing reasonableness, e.g., Origen's ransom theory, Anselm's satisfaction theory, and the related penal substitution theory of the Reformers, and more recently Rene Girard's scapegoat theory.[11] Each of them throws an important light of how we are to understand Christ's death for us. Yet each of them is deficient is some way. For example, some have taught that in their sinning, Adam and Eve sold humanity into the hands of Satan, and Christ's death pays the ransom necessary for its release. But such an idea hardly fits with the biblical idea that Christ has defeated the evil one in conflict rather than in a business deal! Also awkward is a purely penal substitutionary theory which holds that the believer is declared righteous by the transfer of his guilt from himself to Jesus. This would appear not to take account of scriptural passages speaking of the Spirit-led and energized actions of the Christian who participates in the power of the cross. In view of their limitations, perhaps we need to ask whether in fact it is even appropriate for us to seek after a fully rational explanation, that is, one shorn of any particular historical or cultural context. What I am questioning here are explanations of Christ's death on the cross which endeavour to stand outside of human history and take a God's-eye view of things, as it were. It may well be that such an understanding is not in fact *meant* for us.

If we take seriously the idea that it is social reciprocity that best explains our abstract idea of justice—and not the other way round!—*and* the fact that the incarnation and redemption occurred in *human history*, and cannot be understood apart from that history, then we are pushed to the following two conclusions: God's justice is not our justice, for it is

---

11. For a helpful introduction to this problem of providing a description of the meaning of Christ's redemption, see Birot, "God in Christ," 259–85.

always graced, always shaped, by an attachment-like love, and that means that the cross of Christ is always more than any abstract notion of justice. And secondly, we must think of the cross as the *fulfilment* of the preparations God set in place for that event as we find them described in the Old Testament. I am thinking here of the system of animal sacrifices that was at the heart of temple worship and the chief means by which the people's sins could be forgiven. (And note, too, that through the Eucharist, God's new covenant people continue to look to sacrifice for the forgiveness of their sins!) Theories which neglect that *historical* reality obscure something very important about the faith.

In sum, social reciprocity, the foundation for our ideas of justice, has its origins in our evolutionary history while the cross of Christ, too, is part of history, that is, of Israel's. Thus, in reflecting upon God's redemption of the human race, we cannot help but see ourselves as being immersed in history in every sense, and in this history, through the cross and resurrection, all without exception are invited to share.

Reciprocity and Punishment

The basic mechanism of social reciprocity is that beneficial actions should attract a positive response whereas damaging actions should be discouraged by being responded to in negative or pain-inflicting ways. Gratitude is one way we can respond positively; punishment provides a negative response. But what do we mean precisely by a "negative" response? If we have in mind retaliation or revenge, then we need to hear the word of Scripture which tells us that revenge is the prerogative of God (*"Vengeance is mine, says the Lord,"* Rom 12: 19), who alone can judge justly because he knows the heart of man. But if that is the case, where does that leave political authorities who are required to fulfill the duty of punishment on those who offend against the law? Here I would offer one basic point in relation to this complex question: if we wish to follow the way and the spirit of Jesus' teaching on non-retaliation, when we hear that a person has committed a crime, even a serious one, we must be willing to set aside the hope that revenge or retaliation is appropriate and look rather to a different way of dealing with the offender. Of course, some of those who harm others must be kept away from society for its own safety. Beyond that, society can also require them to repair, as far as possible, the damage they have done to victims, as well as that suffered by the wider society, for example, an increased sense of insecurity or loss of peace. That is, instead of retaliation and the "equalizing of suffering," a Christ-based system of justice would seek rather to achieve the *restoration* of that which has been damaged by the offence.

Such a change in our way of thinking is difficult for many believers who have grown up in societies which value the notion of revenge or retaliation. However, I do not believe that we can justify such attitudes in the light of the scriptural witness or of the reflection of believers over the centuries. As we have seen, the changes that Christ made to the way the social reciprocity motive was to operate among his disciples were quite radical, and as his followers today we must be careful not to return to the old ways of treating the motive as a kind of absolute rather than a relative value.

To see what a contemporary Christian source has to say on the matter of punishment, let us consider a passage from the Catholic Catechism, an authoritative description of the Catholic faith. Quoting St. Thomas Aquinas, it notes that, as a general rule, "to desire vengeance in order to do evil to someone who should be punished is illicit," but it is praiseworthy to impose restitution "to correct vices and maintain justice."[12] "Restitution" here means the restoring as far as possible of that which was lost to the victim and to the wider society as a result of a crime. Relevant, too, is the Catechism's discussion of capital punishment, and punishment more generally, by the state. There we read: "Legitimate public authority has the right and the duty to inflict punishment proportionate to the gravity of the offense. Punishment has the primary aim of redressing the disorder introduced by the offense."[13] Here, again, we observe the purpose of punishment by the state as that of repairing the disorder, that is, restitution, resulting from a crime. The text uses the word "inflict," since the offender will experience such restitution as onerous, but this does not warrant the conclusion that it should take the form of revenge.[14]

---

12. *Catechism of the Catholic Church*, para. 2302. The Catechism is a compendium or handbook containing the teaching the Catholic Church on faith and morals.

13. *Catechism of the Catholic Church*, sec. 2266.

14. The Catechism also acknowledges that criminals can be a danger to society and therefore may be legitimately removed from interaction with others. But here again, we must note that the purpose is to protect society, not to inflict suffering on the offender (even though suffering will doubtless result from such isolation). I touch on this theme further in chapter 18.

Social reciprocity operates through a simple rule which tells us to repay like with like. While it has served social groups and nations well enough, aiming as it does to hold them together, it has its limitations. As Jesus has shown, it must be modified in important ways to fit into a Christian framework.

Though the motive of social reciprocity does not drive our major purposes and action-plans in the way that dominance and attachment do, it has had, and continues to have, a profound impact on individuals and on societies and on the way those societies themselves are ordered. In Western societies, this is made clear in the way we have almost universally accepted the principles of justice and fairness. The reality that such seemingly transcendent principles are in fact the outworking of evolutionary adaptations both biological and cultural which have shaped the path toward modern civilization is another sobering reminder of the earth-bound, historical character of human reasoning. This is not to diminish its significance, since it is a kind of pointer to the image of God that we humans bear, that is, our deeper spiritual nature. Yet, it is to say that we easily over-value our reasoning abilities, and it seems that sometimes we place reason on a higher pedestal than the one that we owe the Lord God.

Now our attention turns to a quite different aspect of human nature, the motive which pushes us to reproduce, part of which is the fascinating and powerful force of sexuality.

7

Mating

We come to the last of the four social motives which we humans share with many non-human, animate fellow-creatures: mating. The term "mating" is ambiguous. In a narrow sense, it can refer to the specific act of sexual intercourse, but also to the wider activity of finding a mate or spouse. In a still wider sense—the use I have adopted here—it includes both these things as well as that activity that accompanies mating as such, which is the bonding between the partners and the sharing of the task of raising offspring, the fruit of sexual intercourse.

Mating among the Social Motives

The Relative Importance of the Mating Motive

One might ask why I have placed it last among these four motives. Surely it has a priority above that of the others since, unlike them, it relates directly to the survival of our species. Apart from the more urgent drives for food, drink, and safety—those things that keep us alive—it is mating which preserves our species through the generations and across the millennia.

Yet, while it is true that mating is of predominant importance to us in larger time scales, for the individual it ranks further down the list. This might seem surprising given that, for many people, sex-related thoughts occur quite frequently throughout the day. However, one of the points I have sought to highlight here is that most of the important drivers of our thoughts, attitudes, and actions are those which are hidden from view. Dominance, attachment, and social reciprocity are much more influential as direct contributors to the outworking of our lives. Without an understanding of their operation, we would be left with the false idea that it is a kind of neutral consciousness that we habitually live with, into which sexual thoughts intrude. It is closer to the truth to say that our consciousness is *always* driven by motives; it is never neutral, and the mating drive pushes its way into what is already a busy, motive-driven consciousness.

In terms of relative importance of motives, I need to nuance somewhat what I have just said. As we have seen in chapter 2 in our discussion of the dominance motive, that drive is, in fact, a development or a support system for the mating drive to help it work more efficiently. Looking at dominance in animals, we observe that it ranks males and females according to their reproductive potential, that is, their ability to produce healthy offspring and, in many species, to form a successful bond between male-female pairs. With that ranking in place, it then works to encourage mating between higher-ranked males and females, and to place barriers in the way of pairings among those which are lower ranked. Thus, the gene pool is improved, and the species has a greater likelihood of survival. Humans unconsciously participate in precisely this same process, so we can say that for us, mating *in itself* might be less important than the other motives in terms of how much of the time it controls our behavior, but if we include dominance as a kind of component of mating—even though it has a life of its own[1]—mating consumes the preponderance of our day-to-day energies.

The Hidden Dimension of the Mating Motive

At least on the surface, another characteristic of the mating drive is that it is more "up front" than the other drives. We have seen how the other three social motives operate mostly under the surface of our awareness; we can really only see them when we know about them and examine behavior which we can then interpret as indicators of their workings. With mating, however, it looks like we are dealing with a motive whose triggers are more obvious to us. We see a sexually provocative image, or

---

1. We can see that this is the case if we consider that dominance appears before sexual maturity in humans and continues well past menopause among women. Women who can no longer bear children are still commonly observed to present publicly in a way that accentuates their femininity.

are stimulated through our other senses, and sexual thoughts come to our minds; the connections are more direct. Yet, this is only apparently so. The truth is that *awareness* of such connections between stimulus and conscious response is a process often late in the sequence of stages which make up the activities of our mating drive at any given time.

To see how this is the case, consider the experience we have just described. We are typically confronted with many stimuli of a sexual nature, but not all of them provoke the same level of response, and this is the case even for the same stimulus presented to us at different times. This means that our readiness to be stimulated fluctuates, and this occurs because our mating drive, operating below the level of our awareness, varies in its arousability. This subconscious arousal can come about through external stimuli of which we are completely unaware or through internal processes that are at work in our body. For this reason, we can say that the mating drive, in much of its workings, is no different from the other social motives in that it also operates at a subliminal level. In passing, we may note here that this helps us understand why the mating drive is often so difficult to control. If we limit ourselves to dealing with the explicit stimuli that provoke arousal in our efforts to manage the drive, we are seeking to control it after the horse has bolted, as it were. Other, less direct measures must accompany conscious control if the drive is to be properly integrated into a mature Christian life.

The Evolution of Human Mating

In this chapter I can only deal with the topic of human mating in broad terms. In fact, I will mainly restrict myself to addressing the question of how human males and females enter into a sexual relationship and what that means for long-term relationships. This part of mating has great significance for many believers in our days, so looking at it from an evolutionary point of view can be helpful. In limiting myself to this area, I will have less to say about questions to do with mating in the sense of sexual intercourse itself. This aspect, of course, is an important part of human life, but it will not be the main theme of my discussion.

As with the other motives, so too with mating, if we are to gain a deeper understanding of it, we need to grasp how it has evolved not only in our distant non-human ancestors, but more particularly in that period of the evolution of human-like species from roughly five million years to about 50,000 years ago when what is called behaviorally modern man appeared. This was a time before many characteristics that we consider distinctively human began to develop. Thus, there was no agriculture, no large-scale communities, only very primitive art or sculpture, religious belief or ritual, and certainly no universal moral code as we understand it. All of these things emerged more fully only after the period we are considering.

During this time period, evolutionary pressures were still working to shape the way males and females related to each other. It is important to keep in mind that human creatures lived and loved then without the constraints of a developed morality. Yet, what happened then is still important to us moderns because many of the processes arising in those times continue to exist and have their effect on our thoughts and actions today.

Sexual Strategies Theory

When we reflect upon how, why, and under what circumstances human males and females come together to form mating pairs, it makes sense to think that they do so to their *mutual* or *shared* advantage, that is, that the *same* incentives spur them to bond together, to bear children, and to invest time and effort in raising them. "We're in this together, we both get meaning and a sense of accomplishment in what we are doing, and we share the work between us." This is certainly the case, but only to some extent; it is not the whole story. Here I want to review briefly the processes that would seem to work against this "mutual advantage" view of mating and bring to the fore the fact that men and women have also evolved to have their own gender-specific goals as well as strategies to achieve these goals. These processes have been extensively studied as part of a broader approach called "sexual strategies theory," proposed by David Buss and David Schmitt, which centers around the idea that, as an element of human evolution, men and women have developed ways of entering into both long-term and short-term relations with one another.[2] Its key points relevant to our theme are the following:

1. Both long- and short-term matings have been used by men and women when one or the other strategy (or a mixture of both) has

---

2. Buss and Schmitt, "Sexual Strategies Theory," 204–32. This theoretical formulation drew upon earlier seminal work by Trivers, "Parental Investment," 136–79.

provided reproductive benefits (e.g., passing on one's genes), which have outweighed the costs involved.

2. Men and woman differ in how much effort they each must put into producing children. Men devote more attention than women to short-term mating, that is, having sex and then leaving the woman to bear the consequences. For the man, his unconscious goal is simply to pass on his genes to the next generation.

3. In pursuing a *short-term* mating strategy, men had to deal with four problems: (a) "Do I mate with women of high genetic quality who are hard to attract, or do I settle for many women of lesser quality who are more available?" (b) "How do I know if a woman is available to me?" (c) "How can I tell if a woman is fertile and therefore ready to conceive and bear my child?" and (d) "How can I manage to make women pregnant but not have to stay around to care for the children?"

4. In pursuing a *long-term* mating strategy, men historically have had to answer the following questions: (a) "Which women are going to produce the best quality children for me?" (b) "How can I ensure that any child a woman has with me is actually mine (genetically)?" (c) "How do I know that a prospective partner will be a good mother (so that my children will be more likely to survive)?" and (d) "How can I tell if this potential partner is someone who is willing and able to commit to a long-term mating relationship?"

5. For women adopting a *short-term* mating strategy, she would need to ask: (a) "Does this potential short-term partner have enough resources (wealth, food, etc.) so that I will have security for myself and for my child when he leaves?" and (b), perhaps secondarily, "Is this potential partner of sufficiently high genetic quality to risk raising a child by him without his long-term presence and support?"

6. In taking a *long-term mating* approach a woman would have to deal with the following issues: (a) "How do I know if a potential partner is able and willing to invest his resources in me and our children on a long-term basis?" (b) "How can I tell if he will be a good father?" (c) "Will this man be willing and able to commit to a long-term relationship?" and (d) "Does he have the capacity to protect me and my children from other aggressive males?"

As can be seen from these points, both men and women could engage in either short-term, long-term, or indeed mixed strategies of mating with members of the opposite sex. The questions they faced for these strategies would not have been conscious ones; it is just that their minds would have worked subconsciously in a way that would have addressed them. The issues to be faced had to do with reproductive benefits, i.e., bearing a sizeable number of children, or trying for the best genetic quality of offspring, and therefore of sexual partners, or a combination of both. Important to note also is the *difference* between men and women in what they were to take account of. Women had different concerns to those of men chiefly, but not only, because they had to invest more time and energy in the gestation and nurture of any offspring they bore.

Buss and Schmitt's sexual selection theory highlights the existence of specific short-term and long-term mating strategies in men and women during the early years of human evolutionary development, but it is also the case that they are still operative among modern humans. I will give a few examples of research which illustrates the continuing existence of those subconscious strategies and thus their relevance to us today.

Mating Strategies: Female

It is at the time of fertility, i.e., around the time of ovulation, that women's attitudes unconsciously display several subtle features characteristic of a *short-term mating strategy*. This strategy involves a woman's heightened attraction to men of higher genetic quality than her current partner, i.e., strongly masculine in appearance, facial symmetry, dominant in personality, deeper voice. However, these features are preferred during ovulation *only when evaluating men on the basis of their suitability for short-term mating*. When these same masculine features are evaluated by a woman with a view to a long-term mating strategy, no such fertility cycle shift in perceptions is found.

Surveying a sample of women, researchers found that: (a) women reported greater sexual interest in, and fantasy about, men other than their partners near ovulation than during the luteal [post-fertile] phase of her period; (b) women did not report significantly greater sexual interest in, and fantasy about, their own partners near ovulation; (c) women reported that their partner was both more attentive and more "possessive" near ovulation.[3]

With research of this nature, it is important to keep in mind that the ovulation-specific processes which have been observed are typically not available to the awareness of either males or females. They operate subconsciously rather than forming part of an individual's intentional strategy.

By contrast, when women evaluated a male partner for suitability as a *long-term* mate, a different set of qualities comes to the fore. With a long-term strategy in mind, a woman's mate preferences align more closely with the characteristics that mark out a good *long-term partner*, i.e., reliability, status, resource capability, a personality suited to empathy and support, even if these qualities mean overall less masculinity. But there is a limit to this trade-off, since women still prefer long-term mates who are older, taller, and better resourced than themselves—and these are characteristics that are associated with masculinity.

In sum, then, we observe in women a complex set of subconscious predispositions towards sexual relationships that are correlated with periods of fertility. For a woman, the overarching, unconscious "goals" shaped by evolutionary processes are the following: to maximize the genetic quality of the children she bears, and/or to ensure that a suitable male provides protection and resources together with a contribution to the nurture of her children within a long-term and stable relationship.

Mating Strategies: Male

We observe something of the difference in attitude towards casual sexual relationships between the genders in a classic experiment carried out by the psychologists Russell Clarke and Elaine Hatfield during the 1980s. The study involved a group of women of average attractiveness and engaged by the researchers to carry out a task at a university campus. They had to approach male students on campus, inviting them either to go on a date, to go with them to their apartment, or to go to bed with them. The overwhelming majority of male students were willing to have a sexual liaison with the female proposer. When the researchers reversed the process so that the proposers were male students who had to approach female students, it was found that not one female student accepted such an

---

3. Gangestad et al., "Changes in Women's Sexual Interests," 975–82.

invitation. This strong difference in response between men and woman was in stark contrast to the equal numbers of men and women who accepted an invitation merely for a date rather than for sexual engagement.[4]

Apart from reflecting poorly on the moral fibre of the male subjects, the experiment demonstrates some key features of male sexuality, *understood in evolutionary terms,* as captured by sexual strategies theory. First, a greater willingness to engage in casual sex expresses the fact that there are fewer negative consequences for the man in the case when his partner falls pregnant. Second, men apply lower criteria in determining suitability for a casual liaison. That is, men have evolved to be willing to engage in sex with women of only average attractiveness. (In recent studies it has been found that women were more willing to accept similar invitations if the male proposer was especially attractive, a celebrity, or sexually skilled.[5])

We see, then, that men have evolved to pursue somewhat different strategies in their sexual relations: to maximize the number of genetic offspring a man has while minimizing the drain on his resources, time and commitments; or to ensure that he is the actual father of children he cares for through a long-term, exclusive relationship with a woman who bears his offspring. Note that for both sexes, the continuation of their genes is at the core of their mating strategies, but how this happens is different since females have to invest more time and effort in bringing this about.

What is of interest for our purposes is to note that there appear to have evolved some unsavory "moral" tendencies in both men and women. For men there is the callousness that would impregnate many women but not contribute to the care of his children; among women, there is the willingness to conceive through a male who is not her long-term partner, and then to deceitfully act as if the offspring of that liaison were in fact those of her partner, thus tricking him into thinking that he is helping to raise children who are not the bearers of his genes.

And yet, we need to keep in mind that evolved characteristics which we observe in humans when studied in large numbers, do not necessarily determine the way that we as individuals think and act. Cultural and religious training can work to either support or override the tendencies we see in sexual strategies theory. Thus, in samples of intrinsically motivated

---

4. Clark and Hatfield, "Gender Differences," 39–55. For a recent update of this research see Tappé et al., "Gender Differences in Receptivity," 323–44.

5. Conley, "Perceived Proposer Personality Characteristics," 309–29.

Christians (i.e., those involved in the practice of their faith for intrinsic [religious] rather than social or status reasons) long-term sexual strategies are predominant, as one would hope![6] Religious teaching against premarital and extramarital sex shapes actual behavior.

The Scriptural Witness

Old Testament

The crucial difference in mating practices between, on the one hand, human (and human-like) life as it existed between five million and 50,000 years ago, and, on the other, that which is portrayed in the Scriptures comes down to culture. In the biblical accounts we find agricultural and pastoral societies, cities, established states and institutions, extensive trade, and religious belief and practice. Unlike in earlier times with their less institutionalized practices, the peoples of the scriptural times operated—at least as an ideal—with well-honed rules for bringing about mating pairs. In most cases there might not have been much input from the prospective partners in the decisions that would create a couple. Much would have depended on the families and especially the parents of the bride and groom. And as is the case today in many Middle Eastern cultures, pairings between cousins would have made up the bulk of marriages. Marriage arrangements that are described in the Old Testament are those of Hagar's son (Gen 21:21), Isaac (Gen 24), Judah's son, Er (Gen 38:6), Caleb's daughter, Achsah (Judg 1:12–13), Saul's daughters, Merab and Michal (1 Sam 18:17, 21) and Ruth (Ruth 3:1–4). Yet there are also examples of couples coming together according to their own wishes, for example, Samuel and his wife (Judg 14:1–4), Isaac and Rebecca (Gen 24:57–58), and Esau and his two wives, Judith and Basemath (Gen 26:34–5). So, we can see that the rules did not apply rigidly but allowed for some variation.

When it comes to descriptions of the pairing or courting process, that is, the stages by which a man and woman become husband and wife, what is of particular interest is that typically we do not find descriptions of *actual* betrothals/marriages. The most prominent accounts are those that are *figurative*. Thus, Hosea depicts the Lord God wooing Israel as a renewed and forgiven wife (Hos 2), and Ezekiel describes in even more

---

6. See, for example, Barkan, "Religiosity," 407–17.

detail the Lord's betrothal of his people as a figure of the covenant of Sinai. Even the material found in the Song of Songs might, according to some scholars, have a symbolic sense that relates God and his people to the figures of the lover and his beloved in that text.

Instances of opportunistic mating, that is, adultery, also figure in the Scriptures, though they are always portrayed as morally reprehensible. Thus, David is condemned for having sexual relations with Bathsheba, Uriah's wife, and Hosea's wife, Gomer, is judged similarly for her adultery with other men. Again, we also find numerous figurative examples of unfaithfulness on the part of Israel in its relationship with the Lord.

New Testament

In the New Testament witness, for the most part, we find the same institutions and social customs as operated during the Old Testament period. However, absent are any of the overtly sexualized narratives that we observe in Hosea and Ezekiel. The betrothal of Joseph and Mary is related in sober terms. Paul's advice to believing couples who are contemplating marriage contains nothing of a "romantic" nature, with the focus on the management of sexual passions and the difficulties that married couples would face in those times (1 Cor 7:25–38).

We observe in the Old Testament the existence of betrothal customs that were not particular to the people of God but shared by surrounding cultures and indeed by many societies worldwide. In the New Testament there is little evidence to suggest any significant move away from these customs. Given that this is the case, it comes as no surprise that, when we consider the deeper, biologically evolved features which sexual strategies theory describes, we also observe those features in the biblical approach.

Implicit in Buss and Schmitt's theory is the idea that women must take greater caution in entering a mating relationship due to the much more significant risks such a relationship carries for her. This is witnessed to in Scriptures by the fact that virtually always the active initiative to seek a partner is taken by men rather than women. The man proposes, but it is the woman who decides.

Furthermore, according to the same theory, the shared goal of a man and woman in a mating relationship is the generation of offspring. In a long-term bond, which is the only one that should concern believers, this requires the investment of both parties in the work of nurturing and raising a family. Indeed, the whole evolutionary process of mating aims for this very purpose—marriages are "designed" for the begetting of offspring. Again, we see this mirrored most powerfully in the Scriptures in the joy of giving birth especially among women such as Sarah, Rebecca, Rachel, Hannah, and Elizabeth, each of whom had difficulty conceiving.

Those same processes, so the theory indicates, point towards a specialization in the functions of man and woman in a mating relationship. As we have seen, a key criterion for a woman is: "Can this man provide for me (and protect me) when I am vulnerable?" She is looking, therefore, for a man who is of good build, willing and able to provide a safe environment, resourceful and intelligent, as well as someone who displays the kind of qualities which would make a good husband and father. He, for his part, asks, "Will she be a good mother, and produce healthy offspring, caring for them in their early years?" Though he is not usually conscious of this question, his thoughts and actions (e.g., seeking well-rounded body shape, smooth gait, healthy hair and facial complexion, particular personality characteristics, etc.) suggest that this is precisely what is being sought. Although these matters are rarely addressed in the biblical text (but see, for example, Ezek 16:1–14) what we do find are assumptions about the differing roles to be fulfilled by husbands and wives which closely reflect that which the theory suggests.

Note, for example, the distinctive ways that God relates to Mary and Joseph. Mary receives the visit of the angel because the divine message connects firstly to her as the one who would bear a savior. Joseph, on the other hand, is informed in a dream about the need to take flight to safety in Egypt. His responsibility was to take care of the Holy Family: *"And he rose and took the child and his mother by night and departed to Egypt"* (Matt 2:14). A similar differentiation is observed in the way the Lord, through an angel, relates to Manoah and his wife prior to her giving birth to Samson (Judg 13). The angel appeared to her for matters relating to the pregnancy, whereas hospitality, or how the couple were to engage with the "stranger" (angel), was addressed by Manoah. Finally, we recall that, at the foot of the cross, Jesus entrusts Mary to the beloved disciple so that he might care for her in the absence of her son, and presumably, too, of her deceased husband, Joseph. In each of these examples we are not simply observing the outworking of a particular culture that might, in different circumstances, have been otherwise. More than that, the scriptural accounts speak of the *divine* accommodation to that part of our permanent heritage as creatures which is the specialization of function of men and women in their mating relationships.

Reflections of Faith

Mating and Dominance: Selecting a Spouse

One issue for believers arises from the observation that dominance (gaining high status in order to choose the best partner) appears to be important in the process of mate selection, or, in the Christian scheme of things, marriage. How might the believer, seeking to find a spouse, respond to this? Do we ignore our natural desire for physical beauty and the urge to enter sexual relations with those who are more attractive among the opposite sex? Should we avoid partnering with someone who has a chronic mental illness or a serious physical impairment? We might briefly note two considerations relevant to these questions.

First, as humans we participate with God in the work of creation, that is, the creation which is good, so we must be cautious about bringing into the world those whose life is going to be marred by serious suffering. While Christian teaching encourages large families, it also warns against valuing human births more than spiritual births. Among Catholics, the high esteem in which the consecrated life (e.g., monks, nuns) is held within the faith captures this ordering of values. (There will be no "giving and taking in marriage" in the age to come, so mating will no longer be needed.) All this means that those of us who possess significant defects, transmissible to potential offspring and likely the cause of great trial to children we would have, should think twice before entering marriage. In this case, a believer would be advised to give thought to the work of spiritual fruitfulness as a key direction for his or her life. "How can I exercise my gifts so as to assist in bringing others to faith in Jesus Christ?" might be the question that shapes the life of such a person.

Secondly, for believers who are well suited to marriage, we can agree that it is appropriate to take physical attributes into account when considering who might be suitable to marry, but we must also take note of the reminder of the Scriptures, that spiritual beauty is of equal or more value than that of the body. This means that when it comes to mating, in the new covenant, the realm of the spirit holds a higher place than the values implied by the dominance motive. *"Likewise, wives . . . let your adorning be the hidden person of the heart with the imperishable beauty of a gentle and quiet spirit, which in God's sight is very precious"* (1 Peter 3:4). While the Scriptures do not deny the value of feminine beauty along with the relevant masculine qualities, they qualify them by highlighting the importance of personal and spiritual characteristics that mark the follower of Christ. Physical features are important in choosing a spouse, but more so are maturity of faith, generosity in love, humility of soul, and an inner spiritual strength. In short, the functions which dominance serves in preserving and enhancing species survival can continue to operate in our work of selecting a mate for life, but these must be subordinated to spiritual considerations so that partners not be mismatched or *"unequally yoked"* (2 Cor 6:14).

Mating and Dominance: The Spousal Relationship

In our discussion of dominance, we concluded that, while it might have some legitimate purposes (especially in relation to authority in social relations which we will explore further in chapter 10), it was a force in our makeup that had the capacity to undermine, in a quite insidious manner, the teaching of Christ about humility and love, and against pride, vanity, and selfishness. And yet, when we think about the fundamental mechanisms of mating and why they came to exist in their present form, we are struck by the elements of dominance that are inherent in their operation. Consider the process of entering a mating relationship: the characteristics distinctive of males, that is, possession of a stronger sexual urge, fewer risks in mating, and the very mechanics of the sexual act, make them eminently suited to be the sex which *actively* initiates mating relationships. The male *moves* towards the female; he *enters* her world and her body. She, for her part, in seeking a mate, *displays* rather than approaches; she responsively *invites* and *accommodates*. To her falls the task of weighing up the risks and benefits in a much more considered way than the male because she will bear most or even all the burden of a pregnancy and the nurture of children. Now, reflecting on these obvious differences between the sexes, it would be surprising indeed if nature had arranged the initial phase of mating this way, only to have it all set aside once a long-term relationship had commenced.

In fact, within such a relationship, we do see signs of similar dynamics. The male will normally be occupied with managing the relationship between the outside world and the family, for example, by garnering resources for its survival and protecting his wife and children from harm. Her efforts will be given over to the care and nurture of young children and assisting resource acquisition in ways and to the extent to which her other responsibilities allow. Add to this the masculine features of greater size and strength, and a deeper voice, and we are forced to the conclusion that nature has inserted into mating relationships an element of dominance.

Certainly, such an arrangement was adaptive in the circumstances that humans found themselves in during ancient times. The presence of gender differences in dominance led to success, whereas—presumably—their absence did not. Those mechanisms still exist and operate in modern humans, although in Western cultures there is now strong resistance to their presence within marriage relationships. Our world is vastly different from that of our prehistoric forebears and so there is a mismatch between our biologically evolved dominance motive and our contemporary cultural environment. Fortunately, there is much more for us to consider than this motive.

As we will see in the next chapter when we consider how mating connects with the attachment motive, dominance does not fully define mating bonds, and when viewed in terms of power we can see that both males and females can exert significant power in relating to each other. However, the fact remains that as believers we need to take into account the reality of dominance in the relationship between spouses and not deny its existence as part of our biological heritage. When we consider the matter more fully in chapter 17, however, we will gain a clearer idea of how the elements of dominance can be reoriented to the more socially useful purpose of authority within the marriage relationship.

As we have seen, the core purposes of the mating motive are quite straightforward, working as they do towards the continuation of the species through the transmission of genes. However, the outworking is rather complex and is based on processes that evolved many millions of years ago. The societies in which we now live in are a world away from this past era, and this creates tensions in the way the mating drive expresses itself in our individual lives. For believers, a special tension has to do with the role physical attractiveness plays in selecting a spouse. Another difficulty arises when we try to take account of the obvious relevance of dominance-related behavior in marriages. This latter issue will require further reflection on the mating motive, especially as it connects with the other social motives. Our next chapter will address these connections.

8

Mating: Further Dimensions of the Motive

IN THE PREVIOUS CHAPTER, we considered sexual strategies theory and the place of the dominance motive as it relates to mating. As already suggested, mating, especially as it expresses itself in long-term relationships, involves other motives, including those of attachment and social reciprocity. In what follows I want to round out the discussion of mating with a few ideas about these inter-connections.

Mating and Attachment: How Are They Related?[1]

Unsurprisingly, it has been found that the attachment relationships which shaped us during our early years are a key factor affecting the quality of the long-term mating relationship we call "marriage." Couples who grew up in families in which they developed secure attachments are more likely to stay together in their marriage than those with anxious-insecure or avoidant-insecure attachment interior models. This is understandable when we think of how insecurities can make individuals in a marriage more vulnerable to anxiety, threats, anger, and persistent hostility, that is, all those things which can do damage to the marriage bond.

Furthermore, the strength of attachment is also related to the quality of a couple's sexual relationship.[2] It has been found that securely attached

---

1. For a review of some of the literature on this topic, see Stefanou and McCabe, "Adult Attachment," 2499–2507.

2. For a review of the relevant research, see Feeney, "Adult Romantic Attachment,"

individuals are more likely to indicate satisfaction in sexual relations with their partner as well as in being able to initiate sexual activity (rather than it being initiated by one partner exclusively). They also report fewer "one-night stands" or sexual activity outside their primary relationship. Among avoidantly attached individuals, by contrast, we see a tendency to evade psychological intimacy and therefore to have more "one-night stands" and sex without love.[3] Supporting these findings are those of a Canadian study of couples aged from twenty-one to seventy-five years which found that anxious or avoidant attachment in an individual was linked to lower sexual satisfaction.[4]

Delving a little further into the mechanisms that connect mating and attachment, we can see that the avoidant and anxious patterns of attachment lead the individual to veer in either of two directions: those with avoidant styles are strongly resistant to opening up their self-boundaries to any other person, since their early life experiences demonstrated to them that doing so often led to rejection or unresponsiveness. The resulting self is diminished and tends to engage with others chiefly by using them rather than being fully open with them. This serves to protect their self from hurt. Insecure-anxious attachment, on the other hand, shows itself in individuals who are so needy of emotional support that they lack discernment or self-control in maintaining healthy self-boundaries; they tend to open those boundaries, often too easily, by calling upon others to care for them.

By comparison, in the securely attached individual we find one who is more able to discern when and how far it is appropriate to reveal herself in her relationships and to allow another person entry into her psychological "inner sanctum." It is in romantic bonds especially that such discernment is most important, since secure attachment in an individual gives them the level of trust and confidence needed to open up their self, and later, if marriage ensues, also those aspects of the intimate self that have to do with sexuality.

It would seem that the kind of society we live in will have an influence on how the connection between mating and attachment shows itself. During the period of early human development, before large-scale societies existed, sexual strategies theory suggests that short-term mating

---

456–81.

3. Feeney, "Adult Romantic Attachment," 472.

4. Butzer and Campbell, "Adult Attachment," 141–54. See also Birnbaum et al., "When Sex Is More," 929–43.

would have been common, with many entering sexual relationships without the intention of them being permanent. Later, with the emergence of societies and the morality that strengthened those societies, long-term mating would have been favored through marriage-like institutions. One might imagine that this would have offered better prospects for both male and female gene transmission across generations. Thus, the pathway towards the linking of attachment and mating that we observe in our times would have been established. It must be acknowledged, however, that today in Western societies there are several factors, not least of which is the ready availability of effective contraception, which have weakened that connection.

The Scriptural Witness

The Scriptures are unanimous in affirming the importance of preserving the link between long-term bonding as represented by secure attachment relationships and the process of mating in its broader sense. In the second chapter of Genesis, the foundational character of the male-female relationship within human existence is established. In a truly singular way, men and women are meant for each other: *"This at last is bone of my bones and flesh of my flesh,"* exclaimed Adam, and the text continues: *"Therefore, a man shall leave his father and his mother and hold fast to his wife, and they shall become one flesh. And the man and his wife were both naked and were not ashamed."* (Gen 2:23a, 24–25). Here we see attachment, in its aspects of closeness and vulnerability, linked intimately to sexuality. Following the fall described in Genesis 3, we meet one of its unfortunate consequences: *"Your desire shall be for your husband, and he shall rule over you"* (Gen 3:16). Some of that original mutuality assured by a secure attachment relationship between husband and wife is lost, and into the vacuum enters an excess of dominance.

The damaging pattern set down in the third chapter of Genesis continues to show itself through much of the Scriptures. We see it in the polygamy of many of its major players, e.g., Abraham, Esau, Jacob, Gideon, David, Solomon, and several kings, since having more than one wife is necessarily the acceptance of a weaker attachment relationship with each of the wives. Yet, something of the original ideal appears in the words of the late prophet Malachi, which he addressed to the people of Judah: *"The Lord was witness between you and the wife of your youth, to whom you have been faithless, though she is your companion and your wife by covenant. Did He not make them one, with a portion of the Spirit in their union?"* (Mal 2:14–15a).

Still, by the time of Christ, impoverished attachment relationships within marriage had become institutionalized within Jewish culture, at least if the picture painted by the German Lutheran New Testament scholar Joachim Jeremias is close to the truth: "We have therefore the impression that Judaism in Jesus' time . . . had a very low opinion of women . . . She [was] kept as far as possible shut up away from the outer world, submissive to the power of her father or her husband, and . . . inferior to men from a religious point of view."[5]

In that setting, Jeremias goes on to describe the remarkably different attitude of Jesus towards the marriage relationship. Emphasizing God's original intention for a deep, mutual bond between a husband and wife, he sets aside every legally sanctioned hindrance to its fulfilment. Writes Jeremias, "[Jesus] was not content to stand up for monogamy; he completely forbade divorce when talking to his disciples, and unhesitatingly and fearlessly criticized the Torah for permitting divorce because of the hardness of human hearts."[6]

Elsewhere in the New Testament we come across apostolic teaching which is in line with Jesus' attitudes and teaching. In the letter to the Hebrews, we find the dignity of marriage being affirmed against every attempt to diminish its importance: *"Let marriage be held in honour among all"* (Heb 13:4), while in 1 Peter, following a discussion of leadership in the marriage relationship, we note a concluding affirmation of the equality that is to exist between husband and wife. The author, reminding husbands of the humanity and vulnerability of their wives and the need to care for them, ends with a brief but powerful statement of the basis upon which Christian teaching on marriage stands: *"[Wives] are heirs with you of the grace of life"* (1 Pet 3:7). Such mutual respect also lies behind Paul's teaching about sexual relations in marriage: *"The husband should give to his wife her conjugal rights, and likewise the wife to her husband. For the wife does not have authority over her own body, but the husband does. Likewise, the husband does not have authority over his own body, but the wife does"* (1 Cor 7:3–4). Without that kind of attitude present at the heart of a marriage, the mutual attachment between husband and wife

---

5. Jeremias, *Jerusalem*, 375.
6. Jeremias, *Jerusalem*, 376.

is difficult to sustain. Efforts to be responsive to the sexual needs of the other party, as Paul advises, are a key part of assisting that attachment bond. Conversely, a solid attachment to each other is a firm foundation for a healthy and nurturing sex life.

Although the well-known Ephesians 5 passage on the relation between husbands and wives does not speak explicitly of the sexual relationship, the intermingling of "love" and "bodily" language hints that sexual love was in mind when these words were written. *"Wives, submit to your husbands . . . Husbands, love your wives . . . husbands should love their wives as their own bodies"* (Eph 5:22, 25, 28). Moreover, the comparison of husbandly love with that of Christ for his Church in the text is strongly reminiscent of the imagery found in Ezekiel 16:1–14, a passage suffused with chaste sexuality, where the Lord God, through purification and adornment, prepares Israel to become his bride. In both texts, the emotional bonds of marriage are linked overtly to the imagery of sexual union.

The Scriptures, then, witness to a developing understanding of the relationship between husbands and wives as being one of deep emotional and spiritual mutuality. This bond was built on a mutual attachment relationship but also on the conviction of the New Testament church that *"there is no male and female, for you are all one in Christ Jesus"* (Gal 3:28). In affirming this mutuality between the sexes, therefore, the Scriptures are supportive of the idea that sexual love, and the long-term attachment bond of marriage which is so beneficial for the nurture of children, go hand in hand.

A Reflection of Faith

Insecure Attachment and a Healthy Marriage

For married believers who ponder the connections between mating in its broader sense and attachment, what I have written might lead them to a position of uncertainty and even anxiety about their own marriage. What are the possibilities of a healthy marriage if my attachment history is fraught with damaged or difficult relationships? What am I to make of the emotional distance from my spouse that has crept into our marriage, and does this relate to the cooling of our sexual relations? It seems, too, that such questioning might well be on the increase. It has been found in a large US sample that between 1988 and 2011, that is, over the period of a generation, the percentage of securely attached persons decreasing by 7 percent with a commensurate increase in less secure forms of attachment.[7] This is not a large change, but it is certainly in an undesirable direction. It is not clear what specifically it is due to, but it could be part of a longer-term, generalized cultural weakening of relationships in favor of individual autonomy (see chapter 11 for further reflections on this change).

Earlier we briefly considered the question of our attachment history in connection with our attachment to God. Focusing here on couples, we note that adjustments or changes to attachment security of one partner are usually reflected in that of the other.[8] Thus, for example, a movement in the direction towards a more secure attachment style in one spouse is commonly reflected in similar changes in the other. This reminds us that our sense of psychological security depends in large part upon our relationships. Growing a healthy and close connection with our spouse opens the way to improvements in attachment security. However, accomplishing that sort of growth is not as straightforward as it might seem. Efforts to change attachment style by altering one's own personal qualities or habits, *apart from changes in one's relationships*, have limited effect. Because attachment quality is *relatively* stable over the span of years and resistant to change, our individual efforts at change usually run out of energy before we see any positive changes. The task, then, is one for a couple together to pursue rather than an individual.

Interestingly, other relationships can be of use in the work of strengthening couple attachment. For example, it has been observed that partial improvements in attachment style can occur within the relationship that exists between client and therapist in psychotherapy. Such relationships have been likened to an abbreviated, diluted form of attachment. We might wonder how this could happen in what is typically a short-term relationship. We know that successful therapy outcomes such as reduced anxiety, improved mood, and the like are more likely when there is a strong therapist-client bond.[9] So what appears to be happening in therapy is that its positive effects can flow on to more long-term relationships such as marriages. For example, if a woman grows in her sense

---

7. Konrath et al., "Changes in Adult Attachment Styles," 326–48.

8. Hudson et al., "Coregulation," 845–57.

9. For more recent examples of this kind of evidence, see Zuroff and Blatt, "The Therapeutic Relationship," 199–206; Falkenström et al., "Therapeutic Alliance," 317–28.

of security through contact with her therapist, she can become a better "safe haven" for her husband, and this can also lead to him becoming the same to her. It is as if the therapeutic relationship takes some of the pressure off the marriage and gives some room for couples to interact more positively with each other.

Coming to recognize and understand the attachment processes which have shaped our lives can be a sobering experience. To realize that constraints on how we live our adult life have been laid down during the first three years of our life, for example and that we do not have full, conscious control over any deficiencies we find in ourselves can prompt us to feel somewhat trapped, especially if we sense that we are one of those 40 percent or more of the population who have some degree of insecure attachment. Yet, as I have noted, marriages can be a source of change for the better, and even when the other party themselves has problems with attachment, outside help can pave the way for improvements in both marital attachment and an improved physical relationship.

We need also to consider that even securely attached individuals, as adults, frequently do not *feel* secure, that is, in the existential sense. Life itself, to the extent that its origins and its destiny are a mystery, and the way we conduct our lives, with our unloving actions and our failures to love, all this produces uncertainties for us in our relationship with God. And no amount of support from other individual human beings (who themselves are in the same quandary) can fully allay those anxieties. Thus, we have no option but to humbly and, in our vulnerability, open ourselves up to the One who offers us what we might call "existential security," that security that comes from a close relationship with Jesus Christ.

Mating and Social Reciprocity

Recall that the function of the social reciprocity motive is to make sure pairs and larger groups of people work well together, not least by keeping the relationships in them fair and balanced. Whereas dominance is based on differences between people, and attachment is a kind of hidden glue for relationships, reciprocity operates in a more open manner to keep groups alive, mostly on the assumption of equal status. When we look at the mating relationship of marriage through the lens of reciprocity, we can see how important it is to the health of such a bond. Benefits that each bestows upon the other will need to be at least roughly equal over the long term. It is a serious threat to a relationship for one party, in a sustained manner, to provide benefits to the other without there being reciprocity between them (due to the other's sense of entitlement or their neglect). We find this issue played out in marriages in the question of who carries out which tasks around the house. In times when husbands committed most of their time to their employment outside of the home, women reciprocated by managing the household and keeping it running, this being more suited to them given their responsibilities for the children. The relationship was considered—and probably was—mutually beneficial. However, as many occupations became, for men, opportunities for self-advancement rather than onerous and unfulfilling, the household equation came to be viewed as unbalanced. The wife was seen as carrying more of the overall burden than the husband. Add to this the growing attraction for women of the idea of paid employment and the resulting reduction in number of children born to a couple, and we find that the housework arrangements of former times now seem unfair.

Thinking about the matter of reciprocity in marriage more generally, we know that imbalances can arise not only in the dividing up of household chores, but also in how the work of raising children is shared, what are the relative contributions to the household finances or how that money is spent, or in how couples relate in the bedroom. These days there appears to be less tolerance for persistent imbalance in a relationship, and this is encouraged by a reduction in both legal impediments and negative social attitudes to separation and divorce. No longer do individuals in an unbalanced marriage feel that they must persevere in their relationship but can now decide to leave their spouse and perhaps enter a new marriage. Yet, the answer to the question of the best way to deal with the changes I have described is not obvious, since the marriage relationship typically has complexities not found in other social bonds. I will offer some further thoughts on this below in the section, "A Reflection of Faith."

The Scriptural Witness

What signs can we discern that the biblical witness has considered the way mating—or in this case, marriage—interacts with the motive of reciprocity? The most obvious indications of this awareness are in the contractual nature of the marriage relationship. Since marriage in biblical times was as much a matter of two families entering into a relationship as of two individuals, the focus of mutual benefit was, in large part, on the families themselves. How would this prospective union affect us as a family? would be the key question. Negotiations could be lengthy and often involved payment of some kind, e.g., Jacob and Hamor (Gen 34:12); David and Saul (1 Sam 18:17, 27). By contrast, there was less interest in reciprocity between husband and wife. A rough and ready balance was understood to exist between the husband fulfilling his obligations to provide for his wife and do what he could to help her to bear and to raise children, while she for her part would carry out whatever else was needed for family life to run smoothly. Sometimes, as in the good wife of Proverbs 31, we see a greater degree of mutuality, but overall, by Jesus' time, we would have to conclude, following the evidence of Jeremias,[10] that once the betrothal negotiations had been settled, cultural expectations about the respective roles of husband and wife shaped their relationship more than the pursuit of a balanced, reciprocally beneficially way of life together.

The New Testament rarely describes any aspects of specific married couples, so it is difficult to gain an impression of how reciprocity might touch on the lives of believing husbands and wives. One example would be that of the Roman Jewish-Christians Aquila and his wife, Priscilla, who had contact with Paul. What is said of them in the book of Acts gives little away as to their relationship, but something unusual about the way they are referred to is the fact that two of the three times they are mentioned she is named before her husband. It is not clear why this is so, but at the very least it indicates that Priscilla is not the kind of wife who hides in her husband's shadow. In fact, women figure quite prominently as coworkers with Paul in his missionary activity, and while we do not know whether they are married, they certainly are not confined to domestic living nor always accompanied by a responsible male. Add to this the strong reciprocity of Paul's teaching about the sexual rights and obligations of husbands and wives (1 Cor 7:3–4), and our best guess is that at least within the fledgling Christian communities of which we have evidence, reciprocity would have more strongly shaped the marriage relations of believers than was the case, for example, in the traditional Jewish communities of Galilee in Jesus' early years.

---

10. Jeremias, *Jerusalem*, 359–76.

A Reflection of Faith

Reciprocity in Contemporary Marriage

As believers, what are we to make of the major chasm between contemporary and biblical understandings of how the principle of justice is applied to the marriage relationship? In our own time, because social norms about marriage have changed significantly over a period of about two generations and continue to show movement, what counts as balanced in one decade can seem decidedly unfair in the next. That makes it difficult to settle upon ways of operating that would be of lasting value. But the change we see in our times is not only to do with wives taking up employment outside the home but perhaps just as much to do with the influence of feminist notions of equality. Equality between the sexes as commonly understood in contemporary Western societies requires that men and women actively work to avoid specialization in their marriage. Nothing is to be linked to "male" or "female" because to do so, according to this way of thinking, is to restrict the freedom especially of women but also of men to shape their lives as they see fit without the constraints of gender expectations. Managing domestic life becomes a matter of spouses negotiating arrangements regarding the chores to be carried out, continuously monitoring "fairness," and, if finances allow, outsourcing tasks such as cleaning, child-minding, laundry, and even food preparation. For, by having other people carry out this work, the scope for conflict between spouses is reduced, and there is the added bonus that more time is made available for each party to get on with their life outside the home.

The "reasonableness" of this way of thinking, however, masks a failure to recognize the way we humans evolved and the fundamental motives which drive us. Nature has not produced specialization in how husbands and wives function within a family without good "reason." The whole mating process is a demanding one, requiring much effort on the part of our mating motive if it is to achieve its "goal" of passing on genes not just to offspring but to the offspring of those offspring! Many of the personal characteristics we instil in our children are precisely those qualities that their prospective partners will look for when it comes their time to marry and have their own family. If our sons and daughters observe us as parents investing as little time as possible in home life and all for the sake of our individual careers; if they grow up with a weak sense of what it means to be a male and an female, to be a husband and a wife;

if there are few signs of generosity and sacrifice for the sake of others, and too great a focus on "fairness"; if there is little respect for the mundane labor that comes with a full commitment to domestic life; then the chances are that the deep bonds of secure attachment will not form, the risks of family breakdown will increase, and our children's desire to form their own family in the future and invest fully in its life will be feeble. Our family line, more than likely, will become one of the millions that have not adapted to the demands of our environment or of our biological nature and have died out. This might not be a concern to those who have lost any deep sense of meaning in their lives and so have no interest in future generations. But to those who possess a vigor, a life direction, and a genuine sense of hope for the future, a different way of thinking about married and family life is needed. Reciprocity and its offshoots, fairness and equality, must mean something different to what we have been told.

Taking account of *both* the constraints of our mating drive and the demands of the reciprocity motive leads to the idea that married life ought to be *both* fair *and* different for husbands and wives. Neither should carry more of the overall burden of responsibility and work that go to make up domestic life. Tasks to which he is most suited should become part of his male identity and those that she is skilled in will contribute to her female identity. Couples are encouraged to embrace these specializations rather than flee from them. At times, the load might fall more on one spouse than the other, as circumstances demand, but over the years, this should balance out so that neither party feels resentful of the other.

As an example of this "balance over time" principle, we might point to the matter of raising children, and especially boys. A common mistake in modern societies is to task the mother with primary responsibility for the development of her sons even into their adolescent years. This is an excessive burden on the mother and hampers the growth of a strong and mature masculine identity in her sons. To overcome this problem, fathers—who are encouraged to involve themselves in the care of their children from birth—should make a special effort from the years of late childhood to take the pressure off their wives and become the main, though not exclusive, carer of their sons. Not only is this arrangement fairer but it also benefits from the particular strengths of fathers and works towards better psychological outcomes for sons.

If we want to give a label to the form of married life I have described, we might call it "equality of value" or "equality of dignity." Its strength, in comparison to a feminist notion of "equality," is that it takes better account of our human nature. It would appear, also, to be more in keeping with the general tenor of the Scriptures.

In concluding our reflections on the mating motive, we have reached the point where our attention moves away from the so-called "biological" motives, and we will now consider a quite different driver of our thoughts and behavior: the conscience.

9

Conscience

AT ITS SIMPLEST, the idea of conscience is that of a kind of "voice" in our minds which *obliges* us to act or to refrain from acting in a particular situation. Where it differs from other motives is that, at least to some extent, it works against what we *want* to do. If we pause to think about that, it seems a remarkable thing: that we have within us a power that can work against what we desire. That does not really make sense! And yet, it is there, and can be extremely powerful, even to the point of pushing a person to accept their own death rather than offend their conscience, as in the case of martyrdom. Let us considers its various dimensions.

The Human Motive of Conscience

Its Development

To understand the character of conscience as a motive, we need to look briefly at its origins in childhood.[1] From an early age, young children are trained by their parents to act in socially useful ways, ways which are useful to the child, but also which assist other family members or even the family as a whole. If a young girl is taking too long to get ready for a family outing, she can cause problems for everyone else. That would be reason enough for her parents to reprimand her. Such discipline usually

---

1. Much of what follows on the development of conscience is based on the pioneering work in this area of the Polish-American psychologist Grazyna Kochanska and her team at the University of Iowa. See, for example, Kochanska and Aksan, "Conscience in Childhood," 299–310.

works because children in their early years are generally—though not always—responsive to their parents' approval and try to avoid their disapproval. For this reason, they learn to act according to their parents' wishes for them and, in so doing, acquire the capacity to take account of others.

An important condition, however, must be in place for this arrangement to be successful. A child will be amenable to the guidance of her parents only if she is attached to them, at least to a "good enough" degree. It does not require completely secure attachment, but certainly a level where the child believes that most of the time her parents will respond to her in times of stress or need, whether practical or emotional. Less attached children will not be as responsive to their parents, all things being equal, compared to those whose attachment is stronger and more secure.

There is another condition for a good conscience, and that is a capacity for empathy. This is not usually a problem for most young children because, as we know from observing empathy among some animals, this is an inbuilt ability that we humans carry. Yet, a lack of empathy can arise among those who grow to develop a psychopathic or sociopathic personality. Whatever its root causes, it greatly hinders the acquisition of a working conscience, and what develops in place of a conscience is a sophisticated skill in achieving one's own ends while maintaining the social bonds that will allow that to happen.

Before about the age of two years, children will be compliant on the basis of a simple calculation according to which, under most circumstances, it is better for them if they act that way rather than to adopt a non-compliant attitude. From about the age of about two years onwards, however, an interesting change occurs in children's minds. They begin to *identify* with the values that their parents are seeking to instil in them, e.g., "Don't hit your little sister," "Wash your hands after going to the bathroom," so that they begin to be able to follow such rules even when they know they will not be found out if they fail to do so. It is as if the voice of their parents becomes internalized inside their minds.

In the development of this identification, we also notice that children begin to display genuine guilt and remorse for breaking rules. There is a look on their face, and often a change in body posture, which reveals the presence of this emotion. They learn to say sorry, and to make amends for the harm they have caused. We need to note that guilt is different from shame, which occurs when we have broken social rules or expectations which might not have anything to do with morality at all. Thus, we can feel shame when we are dressed shabbily in public or when we unexpectedly perform poorly on an exam. Guilt is different; it shows that we have done something *morally* wrong, and it is this reality, the "moral," that comes into existence for a young child and which forms in indelible element of their mind for the rest of their lives. Indeed, as adults, we cannot stop thinking about the world in terms of right and wrong. Regardless of how cynical we might become or how jaded our attitude towards life grows, we still accept that some things, such as deliberately slaughtering young babies, are absolutely wrong, and it is impossible that committing such acts could ever, in any possible world, become a good thing to do.

This change in the mind of children, when they learn to act in a way that reflects values and norms issuing from outside of them rather than merely weighing up the costs and benefits of an action, is the beginning of the conscience. And although we say that our conscience responds to an external voice, in fact, in internalizing that voice, at least to some extent it also becomes our own. It is both ours and our parents'. The young child follows her parents' voice which echoes in her mind, but she also, to some degree, *wants* to follow that voice as if it were her own.

A moment's reflection will show that what the "voice" of conscience tells us to do is to take account of the interests and feelings of other people as well as of our own in a way similar to the urgings of the reciprocity motive. It requires a balancing act and therefore calls for the child at times to suppress the acting out of her own desires. For that reason, conscience is different from the other motives we have discussed in that unlike them it is not purely in the interests of the self or of groups with which the self identifies. It is somewhat easier to ignore—at least in the short term—because it demands of us that we empathize with how other people are feeling and include that consideration into our judgments about what to do. A child walking down the street with his father might think, "I want to jump into that puddle" (and see the striking effects which that will have). Here we have the competence (dominance) motive at work. Yet if his conscience is working properly, he might also think, "Dad is dressed in his good clothes and he'll get wet if I jump in the puddle, and that will be worse for him than the pleasure I would gain." Decision: "I won't jump." This restraint is against his desire, but in accord with his conscience.

Conscience as Moral Authority

When they are young, children typically believe that their parents are the source of moral authority. They likewise think that every other adult is a source from which such authority issues. Yet, as they mature, they come to realize that this cannot be the case, since parents themselves look beyond themselves for their own moral guidance. When things are working well, that source will have a religious character, although unfortunately today this is commonly not the case. If there exists a religious dimension, parents will worship and honor God and will seek to live their lives according to what God tells them is the good and the true. They will encourage their children to do the same so that while, in a sense, the parents will continue to serve as moral authorities, in reality they will be merely the mediators or transmitters of the authority that is truly absolute, that is, of God.

What this tells us is that conscience is always *relational*. That means that it never simply exists inside an individual; it always requires an external authority whose voice is internalized. It might not look like that to some people. They might say, "I listen to my gut feeling; that allows me to know right from wrong." What they are really saying is that the voice of their parents—and of other moral authorities in their lives when they were young—continues to speak to them through their conscience, but they do not acknowledge that voice as the true source of their moral feelings. Perhaps due to their lack of religious commitment, they prefer to claim some kind of "instinct" within them as the originator of their moral sense.

Others, who have been influenced by philosophical explanations about morality, believe that we do not need to appeal to a transcendent or divine authority to tell us about right and wrong. They say that it is in fact better to rely for our moral judgments upon practical reasoning that takes account of other people's interests or needs. Thus, they would say, if I want to make a decision about whether to give some of my money to the poor, I will weigh up how much good that act will accomplish for the recipients, and what benefits and losses it will mean for me, and by applying some rule such as "the greatest good for the greatest number of people, with every one's interests being of the same value" I will be able to decide on the "moral" thing to do.

At least two problems arise from this approach: first, if I follow it, there will be no "voice" pushing me to always stick to the rule, and more than likely, I will give it up and pursue my own self-interest when things become difficult. At least a conscience guided by a transcendent moral authority carries with it a strong aversion to acting against that authority even when we are under pressure. Second, when we replace such an authority with a rule like the one which I described, its application can lead to what most people would say are actually immoral decisions. For example, if a situation arises in which inflicting great suffering on one person could lead to some good outcome for other people, an outcome which was calculated to more than compensate for that individual's suffering (thereby fulling "the greatest good for the greatest number of people" rule), then that presumably would be something that would be considered the "moral" thing to do. Yet most people would hold that it would be in fact immoral. This is because at its heart, the moral sense takes account of persons and as such cannot simply be defined by a single abstract rule.

There are other problems with the view of conscience that excludes a transcendent moral authority, but perhaps it is clear enough from what I have noted about how consciences are formed in childhood that for a conscience to operate as a genuine conscience, it needs be part of a relationship with God. Without that, the life of an individual, or if not theirs, then that of their children and grandchildren, will suffer, as will the community in which they live. There does not appear to be any way of avoiding this, since anything less than a religious moral authority does not have the power *over the long term* to ensure that the conscience remains effective as conscience and works as it was designed to do, that is, as something which is *in its very essence* relational. Passing on a healthy and relational conscience to one's children is a gift that will be of great benefit to them, especially during times of hardship and stress.

The Distinctiveness and Purpose of Conscience

In examining the motives of dominance/competence, attachment, social reciprocity, and mating, we have observed that each has roots in our prehuman forebears as well as parallels in many other animals that exist today. Though they manifest themselves in diverse ways depending on the culture, they nonetheless have biological foundations, and I have sometimes referred to them as "biological." And even in my description of conscience above, it would have been clear that the capacities needed for its healthy formation (attachment, reciprocity, empathy) are also grounded in our biology. Yet, the fact remains that conscience itself is a peculiarly human phenomenon, not least because it is based on language and the reasoning ability that requires language. Non-human animals can certainly act empathically. They are also able to make calculations of cause and effect and, to a limited extent, of means and ends. But language and reasoning as the requirements for rule-based action is something distinctively human. That means that conscience and the resultant ability to feel guilt (as distinct from shame) are things that we observe only among human beings.

In view of what I have written so far about conscience, we are now in a better position to discern the purpose of the conscience as something emerging within human history. Whereas mating, dominance, and attachment serve primarily the survival of individuals (although, as we have seen, the latter two do have a group dimension), conscience, like social reciprocity, is specifically concerned with group survival (and through the survival of groups, a better chance of survival for individual members). It works chiefly by taking account of other group members, and in doing so it strengthens relations between individuals in a group, as well as those between an individual and his/her group as a whole.

In the case where a small-scale society, for example, a hunter-gatherer people, has its own tribal gods and has limited contact with external groups, conscience will mostly work well *within* the group, but will often fail when it comes to contacts with untrusted outsiders. With the emergence of large-scale civilizations, and their associated worship of "more powerful" gods, we find general rules of behavior whose scope is universal rather than limited to one's own group or society: "do not do to others (whomever they are) what you would not want done to yourself." It is unfortunately the case that throughout history the putting-into-practice of such rules when applied to those outside of one's group or nation has been submerged by other stronger forces, such as group dominance and attachment that typically view outsiders in negative terms. So, even though conscience has the capacity to achieve its purposes when we interact with *any* person or group, in practice it accomplishes its purposes more effectively when it applies to our relations with our own groups. It strengthens them and repairs damage to relationships when this occurs.

Conscience and the Other Motives

There is another way that conscience differs from the other motives we have discussed. Dominance, attachment, and mating do not like to be ignored for too long, and from time to time they demand to be "fed," as it were. In fact, dominance/competence is continually demanding our attention and is the key motive that energizes our self. Social reciprocity mainly shows itself when its rules are being ignored, and so, in that sense, it is less like the hunger drive than the others. But like them, it is still basically looking out for itself. Conscience, in contrast to these, works so as to take not only the self and its concerns into account but also the interests of others. It does not, therefore, "get hungry," that is, demand attention from time to time for the sake of the self. What it does do is to remain on the alert for actions, *driven by the other motives*, which offend its rules of behavior, and when that happens, it can take over control of the self for a time. If we are caught out having lied to someone, our conscience kicks into action, and we feel guilty. At the same time, the other motives are put on the back burner.

Now, I need to qualify that somewhat, since what I have described is the case of a "typical" person. For a committed believer, things are a little different. For the believer, as he grows in spiritual maturity, the conscience takes a more active role in the running of his life. God calls him to particular tasks or employments, and to some extent these come to define the way he thinks and acts. Carrying out God-given works requires that he be carefully attuned to his conscience, and that means that it has to do more than simply monitor behavior but also serve as its guide. But for all that, it still depends upon the working of the other motives and cannot set them aside because it is not really a fully independent motive in its own right.

Conscience Subverted

Now, the reader might imagine that some people seem to be an exception to this rule. They are fully committed to "doing the right thing" regardless, it seems, of whether or not matters work out well for them in other respects. As diligent people, always careful of the needs of others, ever taking account of the rules of behavior in each situation, they seem to be permanently driven or controlled by the conscience. In their lives, they would seem to contradict what I have said about conscience being not so much the energizing controller but rather the overarching guide of our actions.

We need, however, to consider further this characteristic of the non-conscience motives, especially dominance, attachment, and mating, of being a bit like hunger in needing to be fed from time to time. If this is the case, then dominance—or at least the competence component of it—and attachment have not been permanently silenced in the person who appears to be fully driven by their conscience but are still there beneath the surface. We can see this in the case of attachment, since a strong conscience cannot exist without a healthy attachment motive. Neglecting that latter motive will lead to a distorted or weakened conscience which will show itself in one of two ways: first, the rules of such a conscience will come to be seen as external, as *imposed* on the self by a demanding lawgiver, rather than guides for action given by a loving heavenly Father; thus, no longer will they be identified with what the self wants to do, and they will become a burden to fulfill. Alternatively, the "conscience" behavior might conceal an anxious desire to please God and so to be accepted by him. "I am worried that God will turn away from me if I let up in my efforts to live according to my conscience. I long to be accepted by God but am not confident that this can happen." Here, the conscience itself is taken over by the anxieties of an insecure attachment system. In either case, what is revealed is the need for conscience to work *with* the attachment motive rather than in its place.

When it comes to dominance/competence, as I have discussed above, we humans need to see that we are having an impact on the world and are competent in the skills and abilities which allow that to happen. We can barely live without that kind of experience. A conscience-guided life that does not allow the operations of that motive will soon find itself *taken over* by it. When this happens, an individual will begin to grow proud of his ability to live by his conscience, he will come to compare himself with others, especially those whose actions are not so carefully controlled by their consciences, and eventually his conscience, as the inner experience of relating the God, will wither away because his focus will turn outward to the approval of others. Increasingly, he will become a caricature of the properly conscience-guided individual; that is, he will become a self-righteous, holier-than-thou individual seemingly guided by his absolute moral authority but actually driven by the applause or admiration of others.

The other side of this is that as the conscience of a faithful believer grows in strength and maturity the way he evaluates his life and the activities he is involved in will change in an important way. When the conscience is chiefly the *monitor* of our actions (rather than its guide), our self-esteem is determined by how we fare in expressing our dominance/competence motive. If we do well in some endeavor, we feel good about ourselves, and vice versa when we do poorly. In this case, our self-image is controlled by how other people evaluate our actions because our (dominance) interests are in how skilled, attractive, muscular, or intelligent, etc., we are. But as our conscience takes a more prominent guiding role in our life, we are able to judge our actions more in terms of how God values us and whether or not we have been faithful to his ways and less on the basis of others' opinions. This change leads to a lessening of inner turmoil because with it our self-esteem is not so much tied to the ups and downs that are part of the life of the dominance motive.

A Simulacrum of Conscience

A simulacrum of conscience, that is, a likeness of it but not the real thing, has gradually taken over from the conscience in Western societies. It is worth spending a moment describing this replacement conscience and how it differs from the genuine article.

In my account of conscience above I have emphasized the centrality of its *interpersonal* character, that it always has an external and transcendent moral authority which is the source of its rules and norms of behavior (as well as of thinking and attitudes) to whose authority the individual relates in a personal manner. In the Christian context, we see that, from the human side, the relation is marked by trust, loving respect, and obedience, and from the divine side, graciousness, love, and a persistent call to holiness.

With the widespread loss of convictions about the reality of God or of any transcendent moral authority, many people are forced to find a substitute for the religious conscience. The reason for that is that society needs what that form of conscience provides; it needs a societal norm or way of relating that requires everyone to show some respect for other people. If that were not to exist, society would fall apart. The alternative that Western societies have moved towards is one based on the dominance motive. The dominance hierarchy used here can be described roughly as "adherence to moral values." People cultivate personal values which fit in with this broadly defined dimension, and thus qualities such as being "respectful of others," "principled," "caring," and "personally responsible" and "fair" become part of an individual's self-image. Now, because dominance is the key motive behind this form of "conscience," how someone is perceived by others is the measure used to judge their position on the "moral" hierarchy. I act uprightly and respectfully towards others because I want to be seen to be doing so. If I fail and others know of my failure, I feel shame, and my position on the hierarchy slips down a few notches. Note carefully that the feeling that accompanies "moral" failure is not guilt but shame. Guilt is what we feel before a transcendent moral authority (or for those without such an authority, the voice of their parents); shame is the result of a loss of self-esteem and the esteem communicated by others.

That this alternative regime is a simulacrum of conscience is clear from the fact that the language of conscience is still used. People continue to talk about "their conscience," they say that "their conscience is clear," they give witness to their deep, abiding, and passionate convictions about equality for a minority group or freedom of speech, and they apologize to wronged parties (but only as a way of acknowledging fault and making *social* amends—not as part of a repairing of their relationship with God). Yet what makes up the values of these "consciences" is notoriously fickle, unlike the relatively clear and settled norms associated with a genuine conscience. If society changes its values—and this can happen quite rapidly—"consciences" have to follow suit, and they do so not necessarily out of some inner conviction, but because not to do so is to risk losing standing or rank on the "moral" dominance dimension.

Such a system is vulnerable to self-deception. People can think that they are acting according to their (genuine) conscience, but are, in fact, acting, via the dominance motive, out of self-interest. We can think here of the company executive who has a sudden conversion and comes to a sincere belief that he must become an "ally" of the LGQBT cause. And yet this change might have occurred after the company had sensed that it was beginning to lose status as a progressive participant in its industry. Another example would be the political leader who has been found to have been "linked" but not involved in some corrupt activity, perhaps she was a friend of the wrongdoer, and there are calls for her resignation. Her fellow party members ponder the matter and decide that she is in the wrong and must resign. The unacknowledged concern is that her continued presence as leader might jeopardize the party's reelection. The so-called "right thing to do" turns out to be the expedient thing to do. We can see from these examples that self-deception is much more likely in the simulacrum of conscience because in it there is no clear tension between the two "competing" forces—both are driven by dominance. In its true form, by contrast, conscience typically works against the harms that dominance can cause, and the conflict is experienced as an inner tension which can be articulated and pondered over before God.

The Witness of Scripture

If the Lord God is the believer's absolute moral authority, then it should come as no surprise to find that the Scriptures are replete with evidence which implies the existence of conscience in humans according to what I have described in the above section. Given the abundance of materials which are relevant to this matter, here I can only speak of the biblical picture in a limited way.

Old Testament

The first rule that God communicated to man was: *"Be fruitful and multiply and fill the earth and subdue it and have dominion over the fish of the sea and over the birds of the heavens and over every living thing that moves on the earth"* (Gen 1:28). It is as if the Lord, right from the beginning, was saying, "Now that I have created you, it is your task to continue in existence, and more than that, to flourish as human beings." Later, in the garden, the first *moral* rule is given: *"You may surely eat of every tree of the garden, but of the tree of the knowledge of good and evil you shall not eat, for in the day that you eat of it you shall surely die"* (Gen 2:16b–17). Taken out of context, this rule looks like a bare order from God or an example of heteronomy, that is, a moral law imposed from outside of man. But it must be understood in the light of the earlier divine statement: *"Behold, I have given you every plant yielding seed that is on the face of all the earth, and every tree with seed in its fruit. You shall have them for food"* (Gen 1:29). First God shows himself as the secure provider for mankind and on that basis also the One who establishes moral rules. As we might say, no genuine conscience without a prior attachment bond.

Such a "care-before-commandment" linking of motives is found throughout the Scriptures, whether it be the redemption from Egypt as the foundation for the giving of the law on Sinai, or the central teaching of the Book of Deuteronomy and the historical books that follow it, or the utterances of the Old Testament prophets. It is certainly the case that we sometimes gain the impression from certain biblical texts that this principle has receded into the background as, for example, when we find in sections of the wisdom literature or some of the Psalms, the sentiment expressed in Psalm 17:5, 6: "*My steps have held fast to your paths; my feet have not slipped. . . . O God; incline your ear to me; hear my words.*" Here, the Lord's support is thought of as not prior to but consequent upon the keeping of his law. Yet, the basic principle—that the divine moral order is established within some kind of preexisting relationship of care—is never completely submerged.

The prophets were especially attuned to the link between how God's people related to each other, and how close was their bond with the Lord. "*Ah, sinful nation, a people laden with iniquity, offspring of evildoers, children who deal corruptly! They have forsaken the Lord, they have despised the Holy One of Israel, they are utterly estranged*" (Isa 1:4). When this distancing from God occurs, there is a change in attitude towards his law. It increasingly comes to be seen as a burden, as something externally imposed, because its source, God himself, has been sidelined from the life of the people; he is merely the One who might continue to be worshipped, but in a way that has grown perfunctory. "*And the Lord said: '. . . this people draw near with their mouth and honour me with their lips, while their hearts are far from me'*" (Isa 29:14).

What, then, does it mean for the Lord to care for his people? Mostly, such care was thought to be evident when God assisted his people to dwell in their own land, at peace from both external and internal threats and with sufficient resources for living. Yet, there were times when such care seemed to be rather "thin on the ground." The destruction of the Northern Kingdom in 722 BC, during the period of the monarchy, was the first of a sequence of severe tests of the truth that God cared for his people. And the leaders of the people were sorely tempted in these situations to place their trust in earthly powers rather than in the Lord; in fact, they oftentimes succumbed to such temptations. The prophetic message, however, was the same: seek your security in the Lord. Yet in later reflections upon the experience of the sixth-century exile—another time when the Lord seemed to have abandoned his people—we find that, while the idea of divine care is still preserved, it nevertheless shifts slightly so as to incorporate a more definitive, future manifestation. In the latter parts of the book of Isaiah and in Jeremiah and Ezekiel, we find the prophets speaking about a messianic age—in some ways distinct from that of the present—and a messiah who will come to lead his people to a time of righteousness, justice, and prosperity. As we can see with hindsight, this paved the way for the further and significant changes in the way God's care is understood which we observe in the New Testament.

In sum, then, we can conclude that in the Old Testament the notion of conscience is centered upon the commandments God gave to his people and their commitment to keep those commandments. But such a form of conscience is only effective when the Lord's reliability as the Redeemer and Protector of his people (in their own land and at peace) is established. Through Israel's history, this condition was, however, tested in such a way that God's people began to conceive of and look towards a future in which a more definitive security in their relationship with him would be accomplished.

New Testament

In the Sermon on the Mount (Matt 5–7) we observe Jesus' multifaceted teaching on the need for obedience to the law and even more so his extension and deepening of that law. However, this is interrupted at two points in the text by explicit instruction encouraging Jesus' hearers to place their trust in God. Matthew 5:1—6:24 contains the first kind of teaching—moral instruction—but then, suddenly, we come across the words, *"Therefore I tell you, do not be anxious about your life, what you will eat or what you will drink, nor about your body, what you will put on. Is not life more than food, and the body more than clothing? Look at the birds of the air: they neither sow nor reap nor gather into barns, and yet your heavenly Father feeds them. Are you not of more value than they?"* (Matt 6:25–26). Then the Sermon resumes moral teaching about not judging, but again, at Matthew 7:7 we find another "interruption": *"Ask, and it will be given to you; seek, and you will find; knock, and it will be opened to you . . . If you then, who are evil, know how to give good gifts to your children, how much more will your Father who is in heaven give good things to those who ask him!"* (Matt 7:7, 11). Though the Sermon is more likely to be a later compilation of various collections of teachings handed down among Jesus' disciples, it reflects well the overall tenor of Christ's teaching in the rest of the Gospels. Specifically, it is from within a relationship of forgiveness and the experience of grace and trust in the Lord that God's law can come to be experienced as not something fully outside of ourselves, but that which—at least partially—is interior to us, something we love to follow, "a burden that is light."

It is perhaps in a similar way that we are to understand the cry of the man in Romans 7 who says *"I do not do the good I want, but the evil I do not want is what I keep on doing"* (Rom 7:19). Here, within the heart of the person without Christ, the wanting is in fact a form of knowing, a knowledge of the truth about the good which yet is beyond his powers to accomplish. It is sin which overly externalizes the moral law, as it were. This inner tension is resolved, as Paul writes, through the gift that Christ offers us: *"Who will deliver me from this body of death? Thanks be to God through Jesus Christ our Lord!"* (Rom 7:24–25). Paul spells out the nature of that gift in the following verses: *"For the law of the Spirit of life has set you free in Christ Jesus from the law of sin and death"* (Rom 8:2). It is only by entering into a relationship of trust in Christ through his Spirit that the externality of the law and in its wake the oppression of sin can be rebalanced so as to make way for a deeper grounding of the believer in Christ's love and its consequence of a closer identification with the demands of the law.

This link found in the New Testament between divine care and conscientious obedience to the moral law is further developed through the idea of grace. In it we are to recognize the *always-prior* dimension of God's care for his people, and indeed for all peoples. The good news of Jesus Christ, therefore, is heard as possessing an element of "surprising kindness"; God has acted *"while we were yet sinners"* (Rom 5:8); we were chosen *"before the foundation of the world"* (Eph 1:4); and *"it is God who works in you, both to will and to work for his good pleasure"* (Phil 2:13). The Holy Spirit is understood to be active both in external events and through inner urging and strengthening to make up, as it were, for the limitations believers face in fulfilling the commands of conscience as they are given by God through Jesus Christ.

Cast in the terms of the framework I have proposed, we might say that, in the Scriptures, we observe teachings which parallel and illustrate one of the key emphases of my account of conscience: a sound working conscience requires a "good enough" sense of security in the relationship with an individual's absolute moral authority. Now, there is one further aspect of that account that we also need to trace in the biblical text chiefly because, for much of Christian history, it has been overshadowed by alternative ways of viewing conscience.

In the Scriptures, human conscience is always understood as operating under the personal authority of God. Where does my sense of right and wrong come from? It comes from the Lord. Well, then, where does God's knowledge of right and wrong issue from? Such a question scarcely ever surfaces in the biblical witness, since the Lord is treated as the absolute moral authority, and a personal one at that. During the ministry of Christ, people marvelled at his teaching as one who spoke with authority, seeing in him someone who had a direct link to God rather than a connection developed through his knowledge of the Scriptures and the traditions of its interpretation. At the same time, we find emphasized in John's Gospel the fact that Christ always spoke not on his own authority but of the One who sent him. So, even in Christ, that is, in that human part of Christ that we can understand to some extent (even though he was truly also divine), his conscience operated with an authority, that is, the authority of his heavenly Father. What is true for the Son of God, in his humanity, is surely also the case for us. The truth of moral authority is always found within a personal relationship; it is never some self-sustaining truth in its own right.

One might wonder, however, about Paul's comments in Romans 1:14, 15. There he writes of the moral responsibility of the gentiles, "*who do not have the law*" but "*are a law to themselves.*" Are they really a law unto themselves? As we read on, we find that in their case, "*the work of the law is written on their hearts,*" but also that they possess a conscience which bears witness to the truth of the law. They have thoughts distinct from, and in a sense external to, their own "self" thoughts, and it is this former kind of thought which will *accuse or even excuse them* on the day of judgment. So, even though, for the gentiles, there is no law which has been personally given to them in the same way as with the people of Israel, nevertheless, there is still the voice of conscience echoing inside their minds; they still grow a conscience through their parents, through their society, and through their immersion in religion. Conscience among nonbelievers, therefore, is never simply knowledge about the world that people acquire instinctively or simply through learning about what works and what does not work in life. It comes from outside of ourselves and through personal engagement.

Thus, we can conclude that another essential element of conscience, that is, the fact that it always involves, at some level, the *personal communication* of moral truth, rings true to the way the Scriptures speak of it and illustrate it in describing moral behavior.

Now, as I have already emphasized, we can observe in the conscience not only an *external "voice"* but, in its healthy form, also an *inner desire* to follow one's conscience. Here, I want to highlight an element of Christ's teaching which takes up this reality and applies it to the life of believers in a way that represents a major change in how they come to think about ourselves. For us Christians, following our conscience is no longer, as in the Old Testament, a matter of freely choosing a way of life for ourselves which we then pursue with the understanding that it should be lived within the *limits or constraints* placed upon it by God's law. In Christ, our conscience—hopefully—experiences an ardent desire to follow his call to us in every aspect of life; it is no longer so much a *restraint* on life as its *primary driver*. Put another way, we can say that the life of a believer is not simply a more moral version of that which other (nonbelieving) people pursue; it is fully lived according to the purposes which Christ gives it. That is what the New Testament calls "love." Paul writes, *"Love does no wrong to a neighbour; therefore, love is the fulfilling of the law"* (Rom 13:10). But here Paul is not assuming that love is simply the equivalent of the law so that keeping the law is what defines love. Rather, love can and does go beyond the law because of this strengthened desire to follow one's conscience. And that occurs because we have entered into a deeper experience of love ourselves. *"We love because [God] first loved us"* (1 John 4:19). This allows for our life to be fully and positively lived towards love rather than to an otherwise secular life bound only by "thou shall nots." The new commandment for life can now become this: *"that you love one another: just as I have loved you, you also are to love one another"* (John 13:34).

So, we can see that across the Scriptures, the conscience of God's people has been shaped profoundly by the depth or closeness of the relationship they have had with their Lord. In the incarnation, God has lived with human beings, and in the cross and resurrection of Christ his surprising graciousness has been fully revealed to us. Through the life of the Spirit in the church, this intimate bond opens up the possibility of a conscience which more fully *drives* the life of the believer and more effectively works towards a holy and compassionate way of living. When this happens, it is not simply "sitting on the sidelines" watching the other motives do their job and complaining from time to time but is intimately involved in the direction that our lives take.

Reflections of Faith

Conscience as the Locus of Our Freedom

I remarked earlier that conscience differs profoundly from the other four social motives surveyed in not having its origin in prehuman species, since it requires some capacity for language and rationality. It works because we can follow rules of behavior and also feel guilt when we break those rules. However, whether it be conscience or the other motives, we are still thinking of human actions as driven by non-rational forces, and that way of looking at things appears not to make room for that distinctively human capacity which is our ability to make free choices. How can we be free if that is all there is to us? Even though our experience tells us that we are free, from what I have written so far it certainly appears that that is not the case!

Yet there is more to the story of how we humans work. And it is when we see ourselves as belonging to Christ that we can begin to see that the Creator Lord has taken up the highest, the least self-centered motive we possess, that is, our conscience, and made of it the place where we discover our freedom as humans. Thus, it is precisely in the working of the conscience that we exercise our freedom. As Christians have claimed over the centuries, we are most free when, guided by conscience, we live according to the law of Christ, which is the law of love. To live solely according to the other motives is to be driven by psychological forces which are at their core self-oriented, even though on the surface it may at times appear that our actions are at the service of others. Dominance seeks the good of oneself or one's group at the expense of others; attachment works to sustain the bond between parents and children, between spouses, between the individual and social groups upon which he relies, etc., for the sake of physical and psychological survival of the individual; social reciprocity strengthens social bonds for the preservation of groups, but ultimately in order that group members survive; and mating works to increase the chances of *my* genes continuing in later generations. And even a conscience which operates without a transcendent moral authority is, in the end, at the service of the survival of the group and thus indirectly also of the individual. It is only in a conscience that is guided by rules of conduct whose purpose is not limited to the self and to life in this world that we humans can escape the limitations created by our animal nature. The Lord God, being outside of ourselves and thus beyond the control of our motives, and what is more, outside the whole universe and the forces which shape everything that happens in it, in his perfect freedom, engages with us assuming that we too are free to accept or to reject his guidance. We can say that the freedom of God *evokes or calls out* our human freedom, raising us up beyond the constraints that we operate under as animals, and joins us in a conversation as between free agents. Our conscience is the place where that conversation occurs. We heard the words of our loving Father, and we freely respond to them based on our love for others as well as for ourselves. There we are no longer simply animals; we are at that point also spiritual beings or persons.[2]

How Does Christ Become Our Moral Authority?

The Catholic faith has never taught that it is necessary for the children of believers to undergo a conversion experience in order to become a Christian. According to the tradition of faith, baptism is the entry into the church and into its faith. And yet, the notion of "conversion" does have a significant role in the Catholic understanding of how we are to relate to God. Conversion in this context is something that occurs throughout life. There are many moments of conversion which mark the path of growth in holiness. But the question remains: is there one conversion episode that stands out from the rest? If conscience develops along the lines which I have set out above, it is difficult to imagine that for a young person the transition in their moral authority from parents/society to Christ could ever be imperceptible or without any features of a conversion experience, even if it extends over a period of time.

When they are growing up, young people are usually protected from some of the more challenging aspects of life in Christ. Thus, teaching children before they are psychologically ready to give sacrificially in love to others can be detrimental to them, as can Christ's teachings to turn the other cheek.[3] This means that at some point in their development,

---

2. This is a very brief and rough description of human freedom, and no doubt leaves many questions unanswered. I have offered a fuller account in *Chalcedonian Personalism*, esp. chapter 9.

3. In the Catholic tradition, the need for divine grace in being able to respond to these difficult teachings is assumed in the sacrament of confirmation, which

children of believers will come face-to-face with elements of Christ's teaching which will strike them not so much as contradicting what they had learned from their parents but certainly as a big step beyond their present understanding. It is in this kind of experience that a child comes more fully to adopt the person of Christ as his moral authority and to see his parents for what they are, that is, relative authorities. We can call this a conversion. To be experienced as a conversion, however, there needs to be something more than a change of moral authorities in his life (though this is important in its own right); he needs also to come into a deeper understanding of both the profoundly true character of Christ's words and also of his utter reliability, trustworthiness, and, yes, love. In this requirement we see that changes in a child's attachment schema, in his *emotional* connection to Christ, are to accompany those of conscience.

If such accompaniment does not occur, the believer, who now sees Christ as his moral authority, might seek to live his life more closely to the moral teachings of the faith, but such a life will always have the character of obligation, or duty, of a merely externally sourced law. There was a time in the Catholic Church in Australia and the United States where this was quite a common experience among the faithful. Some have identified Jansenist influences that came over with the Irish Catholics as a source of this distortion but there were likely other more important historical factors at play.[4] And we might even see in the scourge of child sexual (and at times physical) abuse which struck Ireland, Australia, and the US so badly the influence of this same problem, that of seeking to live a life of obedience to Christ without an *emotional* openness to the grace that he offers to us to be able to do so. Tough consciences without the support of true trust in Christ and his grace always create an inner world that, in spite of itself, tends to rebel against the externalized impositions of that conscience.

The Discovery of Our True Self in Christ

A commonly expressed cultural notion is the idea of "finding oneself." A person might use this expression during a time of crisis or loss of

---

strengthens the believer to be able to engage fully in the work of witnessing to Christ.

4. Lawrence J. McCaffery considers Jansenism and other forces in the establishment of the Irish Catholic character of the American church in his article, "Irish Textures in American Catholicism," 1–18. See also Fisher, "Lefebvrism—Jansenism revisited?" 274–86.

direction in their life, or when a marriage relationship is going through difficulties. "I need to get away by myself to find who I really am." The idea carries the assumption that there is a true self, a true way of existing and directing one's life which it is possible to lose sight of but also to find again. To rediscover that true self, or even to find it for the first time, would require a period of withdrawal for reflection and also a setting or context in which one is free of those pressures which normally hold in place an inauthentic self. The value of thinking about the self in this way is that it recognizes the existence and importance of the inner self, that there is more to life than operating at a surface level, and that depth of character and a lively inner experience are central to a well-lived life.

Nevertheless, there are also limitations to such a perspective. These center around the notion that one can find oneself *by oneself*, that finding oneself is a solitary activity. The Christian conviction, by contrast, and one affirmed by experience, is that we only find ourselves within our *relations with others*. The Second Vatican Council document *Gaudium et spes* expressed it this way: "Man, who is the only creature on earth which God willed for itself, cannot fully find himself except through a sincere gift of himself."[5] That is, we find ourselves by the giving of ourselves to another or others, with the implication that by doing so we evoke the giving of something in return—a fuller sense of ourselves, of who we really are. Finding oneself is a relational exercise. But more than that, the task also calls for us to simultaneously relate to God. Since all our interactions with other people, through the operation of conscience, have an engagement with God, our gift of ourselves to another person is also a communication with the Lord himself, who never just receives what we communicate to him but responds to us as well.

Put this way, we might say that throwing ourselves into activities that express care and solidarity with others is a worthy thing to do, but it will only go so far in helping us to know ourselves. It also requires the deeper dimension that operates when we relate that giving of ourselves to the Lord. In fact, we can go further and say that it is precisely in the most open and vulnerable engagement with Christ, the kind which can occur when our conscience is fully active, that we come to experience a sense of self that really does feel like our true self. We are most fully our true self when we stand before Christ with a keen sense of how we have failed him, but also with the assurance that he forgives us and has accepted

---

5. Second Vatican Council, *Gaudium et spes*, 24.

us. When we undergo this experience, we have the sense that our self in other settings is not really our authentic self, and that this present self, fully engaging with Christ, is what we are really like. Again, *Gaudium et spes* speaks succinctly on this matter: "Conscience is the most secret core and sanctuary of a man. There he is alone with God, whose voice echoes in his depths."[6] In the innermost core of man is his conscience; there he finds his true self.

To speak of the true self in this way addresses the question left in abeyance in chapter 2: If our thinking and our self are driven and shaped by the various motives which I have described rather than, for example, by a single drive or inclination toward truth-seeking (as traditional formulations proposed), where is our true self to be found? According to what I have written, it is precisely in the outworking of a sound conscience that operates with an awareness of the presence of Christ that our most genuine self is experienced; there we are our true self, there we are most free.

Conscience and Dominance

In what I have written so far, I have emphasized several times that unless there exists an attachment connection with God, the conscience will be experienced as burdensome rather than as something which, at least to some extent, we *want* to follow when we hear its voice. This is so much the case that we can be confident, when we do have that sense of being burdened by obligations in our life, that our relationship with the Lord (as our security) has been weakened and needs repair for us to regain a well-functioning conscience. A common reason for such a weakening is that we have allowed too much influence to our dominance motive, and an adjustment is called for. This raises the question as to what, more generally, is the relationship between dominance and conscience. I have already mentioned how a strong conscience can limit our dependence on our dominance motive in shaping our self-esteem but there are other aspects to the interaction between the two we need to consider.

These two motives seem by their very natures to work against each other. Whereas conscience always seeks to take others into account, whether it be other humans and their interests or God himself and the honor and worship which is due to him, when I am driven by dominance,

6. Second Vatican Council, *Gaudium et spes*, 16.

in contrast, I seek my advantage over that of other people; I want to benefit myself, and usually to the disadvantage of others. So, the question arises: how can conscience ride "on the top of" dominance? One is pulling one way, and the other in a different direction. Viewed in this manner, we can see why Jesus was especially wary of the dominance motive. Much of his teaching was directed at preventing it from controlling the actions of his followers.

As we saw in chapter 2, the way forward is to call to mind that dominance itself is made up of two processes, a competence foundation upon which is built a fully dominant or competitive element. The latter is the part of the motive that is destructive, the former is not and is indeed an essential dimension of our life. We can gain a sense of pleasure in being competent at something, even when we are acting according to our conscience. The sense of competence we feel in this situation is a foretaste of what we will receive in heaven when we are rewarded for our actions. The Scriptures speak of crowns, or of being placed over much, or given a seat near the front, and in similar terms. All this shows that God takes seriously our responsibility not only for our sins but also for the acts of love we carry out in his strength.[7]

And yet, in any loving action of ours, if we are honest with ourselves, we will acknowledge that it was the Lord who created this opportunity, who is the ultimate source of the mindset we had which helped us carry out the act of love, and who prepared the other person to accept our act. And it seems to be the case that the more we find ourselves acting in a Christlike manner, the more, too, we perceive the workings of the Spirit in our lives, inspiring, enabling, and strengthening us. So, the Book of Revelation speaks of the twenty-four elders around the throne—front seats, you might say!—falling down before God, "*and they cast their crowns before the throne, saying, 'Worthy are you, our Lord and God, to*

---

7. More might be added here concerning the relations between conscience, dominance, and competence, since in their interconnections is determined the form of the Christian life in its moment-by-moment reality. Within the Christian spiritual tradition, the ideal has been promoted of a balance between initiating one's own actions and purposes, on the one hand, and being on the look-out for God's participation in one's life through intervening events, barriers placed in the way of our own actions, or gentle encouragements for our plans and endeavors, on the other. In past centuries, the dangers of leaving things too much up to God, called Quietism, were recognized. Today, the opposite problem of ignoring God's involvement in our lives, what we might call Activism, appears to be much more prevalent. It is one of the many harmful effects of an overly indulged dominance drive.

receive glory and honour and power'" (Rev 4:10–11). As the Catholic Catechism expresses it, "The saints have always had a lively awareness that their merits were pure grace."[8] They grasped the truth that Paul affirmed when challenging the Corinthians: *"What do you have that you did not receive?"* (1 Cor 4:7).

In the time of the Church, perhaps nothing has been more destructive to the witness of believers in Christ than when their dominance motive takes over and controls their conscience. For the glory and honor of God we have sought to wipe out heresy by force ("This is what God would want me as ruler to do in my kingdom"), but we have done so with the thrill of power and control over others moving our hearts (dominance); men have entered the ordained ministry, obeying the call from God (conscience), but the sense of self-worth they often experienced when they found themselves honored by others ("I am not like these laypeople") was frequently dominance-driven; we have studied the Scriptures to show ourselves approved (cf. 2 Tim 2:15) but then we have gloried in our superior knowledge as well as in the lion's share of the talking time we could claim (dominance); we have kept the commandments of the Lord (conscience) but have tut-tutted those who lacked self-control and who frequently fell in their walk of faith ("I thank you, Lord, that I am not like other men"). Behind much seemingly conscience-driven behavior, there lurks plenty of dominance. The tradition uses the term "vainglory" for this kind of thing. It is a vice, and yet one which is singularly neglected, certainly within the wider culture but also—painfully—in Christian circles. This points to the reality that dominance is such a pervasive and powerful motive that it can easily and surreptitiously override that of conscience. For the believer, then, it is the competence component of the dominance motive which must be nurtured and shaped through the lively operation of the conscience; on the other hand, dominance as comparison and competition is the road to division, vainglory, and a weakened relationship with the Lord.

To give an idea of the struggle that even the saints undergo in working towards this connection between dominance and conscience, consider the apostle Paul. His Damascus road call produced in him a powerful change of heart, a conversion to Christ, and a divine calling, all of which were to define the rest of his life. He experienced the reality of the Resurrected One, which created in him a new and fundamental sense

---

8. *Catechism of the Catholic Church*, sec. 2011

of security. As we read the letters he wrote to communities of believers, we can see in them a remarkable sense of care for the spiritual lives of their members, an empathy that made him anxious that they not suffer from the influence of "other gospels," and joy when he heard encouraging news of his churches. All this is to be understood in terms of conscience, attachment, and competence. Yet, there are signs that he still struggled with the effects of the dominance motive. We find this most clearly in the later chapters of his second letter to the Corinthians (2 Cor 10–13). There the struggle is palpable. Paul wrestles with the temptation to give way to dominance. At times he is successful, at other times he appears to succumb. He begins his defense of his ministry by bristling at criticisms he has heard about his manner of relating to his communities. *"I, Paul, myself entreat you, by the meekness and gentleness of Christ—I who am humble when face-to-face with you, but bold towards you when I am away!"* He is aware of the saying that *"he who boasts, let him boast of the Lord,"* but cannot stop himself from boasting about being taken up into the third heaven. He urges his readers to *"bear with a little foolishness"* and is keen to claim that, *"even if I am unskilled in speaking, I am not so in knowledge."* He compares himself favorably to other so-called "apostles." In the end, however, dominance gives way and his justifications for "boasting" are, in fact, reasons for boasting of the Lord, for he speaks chiefly of vulnerabilities on his part from which the Lord saved him. And drawing the letter to a close, we begin to see what is happening under the surface: his concern and love for the Corinthian community begins again to shine through, and his anxiety about having failed Christ if the Corinthian cause should collapse brings him back to his true self. Conscience and attachment win out; dominance recedes; he has fought the fight—and won.

Calling to mind Paul's relationship with believers of the Corinthian and other churches, we can see that another element, that of authority, enters the picture. The question that comes to mind here is, How are conscience and authority linked? This will be the theme of our next chapter.

10

Conscience and Authority

IN EARLIER CHAPTERS, I remarked that discussion of some topics would have to be left until the question of authority had been addressed. Now is the time to do so because it is the conscience motive which centrally has to do with authority. As noted in the previous chapter, a healthy conscience calls for us to accept the absolute moral authority of God, and we look to how that authority expresses itself as a kind of example for how human authority is to be exercised. Now, of course, we ought never to treat the authority that humans hold in the same way as we relate to divine authority, but it will be helpful in thinking about authority in society if we first clarify what we mean by God's absolute authority.

Divine Authority

To call divine authority absolute is not to say that once we have accepted it as a religious moral authority according to our conscience we cannot at some later time reject it and adopt another (religious) authority. This might seem a strange thing to say, given the absolute nature of that authority, but we need to keep in mind that we received our fundamental moral sense not directly from God but from our parents, and we never set that latter form of authority fully aside. It is always there as a basis upon which to evaluate any subsequent question of morality, and that includes even the teachings of our religion. (This does not make our parents' authority absolute, but the *core* or *ground-level* moral rules we learned from them are hardwired in us, as it were.) Thus, it can happen that believers in a particular faith, on further examination of its beliefs, discover things which they feel offend the basic sense of morality which they learned from their parents. This might eventually lead to them setting aside their particular religious faith and seeking moral authority and religious truth elsewhere.

It should also be noted that a similar rejection of an absolute moral authority can occur when a follower comes to the realization that they are not really cared for by their authority/god in a way that reflects the care of their parents. (Remember that such care is a condition for the emergence of a healthy conscience.) Similarly, a follower might observe in another religious faith a level of support for its adherents (ultimately sourced in a deity) which is much superior to that provided by their own. This, too, might prompt them to change religions.

Moving between religions—and thus adopting different absolute moral authorities—is, however, something that is mostly seen within Western societies. Elsewhere the link between family, tribe/community, and religious adherence is typically quite tight, so that cross-religious movement is less common. Conscience and self-identity (through group membership) are so tightly bound together that there are strong constraints against abandoning the faith of one's fathers. But, of course, it does happen, for otherwise the Christian gospel would not have taken root in virtually every country in the world.

So even moral authority that we call absolute can change over time, but when it is accepted as such, it truly is absolute. As Christians, the authority of the God of Jesus Christ is what we rely on for how we think and how we know right and wrong. There is no neutral perspective we can take by which we can judge the authority of the Lord God. By contrast, even though we give human authorities the benefit of the doubt and trust them until they cannot be trusted, every one of them, whether they be political leaders, members of our family, or authorities in science or human wisdom, must be evaluated by comparing them to the truth we have been given from God.[1]

---

1. For Catholics, the case of Church authority is a little more complicated because we believe that the Church's faithfulness to the authoritative word of God is guaranteed *through* the discernment of bishops. They are specifically gifted servants of the word (and more specifically so gifted is the Bishop of Rome), and as such they are authoritative for believers. Thus, the individual believer always makes judgments about the faith within the context of what the Church believes. Catholic faith is always a shared faith. So, when individual church leaders go awry—as sometimes they do—we can rely on the teaching of the Scriptures, the Sacred Tradition, and of the teaching of the Church

Conscience and Human Authority

With this difference between divine and human authority in mind, let us now think about the ways that authority works in human groups.

In line with my earlier description of the development of the conscience, again it is important to emphasize that all human authority relies upon some level of trust between authority and subject. This marks it out as distinct from the exercise of power which can be coerced but does not rely upon trust between the wielder of power and those under his/her control.

Human authority presents in diverse ways. It can take the form of specialized knowledge which others respect and so they can accept as authoritative the judgments from possessors of that knowledge. Most of us do not know our way around the law nor are we well versed in medicine. We therefore usually—at least as a default position—trust the authority of our lawyer or doctor. For young people, parental authority includes an element of "knowledge about the world" which parents possess to a greater extent than their children and which can be drawn upon when exercising authority over children.

But unlike the authority of a lawyer or a doctor, which we can accept or reject as we decide, parental authority also carries with it a power of coercion. As young children, we learned that parents are able to both reward and punish our actions and thus they can exercise control over much of our life. This does not normally present as a problem, since most of the time as children we can see that what our parents are doing aligns well enough with our conscience about what is fair, what is good for the whole family, what is good for our maturing or for our future.

The kind of authority that we experience as children of parents, based as it is on both their expert knowledge and their ability to coerce according to conscience, also operates in contexts outside of our families, for example at school, at work, and at the political level. Most people accept it as part of the smooth ordering of social groups and the wider society. It tends to break down when any of its foundations are undermined. The first foundation of authority, the perceived care of the authority for its subjects we have already noted. When political leaders give the impression that they enjoy the authority they exercise more than they consider the interests of citizens, their authority is weakened. Secondly, if

---

through the ages, knowing that the Lord does not contradict himself and what was authoritatively affirmed in the fourth and sixteenth centuries cannot be denied today.

they are seen to be no more competent that the ordinary person, they will also quickly lose their authority. The same process of breakdown occurs when leaders change their positions too easily or too frequently, indicating that they do not possess a knowledge of their own that people can trust. Thirdly, if the exercise of their authority, even if claimed as being in the interests of the common good, offends the basic moral principles that conscience accepts, again, they will lose the support of the people.

Each of these considerations about human authority makes sense in the light of what I have described as the healthy working of both the conscience and the attachment motives. When these two motives are not working in concert or when one is deficient in some way, the exercise of authority will be difficult, ineffective, or even harmful.

The Witness of Scriptures

In the previous chapter, I considered the biblical witness as it relates to conscience and to the ways the Scriptures view its effective operation. There my focus was upon God as the source of moral authority. I highlighted the linkage we observe in salvation history between God's authority and his care for his people, the relation between conscience and attachment, as it were. Here, I want briefly to address the matter of human authority. What is the broad biblical position? Are there clear trends in how human authority is viewed? Where and how do we find God affirming human authority?

In thinking about God's people as a whole, the major development in the Old Testament occurred at the point when Israel sought to have a king of its own, as the surrounding nations had, rather than leave it to the varied and informal arrangements that applied in pre-monarchical times. Scholars have recognized pro-monarchy and anti-monarchy narratives in the history books of the Old Testament, suggesting that among the elite of the various groups making up the people of Israel there was quite a struggle in reaching agreement on how the Lord viewed the idea of a permanent ruler over his people.[2] At some later point, however, after the

---

2. Compare, for example, 1 Samuel 8: 6–7: "*But when they said, 'Give us a king to lead us,' this displeased Samuel; so he prayed to the Lord. And the Lord told him: 'Listen to all that the people are saying to you; it is not you they have rejected, but they have rejected me as their king,'*" and 1 Samuel 9: 15–16, "*Now the day before Saul came, the Lord had revealed this to Samuel: 'About this time tomorrow I will send you a man from the land of Benjamin. Anoint him ruler over my people Israel; he will deliver them from*

success of the pro-monarchical view, we find the existence of a dominant royal theology which propagated the idea that God's blessing was upon the line of David and that his dynasty was the one which, by covenant, kingly rule over God's people was divinely and perpetually bequeathed. The danger in this idea was always the temptation to sacralize the king, to treat him as a kind of semi-divine figure, as routinely happened in other nations. As one of its functions, the institution of prophecy was a means, established by the Lord, of working against the adoption of such a destructive path among Israel's rulers.

In the prophetic writings of Isaiah and Jeremiah, along with a criticism of Judah's kings, we see a longing for a Davidic king or messiah (that is, anointed one) who would bring about a glorious and secure rule, and following the trauma of the exile, this yearning continued right up until the New Testament period.

The New Testament interprets Jesus of Nazareth as the Christ, the Messiah, or the One anointed by God to rule his people. But this rule turns out to be "not of this world"; it is a spiritual rule, though no less demanding of obedience. Christ's Ascension into heaven and the birth of a new people of God resulted in a view of leadership among God's people which was no longer centered upon political authority but rather on a spiritual and moral authority, one which was (a) divinely sanctioned, for example, the office of bishop as the primary form of leadership in the church, and (b) based upon personal characteristics or charisms, e.g., knowledge of the faith, pastoral disposition, strength of character, piety, etc. With this relinquishing of political authority among God's people, coercive power was generally no longer applicable, although shunning (1 Cor 5:11), excommunication (Matt 18:17), and the power of "binding and loosing" (Matt 16:19, 18:18; John 20:23) were available for use if needed. These were called "spiritual sanctions" and of course only made sense for those who belonged to the church community. They were primarily of a "medicinal" nature, aimed at restoring a sinner to spiritual health. As Paul wrote to the Corinthian believers concerning one such person, *"you should rather turn to forgive and comfort him, or he may be overwhelmed by excessive sorrow"* (2 Cor 2:7; see also 7:8–12). As I have noted earlier (chapter 6), there is, perhaps, a wisdom evidenced here that might be of value in thinking about authority more generally: that coercive punishment is designed to effect restoration in an offender and, by implication,

---

the hand of the Philistines. I have looked on my people, for their cry has reached me."'

in the relationships which have been damaged. As Paul writes: "*Beloved, never avenge yourselves, but leave it to the wrath of God, for it is written, 'Vengeance is mine, I will repay, says the Lord'*" (Rom 12:17). (See chapter 17 for a fuller discussion.)

What about authority in the family—what do the Scriptures have to say about it? In the Old Testament the authority of the husband and father is more assumed than expressed. It is patriarchal in the sense of the father as the "source" (*arche* in Greek) of the marriage and the family and thus the one who *represents* the family to the outside world. But it is patriarchal also in that the husband/father has authority, under God, over the inner life of his family. We can observe such assumptions at play even when they are breached. The story of Ahab and his desire for Naboth's vineyard paints him as despised for his weakness, in contrast to the strength of his wife, Jezebel, who engineers Ahab's acquisition of the plot of land. The narrator highlights the humiliation of Ahab in the light of the actions of his more capable but less scrupulous wife.

In the Book of Proverbs, we find occasional indications pointing to the responsibility of a husband to manage his family, including his wife. "*A foolish son is ruin to his father, and a wife's quarrelling is a continual dripping of rain*" (Prov 19:13); "*An excellent wife is the crown of her husband, but she who brings shame is like rottenness in his bones*" (Prov 12:4).

While parental authority over children is uniformly taught throughout the Scriptures, it is that between a husband and wife that causes most resistance in our day. Since I will discuss this issue more fully in chapter 16, here I will simply note that even though *how* authority within the family is to be exercised is not well specified in the Scriptures, what they do tell us is that there is a part to play for authority in the divinely authorized arrangements for marriage.

Other settings for the exercise of authority are also addressed in the Scriptures. We can think here of the relationship of employer and employee and its extension to the institution of slavery. We see, too, authority exercised by those who are teachers or rabbis. In relation to civic institutions, the author of 1 Peter (1 Pet 2) exhorts his readers to ensure that their public behavior does not bring the Christian faith into disrepute. He then goes on to write: "*Be subject for the Lord's sake to every human institution, whether it be to the emperor as supreme, or to governors as sent by him to punish those who do evil and to praise those who do good*" (vv. 13–14). What reason does he offer? "*For this is the will of God, that by doing good you should put to silence the ignorance of foolish people*" (v.

15). He concludes: *"Honour everyone. Love the brotherhood. Fear God. Honour the emperor"* (v. 17).

Here, we can see that it is obedience to God in our conscience that binds us in our subjection to human institutions. These are not authorities in parallel with the authority of God but rather subordinate to him. In relation to political powers, most of the time, the laws of legitimate authority bind in conscience; occasionally, when they coerce us into acting counter to Christ, we are bound to follow our true Master. It is likewise with other institutions, marriage, the family, our work, and also with the authority of experts; each of them carries authority from God, but only within the limits which he approves.

Reflections of Faith

Human Authority: Finding a More Balanced Attitude

Those of us who are believers brought up in Western societies have had great difficulty in arriving at a convincing and convinced attitude towards authorities of all kinds. If we belong to the group who were young in the first half of the twentieth century, then we were raised so as to be respectful of those in authority, and that included the "authority" of social norms. The boss was obeyed, children were "seen and not heard," and divorcées were looked down on for having offended the institution of marriage. This approach no doubt helped keep society together, but it may also have led to much suffering when authority was poorly exercised. Those growing up during the past fifty years or so have seen a dramatic change in secular views on authority, and today there is much greater distrust of those who hold positions of leadership, whether it be politicians, police, the courts, teachers, and even parents. This has likely resulted in less bullying and abuse of authority but at the expense of social cohesion. I imagine most people would accept that their society is growing increasingly fragmented even as more people are being protected from abuses of authority.

Mostly, Christians have fitted in with these changes. We are as ready as our secular neighbors to criticize court judgments without knowing all the facts. We willingly expose ourselves to the populist anti-authority attitudes that are so common, for example, on the evening TV news. As believing parents, along with the rest of society, we struggle to know how to raise children in a way that results in them becoming good citizens as well as people of character; for us, perhaps even more bewildering is the task of helping our children become convinced and active Christians. Our example as parents is no longer authoritative or compelling. On the question of political authority, whether we are believers or nonbelievers, most of us think we could do a better job of running our country than those who are our current leaders. That this last statement is not intended as an exaggeration but a statement of sober observation is perhaps the first hint that our current perceptions about ourselves and about authority are seriously distorted.

Many who have thought about this crisis of authority have argued that even though it might to be a relatively recent phenomenon, underlying it is probably a centuries-long, whole-of-culture movement which has paved the way for the crisis to develop. This idea of a much longer-term tide of history at work makes good sense when we consider that difficulties in the exercise of authority are simply one among a host of unsettling society-wide changes that people have recognized in recent decades. It seems as though our whole Western culture has been moving slowly in a particular direction over the centuries with a momentum all its own, and while many still talk about the pendulum that will swing back soon, increasingly it does not look like that will happen. Thinking about this in terms of the five key social motives we have considered, my own hunch is that our culture has empowered the motive of dominance (as comparison and competition) and along with that has weakened or suppressed that of attachment. This effect on attachment also means that conscience has become increasingly compromised (because it depends on the attachment motive). If it is the case that two of the three most important drivers of human behavior have been overshadowed by the dominance of dominance, then much of what has happened in Western nations during our lifetimes begins to make sense. However, to say that is to immediately raise the question as to *why* the unbalancing I have described should have occurred at this point in history. In the next chapter, which considers how the motives have been affected by historical processes, I offer a few observations in response to this question.

Whatever the deeper causes of the predicament we face concerning authority, the reality is that as believers we must address this issue in the best way we know, which is through the Scriptures and with the help of other believers. The more we immerse ourselves in the biblical mindset, the greater capacity we will have to undo the false messages which our culture has insinuated into our subconscious mind. The Old Testament gives us a fundamental conviction about God's authority and how important it is to obey him. It also teaches us how weak is unaided human nature in being able, with full heart, to remain obedient to the Lord. In the New Testament, these basic truths are developed in the light of the cross, and a reliable picture emerges of how authority, attachment, and dominance are to relate to each other. Keep in mind that without a serious and sustained commitment to finding one's way into New Testament thinking about authority, we will not be able to escape the prison of our cultural understanding of this matter.

One of the most important truths of the Scriptures on this theme is that we are to see ourselves as pilgrims in this world, that it is not our ultimate home: *"For here we have no lasting city, but we seek the city that is to come"* (Heb 13:14). To continually keep this at the back of our mind allows us to avoid treating matters to do with authority as more important than they really are. Authorities will abuse their authority and treat us in ways that diminish us. We know this. But our earthly self is not ultimately important. As the Scriptures urge us: *"Set your minds on things that are above, not on things that are on earth. For you have died, and your life is hidden with Christ in God. When Christ who is your life appears, then you also will appear with him in glory"* (Col 3:2–4). This reminds us of the true center of our self. But to realize that and to live by it is a hard-won and life-long lesson.

Another idea found in the Scriptures is that God, in calling individuals to positions of authority, commonly works against the very human belief that authority must be closely connected with dominance. By that, I mean the false idea that those who gain positions of authority are there because they are fundamentally better persons than you or I. Sadly, this distortion has been a hallmark of authority in the church at many points in her life. However, it is not God's way. Consider the selection of Israel's first king, recounted in the First Book of Samuel. There the sons of Jesse are paraded before the prophet Samuel, who thinks that they would make ideal kings because of their bearing, their build, and such. But God rejects each of them. Only the youngest son, David, the shepherd boy who still bears the ruddiness of youth, is anointed for the future work of the king of Judah and Israel. Likewise, we find those who will carry the authority of apostleship, the men who will become the foundation stones of the kingdom of God, to be a rather inconsequential, non-dominant group of disciples. Then there is our Lord himself, again, a "nobody" from the back blocks of Galilee, a region far away from the center of power which was Jerusalem. And yet upon him, as it turns out, rests all authority, dominion, and power. In God's approach, authority and dominance do not necessarily coincide (although competence and certain features associated with dominance, e.g., height, voice, and manner, are useful in the exercise of authority). This means that the believer under earthly authority respects that authority as being at least permitted by God, and in many cases willed by him, and is willing to acknowledge the gifts that a person brings to bear to that task. However, these attitudes will not translate into an obsequiousness that fawns upon leaders and acts in ways that diminish one's own dignity.

A peaceful attitude towards authority sees it always in the larger scheme of things. In obedience to God, it submits to legitimate authority and as a default, will trust it and avoid a suspicious or jaundiced attitude towards it. Such a disposition will also be on the lookout for a preciousness or defensiveness within oneself. Along with this, it will know that it is obedience to the *office* of the one in authority, rather than to the *person* who holds that position, which counts. The person themselves can show serious defects in character and judgment, and as followers we need not be blind to these. But we are called to follow these people as officebearers, not as human beings.

How Are Believers to Exercise Authority?

Jesus gives us the basic rule for how believers are to be authorities. To his disciples he said, *"You know that those who are considered rulers of the Gentiles lord it over them, and their great ones exercise authority over them. But it shall not be so among you. But whoever would be great among you must be your servant, and whoever would be first among you must be slave of all. For even the Son of Man came not to be served but to serve, and to give his life as a ransom for many"* (Mark 10:42–45).

This is often presented in terms of a contrast between being a servant versus not being a servant. The commonly heard phrase is "servant leadership." I have found this approach mostly unsatisfying, mainly because it is not clear how we are to distinguish the different behaviors and attitudes of "chiefs and Indians." In other words, it sheds no light on what a leader as distinct from a follower is to do—both should act in the service of others! Hardly more helpful is the advice that a leader is to serve the interests of all his followers, not just of any particular individual (himself included) or group. Again, for groups of believers, all should think that way, not only the leaders!

Perhaps a more useful approach is to rephrase the question in this way: What characteristics should the leader-follower relationship display? In thinking about the matter like this, we subvert the powerful cultural assumption that the main problem in groups, societies, and nations today is with leaders rather than it being a problem also with those who are led. Leaders today, whatever group of people they lead, often have extraordinary difficulty in carrying out their responsibilities because those who are led do not imagine that they are just as responsible for monitoring their own behavior in relation to their leaders as are leaders to them. With that in mind, I would offer the following ideas about the leader-follower relationship in light of what has been said about conscience and its relation to other motives:

First, perhaps the most important consideration for a Christian approach to authority has to do with how the dominance and conscience motives are brought to bear on the matter. In chapter 2 we saw how certain qualities, attitudes, and behaviors signal dominance and submission in a relationship. Dominance is shown by a person taking the initiative, leading the interaction, displaying such qualities as a less anxious/freer emotional tone, a willingness to correct others, as well as by such physical characteristics as a deeper voice, less rounded facial features, and having a stronger/taller build. All these serve the purpose of signalling how the relationship is to proceed. If the dominance of one party is accepted by both, then things will run smoother than if it is contested and has to be established between them. The usual outcome of dominance in a relationship is that one of the two—the dominant one—will gain more benefits than the one who must submit to him/her.

Now, when it comes to Christian authority, we can say that leaders are to draw upon some dominance-signalling *behaviors and characteristics* when they engage with their followers so that the latter will be more willing to be responsive to their leadership. However, when it comes to the typical *benefits* of dominance mentioned above, it is important that Christ-inspired leaders not seek after them. Thus, they should not assume the right to dominate conversations or take advantage of their followers' tendency to give them undue attention. Nor should they interact mainly with higher-status members of their group or accept any of the other spoils that typically accrue to a dominant person. Let us consider Jesus' comments on authority in this light. For him, being a servant leader would mean not taking advantage of a dominance/submission relationship to advance one's own interests but rather to use it for the sake of others in one's group. Such a leader, in their interactions with individual group members or with the group as a whole, will seek the good—and that means also the social good—of the others. To achieve this requires a strong conscience on the part of leaders, one which is closely attuned to the example and teaching of Christ, since dominance, as we have observed, is an immensely powerful motive which has the tendency to override conscience.

There is a reciprocal dimension to this arrangement that calls for responsibility on the part of followers, and here believers must be on their guard. The "natural" tendency for them is to fit into the submissive role which, in the normal operation of dominance relationships, requires that they provide the dominant party with the relevant social benefits or goods, or at least accept their appropriation. However, in a Christian authority relationship, to do so is to cause harm to leaders because such action serves to tempt them towards self-indulgence and pride and thus to failure as a leader. Followers, therefore, are called to preserve a tension between accepting their position as follower but at the same time not being drawn into a passivity and acquiescence that would hinder their sense of responsibility for themselves and for the other members of the group. Leaders might take much of the initiative in a group, but followers will actively support such initiatives and offer their own ideas to the group. Leaders will consider the interests of the group, but so too will followers, in their case, especially avoiding the temptation to freeloading, or taking without giving to a group. Finally, whereas leaders, *as leaders*, are to serve the other members in advancing the purposes of the group, followers will model respectful behavior when interacting with their leaders, not least as a way of assisting the latter in their task.

Secondly, among the other motives that of attachment has a not insignificant, beneath-the-surface part to play in the exercise of Christian authority. In some large-scale groups, for example nations or religious denominations, as well as in families in which close personal relationships are the norm, those in authority must take account of the sense of security among members which can be undermined both by external and internal threats to group cohesion. In this case, the qualities of good parents, that is, in their role as attachment figures, are also called for in those who lead nations or religious groups. Communicating a sense of assurance, demonstrating competence and resoluteness in dealing with threats, and a dedication to maintaining the security of the group; these are the essential tasks of those in authority in such circumstances. The British wartime prime minister Winston Churchill encapsulates this kind of leadership and authority in the secular realm, while a spiritual leader such as St. John Paul II, who became a rock of spiritual security for so many Catholics and other believers during his quarter-century as pope, is an example of such a leader of the faithful. Each in their own way was able to respond to the attachment needs of their people during times of great threat.

For any social or political group in which safety and security play an important part, a warm, non-defensive, and emotionally responsive style is needed, but also one which communicates conviction and strength. Conversely, group members themselves can do much to assist their leaders in this regard by discouraging inflammatory or unreasonably disturbing comments by other members. The communicative tone of a group can be as much the result of followers' actions as it is that of leaders.

At the conclusion of this two-chapter section on conscience, I hope that it is apparent to the reader that, more than the other four motives, that of conscience determines how much our actions reveal the dignity which God has given us as human beings. While the Catholic Catechism speaks of the human heart in the following ways, it could equally be describing our conscience: "[The human heart] is the place of truth, where we choose life or death. It is the place of encounter, because as image of God we live in relation: it is the place of covenant."[3] At its best, it is that which sets us humans apart; we are more than our history, our evolution, or our biology.

---

3. *Catechism of the Catholic Church*, sec. 2563.

11

Human Motivation and Historical Forces

THUS FAR IN THIS BOOK, we have discussed social motives which are part of our human nature. Earlier I also remarked that there are other motives, some less social and some less important, that go to make up who we are as human beings. For example, we possess a powerful motive towards what might be called "harm avoidance," that is, the preservation of our health and life. We know that this works strongly when we drive a car and keep a lookout for danger, or when we seek to avoid sicknesses or diseases. Its workings help explain the enthusiasm for gym workouts and the particular care we take in monitoring our diet. Another less powerful motive is that of curiosity, which kicks in particularly when we find ourselves in a new situation or confronted with an area of knowledge unfamiliar to us and need to gain a sense of the "lay of the land." Apart from our conscience, these, along with the other major motives we have discussed, are not specific to our species, since we observe them in various forms among non-human animals. All of this is very "biological!" Now, there is another side to our life—and like conscience, it is distinctively human—which talk of motives takes little account of, but which we must consider if our story is to cover the major features of those forces which drive human behavior. We might think of this other aspect as the *history* side of things. If we have so far been looking at our "nature" as humans, now we must consider our "history," or how the motives change over time in the ways they express themselves.[1]

1. Giving only one chapter to a discussion of the historical and cultural dimensions

Social Motives through History

Human motives are part of the hugely complex biological processes that make up our physical and psychological being. And yet we know, too, that humans change over periods of decades and centuries, admittedly only in minimal ways in our biology or basic psychology, but very much in the way these parts of our nature are manifested. Think, for example, of the dominance/competence motive and how the era of the mobile phone with all the possibilities afforded by that technology has changed how we express that motive. The excitement of being able to do many new things using phone apps is something that was unknown even as recently as the late 1990s. The ability to speak from my home in Melbourne, Australia, to another person who is out wandering in the country in rural Scotland, on the other side of the world, is an example of just how greatly expanded are the possibilities of action for the average person today. And there have been several other historical changes within our own lifetime which likewise have worked to alter the way our core motives are expressed. In short, it is clear that we must take account of history and the changes that come with the passage of years in our description of human motives. In doing so, our focus will be on the motives of attachment and dominance/competence since, as we have seen already, it is the relationship between these two which appears to have the most profound effects on how we think as well as the forms which Western societies have taken. Yet, as we will see, cultural changes have also left their mark on how other motives work.

Now, because there have been a vast number of changes in our times which have affected the way we exercise our motives, first, what I will do here is to give a description of two such ways simply to illustrate the effects of history on our motives. As examples, I have chosen to discuss (a) the move towards greater convenience, and (b) the growing tendency to try to extract and distil the pleasure that comes with fulfilling a motive. Following that, I will consider a third, and what I believe is a mostly unacknowledged but remarkably powerful shift occurring in Western society, one which perhaps lies at the root of most of the other changes of which we can think. Indeed, it might be one of the major factors in

---

of human motivation does not signal their relative lack of importance but rather the limits of my own competence. Just how illuminating for an understanding of human behavior such analyses can be is shown by a work such as that of Joseph Henrich, *The Weirdest People in the World.*

bringing about the imbalance between dominance, attachment, and conscience that I have mentioned in previous chapters: I am referring—perhaps surprisingly—to the movement towards smaller families.

Technology and the Attraction of Ease

Consider the development of footwear in Western societies. For many centuries, leather was almost the sole material used to manufacture shoes. It possesses properties that make it useful for such a purpose. And yet, for all its value, it has its limitations. In times past, with new shoes, over a period of weeks and months, feet had to accustom themselves to the form of the shoes, and this could be painful. Leather soles, too, could be slippery on smooth surfaces, and leather footwear could leave one's feet tired and sore at the end of a day of walking. In all these respects, modern forms of shoe, both in the ways leather itself is processed and in the new materials used, have made big improvements; long-standing problems have been solved. Only the most doggedly conservative person would resist the notion that this is an example of progress.

Yet, other forms of improvement in contemporary societies are more ambiguous. Take, as an example, the electric tumble clothes dryer. With it, no longer is a person required to hang out washing on a clothesline and hope that the weather will be kind enough to allow it to dry. Modern clothes dryers leave washing feeling soft and fluffy and generally take much less time to do their work than does the traditional way of drying clothes. We can see here straightforward evidence of convenience. And yet, not all is positive. The heavy use of electricity of a clothes dryer still translates into a significant increase in the release of CO_2 into the atmosphere and, furthermore, it is commonly the case that clothing does not last as long through frequent tumble drying. But there is another often-hidden issue that the use of clothes dryers and other technologies raises, and that is the question: Is convenience *always* a human good? Does making something easy in and of itself mean actual improvement in the way we live?

This might seem like a silly question, since our culture has routinely affirmed or at least assumed that convenience is virtually an unalloyed good. How could it be otherwise? Ease and convenience provide us with more time to do other more meaningful activities. Yet it is reasonable for us to question such an assumption. The following example makes the point well.

The Institute for Advanced Study at Princeton University in Princeton, New Jersey, was established in the 1930s to discover new knowledge for its own sake. Scientists and scholars invited to be part of the institute have no teaching responsibilities, no research contracts, and have lifetime tenure. A perfectly convenient setup, one might say. All they are there for is to advance human knowledge. We might call this the ideal setting for such a purpose, and it is true that many of the greatest minds of the past century, including Albert Einstein, Robert Oppenheimer, and Kurt Gödel, have been associated with the center. And yet, it is not at all clear that it has been the time spent at the IAS which has led to the great achievements of these people. Richard Feynman, a famous physicist, once remarked:

> When I was at Princeton in the 1940s, I could see what happened to those great minds at the Institute for Advanced Study who had been specially selected for their tremendous brains and were now given this opportunity to sit in this lovely house by the woods there, with no classes to teach, with no obligations whatsoever. These poor bastards could now sit and think clearly all by themselves, okay? So, they don't get any ideas for a while: They have every opportunity to do something, and they're not getting any ideas. I believe that in a situation like this a kind of guilt or depression worms inside of you, and you begin to *worry* about not getting any ideas. And nothing happens. Still no ideas come. Nothing happens because there's not enough *real* activity and challenge: You're not in contact with the experimental guys. You don't have to think how to answer questions from the students. Nothing![2]

What Feynman writes here points to a phenomenon that many before him have observed: humans work better when they operate with moderate rather than low levels of inconvenience. Not all ease is good ease. Expressed in the language of motives, we might say that having things exactly right so that we can pursue the goals which we set in line with our social motives is not always a good thing. Some inconvenience is needed to energize our motives. Also, in working towards our goals, if the path is made too easy for us, our growth in virtue and character will be hindered. Perhaps the oft-mentioned increases in depression and the

---

2. Feynman and Leighton, *Surely You're Joking*.

burgeoning use of anti-depressants across Western nations might have some connection with this historical change in the way we unthinkingly adopt convenient technologies to achieve the fulfilment of our motives.

Extracting Pleasures from the Operation of Motives

Another cultural change affecting the expression of the key motives is our success in distilling and "bottling" those rewarding experiences that accompany the achievement of our motivated activities. For example, we can know the joy of being able to play an impressive-sounding piano piece simply by learning the melody line and having the complex accompaniment added by our digital instrument. Once we are able to capture and control such pleasures, no longer are we required to endure the delay in gratification that trial-and-error or hours of practice force on us. Consider how widespread are the following examples of the distillation and control of pleasures associated with social motives.

Think about the recent focus upon fine eating that has spawned celebrity restaurants, exotic cuisines, popular TV shows, and innumerable cooking books. In Australia we took over the British diet of predictable variations of meat-and-vegetable combinations with the occasional more adventurous meal out. But now, in its place, variety, novelty, new tastes, and a diverse range of cooking styles and techniques are the routine expectation for the average diet. In this development, the joy of eating has been distilled and intensified to a remarkable degree.

Similar concentrations of pleasure associated with the range of human motives can be observed outside the dining room or restaurant. When in the past alcoholic drinks helped lubricate social interaction among people, this has at least partly given way to a less social purpose of seeking out the experience of drunkenness that no longer bothers with the constraints that friends and family placed on drinking to excess. More efficient and intense still is the experience of recreational drugs that are so concentrated in their effect that for many users everyday life can come to seem colorless and lifeless. Also, the sexual relationship that can be both ho-hum and routine but also exciting and satisfying within marriage can today be enhanced through the use of pornography, sex toys, BDSM, swinging groups, and other supercharged forms of sexual pleasure. As a final example, we might note the distillation of human pleasure in the domain of romantic relationships. The tension between exhilarating expectation and anxious uncertainty that marked the process of courting in the past has given way to rapid friendship-making (e.g., speed-dating) and early sexual encounters that again concentrate the positive experiences and lessen the negative. Unfortunately, these also diminish the drama of the full process and reduce them to the banal, bare bones of romantic linking up.

These are just some of the means Western culture has used to separate off the pleasures connected with motives from the effort involved in exercising them. The expert piano player, the fluent non-native speaker of French, the skilled karate exponent, all invested at least 10,000 hours of training and practice to reach their level of competence and the enjoyment that comes with it. The older husband and wife spent many hours together getting to know each other at an intimate psychological level and, beyond that, spent years learning the character and ways of their partner before they could arrive at that level of deep trust and security in their marriage which represents the earthly fulfilment of the attachment drive. The lifelong task of growing, refining, and integrating one's conscience into the life of faith, which involves a careful and assiduous use of advice from saints and other experts, is able to bring the mature believer to a sense of peace that is resistant to almost any adversity that might come their way. To extract the sense of enjoyment and calm that is the welcome *side-effect* of the successful outworking of human motives, and to make that sense or experience an end in itself, is another feature of the history of Western societies, one which marks a notable change in the way we express our fundamental motives.[3]

---

3. Perhaps here it is appropriate to offer a comment about how these two historical processes, the pursuit of convenience and the distillation and over-valuing of pleasure, connect with the Christian tradition. One of the pair of values that believers are required to balance is that between the cultivation of a longing for seeing the Lord face-to-face and investing energies in the tasks presented by this earthly life. In former times, especially when life was burdensome and often short, the problem of finding a balance was not so pressing, since reminders of the age to come were a common part of everyday life. However, in our times, earthly conveniences and pleasures are so prevalent in the lives of most Western believers that we struggle to find a lively hope of eternal life. This life seems just too good to let go of. But the Scriptures have given us sound advice on this: *"Do not love the world or the things of the world. If anyone loves the world, the love of the Father is not in him . . . the world is passing away along with its desires"* (1 John 2: 15, 17). This would suggest that we Christians ought to be cautious of convenience and pleasure in the sense that we must not grow too attached to them. The ascetical tradition contains much wisdom as to how this caution might be exercised. See chapter 14 for further discussion of this point.

Low Fertility Rates and Human Motives[4]

A final historical process, one which I believe goes to the root of many of the other changes touching on the way motives show themselves within Western culture, relates to family size. Modern Western societies are extraordinarily complex, and the forces pushing them this way and that are difficult to tease out from each other. Technology and wealth are certainly key—and perhaps fundamental—forces of this kind, but another candidate has been discussed in recent decades which may turn out to be equally fundamental, and that is the factor of fertility. The fertility level of a nation is an indicator of how many children, on average, the female citizens of child-bearing age will likely have. Of course, over the centuries there is variation in this number due to events such as plagues, famine, and wars. But looked at over longer periods of time, on average, women have given birth to more than four and often up to six or eight children. One might think that this would lead to massive growth in populations, yet this has not generally been the case, since the rate at which people die has also been high. Death of infants within the first year of their birth has been a particular factor that has worked against rapid population growth.

In recent centuries, however, something quite unprecedented, as far as we know, has occurred in many nations around the world, beginning with those in Europe. Towards the middle of the nineteenth century, France's fertility rate began to decline and has shown no signs of being restored to its former levels ever since. Other nations soon followed suit. England, then many other European nations, also saw their rates of fertility begin a downward slide, and like France remain today at historically low levels. Such patterns have now been observed among all nations across the world except for some developing African countries, and it is expected that they, too, will soon take the same pathway.

Apart from this steady decline, another phenomenon has been noticed in the fertility rates of many nations after about the year 1960. Those countries which were early on the path to low fertility generally plateaued at a rate of just above two children per woman, this figure meaning that population levels would be stable due to the replacement of each generation with roughly the same number of people in the next. However, after the 1960s, these same nations saw a further loss of fertility so that many of

---

4. For a discussion of the ideas linked to this theme, see Newson and Richerson, "Why Do People Become Modern?" 117–58; Newson et al., "Why Are Modern Families Small?" 360–75; also, Patterson, "A Cultural Evolutionary Approach."

them recorded scores between 1.0 and 1.5 children, well below the level needed for replacement. What appeared to be happening here was that, with the availability of affordable and effective contraception, couples could exercise greater control over the size of their family, and this led to the further reduction in the number of children. Today almost all nations with advanced economies have fertility rates which are below, and often well below, replacement level. Their populations would be on a pathway towards extinction were it not for replenishment through immigration.

What are the suggested causes for this phenomenon? Something like the following account has been well argued. The Industrial Revolution in Europe had the effect of drawing sizeable portions of a nation's rural population to live in the cities, which grew as a result of the employment opportunities arising from flourishing manufacturing industries. Cities grew, and rural areas declined. For families on farms in those times, once children reached a certain age, they became useful in helping out with the farming work, or, to put it another way, they became a net benefit to their parents. This was not so much the case in towns and cities, where the parents' work was mostly away from the home. With the introduction of labor laws preventing the exploitation of young children, this difference became even more pronounced. Added to this, it made sense for the women in urban families to reduce the number of children they bore so that they could take up employment and contribute to the family income. And whereas the "female" social world in established rural settings typically contributed significantly to the well-being of the community, the necessity of the urban breadwinner (usually male) to follow wherever employment lead meant that this "female" world could not take hold as easily since it commonly suffered frequent disruption. All this resulted in work outside the home having for women an enhanced value because it was a marker of status ("People are willing to pay for my work") and personal freedom ("I have my own money to spend"). Living in cities, no longer were women forced to spend their lives bearing and raising children in often isolated social situations. We should note that this move towards greater female participation in paid employment took many decades to show itself clearly after fertility rates began to decline, but it has been a reality common to industrialized nations.

We can see from these processes that, due to the growth in general wealth arising from the Industrial Revolution and the movement of large numbers of citizens from farms to cities, the incentives which traditionally pushed husbands and wives to have large numbers of children no longer operated, and in their place were pressures to keep families small. Once this reduction in fertility took hold, there was little that could be done to reverse it even if governments had wanted to do so. In fact, several nations have attempted to do so, yet even with the capacities of a modern state such as Singapore, which has worked hard to raise numbers of births, there has been little success. For this reason, nations have had to resort to relying upon large numbers of immigrants to grow their populations and thus their economies. For example, Australia's extraordinary phase of virtually uninterrupted economic growth in the two decades after roughly the year 2000 can be put down—at least in large part—to the elevated levels of migrant intake that marked that period.

What are some of the changes in the way motives have shown themselves in societies which have witnessed reduced fertility levels? Growth in the overall wealth of a nation, the opportunities for career advancement that are available especially in large cities, and the greatly increased power of governments to provide many forms of security to their citizens, e.g., law and order, education and employment, medical services and social welfare, all these have combined to enhance the dominance/competence motive among large segments of Western society and to weaken attachment connections which families and the church have traditionally provided. We raise our children to be independent more than dependent, to be competent and if possible successful more than focussed on deep and sustained social relationships and competitive more than cooperative. And because we are so fully immersed in this culture of the predominance of dominance, we are incapable of seeing its harmful effects. To do that would require us to spend some time in another, non-Western culture and then observe our own culture from outside, as it were. Certainly, such cultures will have their own difficulties with the dominance motive, but they will be different to those of our own, and for that reason we could more easily see Western culture for what it is.

Think, for example, about young married couples planning their future life together. Today they would probably come from small families themselves, perhaps with one sibling or even none. It is increasingly likely that they would have both received post-secondary qualifications which they would not want to squander. They would like to live in a house that they own and more generally to achieve financial security. She sees a fruitful career path before her and is therefore reluctant to compromise it by taking time out for children. And yet they would both like to have children; indeed, most couples do. But they are conscious, too, that they live in what appears to be an already overpopulated world and they fear for the long-term effects of too many humans on the planet and its available resources. Finally, at a deeper, probably subconscious level, they have been touched by the sense of hopelessness which pervades our culture and wonder whether it a good thing to bring another human being/consciousness into the world with all its turmoil and indeed its meaninglessness. To override these considerations so as to find a justification for having children requires something very powerful, and that is what most couples—including even many of those with religious convictions—do not possess.

Let us imagine that our imaginary couple decides to have a child. It happens when the wife is about thirty years of age, established in her career path, so that she is able to take off a year from her employment to care for her infant daughter. Both parents invest much time and effort in her development, giving her every opportunity to flourish. Given that she is the sole focus of her parents' attention, she will probably be spoiled in the sense of having her desires catered for in a way that would not be possible in a larger family. However, at twelve months of age, she will have to adapt emotionally to the stress of full-time childcare, since her mother has to return to work to keep her career moving forward. This will be simply one element of a wider encouragement towards the child's independence. Indeed, independence, self-reliance, a keen desire to achieve, social confidence, individualism, and a strong personal identity will be the values her parents will seek to instil in her. These are values closely linked to the dominance/competence motive. On the other hand, those associated with the attachment system—dependence, reliance on others, vulnerability, consideration of others, group-focused—are much less on the horizon.

We can see, then, that low fertility rates appear to be a fundamental factor in shaping the way that both the dominance and attachment motives express themselves in contemporary Western culture. This is a historically long-term process, and the problems it presents to us are ones for which we have not yet found adequate solutions. Part of the reason for that failure is the fact that our solution-seeking is itself driven by the dominance motive which is loath to propose courses of action which would limit its own power however necessary that might be. Solutions therefore must come from thinking that is guided not by dominance but by conscience. Needless to say, such solutions would be a very bitter pill to swallow for most Westerners who are so powerfully committed—one might say even addicted—to the cultivation of the dominance motive.

A cluster of possibilities such as the following might be required to restore the fertility rate of a Western nation to population replacement level: educating believers about the scriptural injunction to be fruitful and multiply as well as the blessing that can come from having children; prioritizing pastoral care for families so that couples with children are intentionally supported in the task of nurturing their spiritual and psychological well-being; an emphasis in church teaching about gender complementarity and training which helps couples to resist the typically destructive ideas of female empowerment and equity; developing an influential *feminine* social world that might better support women who opt to care full-time for their children and thus delay their re-entry into employment; and finally substantial government financial support for couples who have more than one child. As the reader will immediately note, none of these is particularly attractive, and some are positively anathema to the dominance-controlled mind! Yet a strong partnership between church and family, one which will grow both the family *and* the church, offers the best chance of helping contemporary society to find some measure of balance in what is at present a seriously distorted mix of social motives.

In this chapter I have identified a few historical factors which I believe have played a significant part in shaping the expression of human motives in our time. Each is deeply entrenched in our ways of thinking. So how we face the challenges they present to us as believers will depend crucially on whether we are open to the witness of the Scriptures and the leading of the Spirit in these matters. My sense is that the path forward will be a difficult one for people of faith.

Conclusion to Part I

WE HAVE REACHED THE end of part I. My aim has been to lay out before the reader a relatively simplified framework that shows how the main social motives that we have been given by our Creator work to drive us towards various ways of thought and types of actions. I began with the dominance motive because it is by far the most influential in shaping our longer-term purposes as well as much of our daily activity. It is also the one about which our Lord most strongly warned his disciples, encouraging them to find a path towards humility and away from pride and vainglory. I then brought into the picture the motive of attachment and attempted to show that it is the system that operates beneath the horizon, below our awareness, but for all that, I argued that it is much more significant in our lives than we might imagine. For both these motives, I distinguished between how they touched us, on the one hand, as individuals and, on the other, when we view ourselves as members of social groups. Then followed a discussion of social reciprocity and its power to drive our sense of right relations with other people, our appreciation of the need for mutual respect for each other, and for the demands of a just ordering of our communities. A brief treatment of mating, the last of the self-oriented motives, raised questions about how men and women form sexual partnerships, that is, marriage relations, and how their different gendered qualities push them towards distinctive ways of relating as husbands and wives.

The last motive, conscience, was described in terms of a personal relation with God rather than simply as a body of practical knowledge about what works in life and what does not. Conscience was described as organizing the other motives or at least ensuring that they do not go their own way, and from this perspective it could be seen as a motive which always works in concert with other motives, that is, it does not operate by itself but requires one or more of the others to give it something to work on.

Throughout this first part, I have also sought to show that the Scriptures take account of the above elements of our makeup when they relate how the Lord engages with us. And more than that, they give teaching which helps us to move beyond a mere description of human motivation so as to enlighten us as to what we need to be on our guard about and how we are to make that structure work in our lives.

Following the description of each motive and the relevant biblical teaching, I have dealt with some questions that arise immediately from a reflection on that material, and which generally required discussion drawing only upon consideration of one or two of the motives.

To round out the work of part I, in the closing chapter (chapter 11) I discussed some of the ways in which historical forces, especially during the past century or more, have led to changes in the way our motives are expressed, particularly in relation to the dominance and attachment systems.

In part II, my aim is to help the reader deepen his or her grasp of the power of an understanding of the principles set out in part I by providing examples of how they might apply in a select range of topics of everyday interest. The goal for the second part, then, is to show how conceiving of human motivation as I have done in part I might be used in significant areas of life.

Part II

Wider Perspectives

Some Implications for Faith
An Introduction

THE MATERIAL CONTAINED IN part I seeks to provide a framework for understanding some of the major dynamics of the human heart and in particular those forces or motives which drive our conduct. In theology this material belongs to what is called "theological anthropology" or "anthropology" for short, and I will sometimes refer to it in those terms.

In the framework I have presented, the forces I describe are, for the most part, beyond our normal awareness, and it is only with difficulty that what I wrote about them can be digested and made part of one's thinking. The attentive reader of part I will have observed that it contains a number of ideas which run counter to everyday thinking about ourselves, and these take some effort on the reader's part to make them useful in daily life. In order to assist this process, in the eight essays of part II, I attempt to use the matter of part I to shed what I hope will be some new light on issues that are often problematic for us believers who live in Western societies. What I seek to illuminate are the deeper psychological processes that are at work when we think about these issues; for example, what is it that underlies a person's belief or disbelief in God? On such a question, the reader is forewarned that I will not be bringing forth arguments in favor of that belief of the kind that Christian theologians have already well argued. Instead, I will be thinking about religious belief as a psychological phenomenon: What is it about our motives which pushes us towards or away from such belief, and how does faith in God relate to optimal *human* functioning? From a Christian perspective one would expect that the Creator God would have shaped mankind in such a way that a healthy relation with him would correspond to a similarly healthy human psychology. I will be exploring this connection. But the reader is urged to remember that such links do not replace the sensible reasons given by Christian faith for the beliefs it holds. These are primary; what I offer is more of a support or a help to such belief. A similar caution is needed when reading the other essays in this part of the book. The faith found in the Scriptures and which has been handed down to us from the apostles comes first; understanding ourselves in relation to that faith can be a help to us, but it is only that. It can never replace our understanding of the faith as given to us by the Lord.

Yet, even beyond this, I have been conscious while preparing the material included here that neither sound reasons for holding to Christian beliefs nor the support for these beliefs which the study of the psychology of man can offer is truly central to the whole question of Christian faith. The true core of such faith is the encounter with Christ to which he calls every human being. As Pope Benedict XVI once expressed it: "There is nothing more beautiful than to be surprised by the Gospel, by the encounter with Christ. There is nothing more beautiful than to know him and to speak to others of our friendship with him."[1] Apart from that encounter, everything else that I have written here just sits on the sidelines. It can be helpful for those whose hearts are even a little bit open to the invitation Christ offers him or her, for it can help ease perplexities and untie the shackles of false convictions that we may have accepted in the past. But it cannot substitute for a genuine encounter with Christ. A faith based solely on rationality and scientific understanding is not faith at all. Only Christ can open our eyes in the way they need to be opened!

So, with that in mind, I invite you to consider the material in the essays of part II. If it is of any help, my hope is that it will impel the reader towards an ever more open and trusting attitude towards the One who, I believe, is the fulfilment of our deepest desires, yearnings, and, yes, motives, Jesus Christ.

---

1. Benedict XVI, "Homily."

12

"Lord, I Believe in You: Help Me in My Unbelief!"

CONSIDERED AS A WORLDWIDE phenomenon, belief in God is growing faster than unbelief.[1] Yet most readers of this book will live in countries where belief has been in decline for several decades. In my own nation of Australia over a period of approximately a century from 1911 to 2016, religious affiliation has shrunk from 96 percent to about 60 percent. And these figures mask the fact that many who identify with a religion do not in fact hold to a belief in God. It seems that among nations that are the most advanced and sophisticated such belief is on a pathway to insignificance. And yet, like many of the changes and trends that appear in Western nations, this one, too—at least in the long term—might not be as unrelenting as it might seem to us from our perspective. Let us consider the phenomenon of the loss of faith from both a Christian perspective and in the light of the anthropology I have offered the reader in part I.

In the Christian conception of things, we do not typically arrive at a faith in Jesus Christ from the bottom up, that is, from pondering reality and the drama of human life and then, by dint of sound reasoning, reach the endpoint of a Christian faith. Instead, we hear the Good News of Jesus Christ, we are confronted by him through his personal address to us as individuals, and we either respond in faith and trust, or turn away from him. Only after our acceptance of his message and then, only over time, do we come to make sense of the rest of our lives, including our

---

1. Pew Research Center, "The Future of World Religions."

former beliefs about God, but that happens primarily through the lens of our faith.

And yet, when believers think about others who do not share their faith—and here I am thinking of those who have full confidence in their unbelief and the unreasonableness of Christian faith—they, that is, believers, can experience unsettling challenges to their own understanding. The stridency of those who oppose our faith, together with the mostly unspoken antagonism of our secular governments, are a burden for us and often result in us doubting our faith.

Furthermore, our Western secularized culture has no real incentive to question itself about the basis of its own way of thinking; it seems to be quite confident of its "unfaith" position and so feels no need to make it the focus of intensive questioning. For this reason, the majority of secular people are closed to a consideration of the invitation that Jesus Christ offers them. In this chapter, I want to deal with both these matters by considering religious belief in the light of the theological anthropology of part I. In doing so, I hope to provide some food for thought both for those who are already Christians, and for those who do not yet believe in Christ.

The Collapse of Belief and Its Causes

When thinking about the decline of belief in God which I have noted, one might be tempted to explain this as the result of an ever-wider appreciation of the use of reason when thinking about these things and a gradual turning away from ways of thought based on fear or ignorance. In this case, one would expect a relatively consistent decline wherever Western cultural influences are apparent. Across the board, there would be an overall loss of faith. Yet, this is not what we find. Rather, the trends in belief and unbelief have not been uniform. According to the World Values Survey, which has surveyed belief in God over a period of decades, there are some nations whose peoples have retained high levels of religious belief in spite of Western influences.[2] Examples include the wealthy gulf states, which possess an overwhelming majority of Islamic believers, almost all of whom hold to a belief in God.

Furthermore, some nations have even grown in their religious belief, notably, some of the nations which belonged to the Soviet sphere of

2. World Values Survey, "WVS Online."

influence (Ukraine, Belarus, Armenia, Georgia, Russia). In these countries, it would appear that, after the collapse of the communist era, with its atheistic indoctrination, the religious faith of many citizens has revived, and that has happened even in the face of the greater exposure to Western influences which came about after the collapse. If sustained influence from Western, reason-based culture is the major factor in the decline of belief in God, then such resurgences should not have happened. The fact that they have suggests that religious belief is open to other factors of which we are less aware (or which are less well publicized).

One of those factors that has been proposed is the level of security that governments provide to their citizens.[3] As was noted in chapter 4, with an extensive and well-funded social security safety net, effective hospital and medical services, a rule of law that mostly works well, and other services that help people feel secure, it has been found that a nation's people typically express lower levels of belief in God. If religious belief is mainly about finding a sense of security in a loving and all-powerful God, then its replacement with a more tangible source of material and psychological security, that is, the advanced Western state, would, it is argued, lead to a loss of religious faith since such would no longer be needed.

Of course, it is difficult to be sure about this, since the nations which take special care in looking after their citizens in these ways—mainly Scandinavian and Northern European nations—also have governments which present themselves as truly secular or non-religious, and this could also have its own effect on religious belief. That is, this theory might be throwing together two things that should be distinguished: the security provided by the state, and the state's powerful example of atheism.

Just how important for religious belief is this second factor can be seen from the recent example of Hungary. Since 2010, the government led by Viktor Orbán, in marked contrast to previous political leadership in that nation, has identified itself as Christian and has sought to implement policies that reflect that identity. During the period from 2011 to 2015, that is, a mere four years, the number of Hungarians who claimed an affiliation with Christianity increased from 55 percent to 76 percent even while living standards, and presumably also the security provided by the state, increased during that time.[4] Granted, this is only suggestive

3. Norris and Inglehart, *Sacred and Secular*. But see also Inglehart's more recent thoughts on this topic which parallel that which I present below: Inglehart, *Religion's Sudden Decline*.

4. For the 2011 census data see Government of Hungary, "Population Census

rather than compelling evidence, but it does raise questions about the idea that merely by reducing a people's anxieties about their access to basic needs in life one will necessarily also find a loss of religious belief.

Considering this matter more generally, we might note that sociologists have identified two processes which are regarded as having a major impact on beliefs and behaviors in a population, and importantly each of them has little connection with the power of reason: first, the practices and beliefs of *high-status* groups and individuals in a society, and secondly, what the *majority* of people in a society think and do.[5] Since Western governments are almost always secular and, by and large, trusted by their citizens, they too fit the category of being high-status influencers. The power of the secularity of elite groups works its way through a certain percentage of a nation's populace, and they come to think like their high-status leaders. Then the second process begins to kick in, with the result that, after a period of time, what was once a minority belief, for example non-religious belief, soon becomes a majority one, and conversely religious belief typically reduces to a small percentage of the population. Today, in the face of these two processes, the number of committed Christian believers in such nations as Sweden, France, and Belgium has dropped to about 5–10 percent, even though a weak belief in God is more widely confessed.[6]

Thus, the decline in religious belief in many Western nations cannot be mainly due to the advance of reason, with its power to dissolve beliefs based on so-called "fear and superstition." Other "non-rational" factors seem to be at play: a people's sense of security, which a competent and technologically advanced government can provide, and the persuasive power of elites and governments as well as that of majority opinions and

---

2011: National Data." The 2015 data are from Pew Research Center, "Religious Belief."

5. Henrich, "Cultural Transmission."

6. It is worth noting here that the Christian faith would reject the views of both high-status groups and of the majority as sources of primary influence for the believer. Neither intelligence nor "following the crowd" are privileged ways of coming to a faith in Christ. The apostle Paul affirmed this when he wrote to the Corinthian Christians: *"For consider your calling, brothers: not many of you were wise according to worldly standards, not many were powerful, not many were of noble birth. But God chose what is foolish in the world to shame the wise; God chose what is weak in the world to shame the strong; God chose what is low and despised in the world, even things that are not, to bring to nothing things that are, so that no human being might boast in the presence of God"* (1 Cor 1: 26–29). Intelligence and status, those things which we think of as an advantage in all walks of life, are of no special use when it comes to grasping the truth which Jesus Christ offers.

practices. But now the questions that arise at this point are these: What is it that brings about these processes more in some nations and cultures than in others? Why have governments and cultural elites themselves become non-religious? And what is pushing the bulk of many populations to do likewise? These questions require us first to take account of the ideas about motivation which I proposed in part I.

But before beginning that analysis, I want to conclude this first section by making a comment about our use of reason in thinking about belief in God because it is easy to lose sight of that side of things when we are dealing mainly with motives and causes of our ideas and less about the reasons we have for holding them.

When it comes to belief in God, rational considerations are important; we cannot simply set them aside as irrelevant. The Christian faith is well able to provide sound reasons for its beliefs, even if those reasons are not ironclad in terms of their persuasive power. Believers recognize that those without religious faith also have reasons which for them at least are convincing. We have seen, however, that the cultural climate of thought we Westerners find ourselves in at present is fully as important as the relative strength of arguments about these matters in pushing us towards faith or away from it. In our cultural situation, arguments that would be credible in other contexts no longer have the same effect on us. It is this that we must now explore.

Belief and Motives

Distortions of Dominance and Attachment—a Reprise

In part I, I suggested that a core dynamic driving our culture is an imbalance between the dominance/competence and the attachment motives. The first has come to exercise greater control over human behavior and thought at the expense of the second. That means that people typically invest an enormous amount of effort in maintaining or advancing their status or in seeking attention from others or in pursuing influence or power over others. We think of ourselves as "can do" people, individuals for whom no problem is immune to some kind of solution; that the only approach any issue in life requires for its solution is for it to be calmly, rationally, and carefully analyzed, broken down into parts, and each of those parts dealt with, step-by-step and with persistence. This is the classic mindset of the dominance motive. It generates a society composed of millions of individual problem-solvers each working at his or her own problems and, if need be, coordinating with others either to deal with larger problems beyond the capacity of any individual or to allow each individual the maximum freedom to solve problems without harming others' freedom. This second reason for coordinating—allowing others their own freedom—is particularly difficult to accomplish. Recall that the dominance motive is, of its very nature, comparative, so that if I win something someone else necessarily loses in some respect. If I get more attention from others, someone will get less. If I win the Nobel Peace Prize, all those who were nominated and harbored the desire to win the award lost, or at best achieved the consolation prize of being nominated. The tension between the pursuit of one's own goals and allowing others the full freedom to work at their own goals is ever-present and has an inherently corrosive effect upon society.

This is where attachment comes into the picture. As we have seen, attachment shows itself primarily within families, that is, between husbands and wives, between parents and their children, and to a lesser extent between siblings and within wider family circles. Outside of the family, attachment also expresses itself in the individual's relationship with God and with the church community, and, in weakened form, with other social groups and with the government. When operating well, its effect is to bind people together in ways which discourage conflict and keep in check fears and anxieties that would provoke it or otherwise harm psychological well-being. On the other hand, when the attachment system is put under stress or weakened, there can be profoundly damaging effects which are felt right across a society. Examples of some of these effects might include the following: nuclear families and larger family groups grow weaker; other social networks become isolated from each other; male-female relationships lived out in marriage or de facto relationships become unstable; larger portions of society live by themselves; loneliness, anxiety, and depression increase significantly; the parent-child relationship becomes more difficult to manage; politics becomes more polarized; and divisions within a society, especially the tensions inherent in dominance relationships, become more toxic.

In describing the two motives as I have, I think you will see that the dominance system is having the best of it in Western societies while the attachment motive is under serious pressure. What is more, with advanced societies mostly made up either of individual adults living by themselves or of families with on average about one-and-half children, there is not much scope for the attachment motive to flourish even if it were otherwise in a healthy condition. At the level of the individual, what happens is that the dominance drive works to suppress the person's responsiveness to attachment concerns or at least make him or her less attuned to them. For a dominance-driven citizen in a Western society, the previous paragraph's list of society-wide harms brought about by a weakened attachment system would not provoke much thought or concern; the individual would likely respond that while some of those consequences are unfortunate, overall, it is not a disaster because it means that individuals end up with more freedom for themselves and are less bound by relationships that might otherwise tie them down. Such a mindset reveals an inability to recognize a core feature of the structure of the human mind, that is, the need to deal with fear and anxiety, whatever its source, through binding ourselves *emotionally* to others.

Attachment and Religious Belief

Now, let us go back to our original problem: belief in God. At least for thinking Christian believers, such a belief has partly to do with the need to make sense of their own lives and reality more generally. While any idea of God we have will necessarily be all too human, at least believing in God allows us to think of reality as having a kind of anchor, so that reality—in its deeply confronting power—is not just hanging there, in its bare existence. This idea reminds us of the attachment motive which in a young child triggers terror in any situation where his mother, the very ground of his being, is not available to him in times of threat or uncertainty. We saw in part I that this vulnerability to threat and anxiety, and our need to link ourselves at our very core to another, never leaves us; it remains with us throughout our life. When we are faced with what is called "existential anxiety," the anxiety we feel when we come face-to-face with reality, we can see how a belief in God is an appropriate response to this situation. The suppression of the attachment motive by that of dominance causes many people in Western societies to avoid confronting existential concerns. They commonly do this by means of thought-stopping, a mechanism that prevents an unpleasant thought from allowing the individual to experience it in its full significance.

There is another aspect of the dominance motive that makes religious belief difficult especially for well-educated people in Western societies, and that has to do with a particular effect of what I have described as the problem-solving mindset. If we have had success at applying this mindset to many real-world problems, it becomes the go-to approach when we examine a new situation that calls for our attention. That leads us to think that everything is analyzable, and that includes even our relationships with other persons. The effect of this is that we come to think that the world outside of ourselves is at its root *impersonal*, that it can be dealt with using impersonal thinking techniques. And our immediate response to someone who tells us that we are viewing the world in fully impersonal terms is that, well, ultimately, it *is* impersonal. In other words, it is very difficult for us to even imagine that the world is, at its very foundations, *personal* rather than impersonal. Only by opening ourselves up to the demands of our attachment motive—which, we should note, is inherently personal—will it even be possible for us to imagine a reality different from the one our dominance motive has shaped for us.

The "impersonal" mindset I have described, not surprisingly, also afflicts many believers in the form of a puzzlement as to why the Lord God does not show his hand more clearly in the events of their lives. They are often reminded by their church leaders that God has given them so much for which they might be thankful: their life, a society in which they are cared for, loving relationships, and supremely the gift of grace resulting from the sacrifice of the cross. But calling these things to mind does not seem to provide a satisfying answer to their unease about God's seeming absence. They know that they are called to faith and that faith relies by its very nature on trust in another rather than on ironclad rational guarantees. But still, the doubts remain.

This difficulty, however, is more a matter of the condition of the believer's mind rather than of any presumed failures on God's part. In short, it arises primarily in a consciousness that is controlled by the dominance motive. We tend to find that such a difficulty recedes into insignificance when one's mindset is being nourished by that of the attachment motive. When the latter is operating, say, through full immersion within the church's worship or in genuine and deep fellowship with other believers, one loses the hankering after certainty that characterizes dominance-driven thoughts about God. The apostle Paul's comment, that *"we walk by faith not by sight"* (1 Cor 5:7), that is, progress in true life comes primarily through trust in Christ, is profoundly true.

In our discussion so far, I hope you are able to see the point I am making: what we imagine are beliefs based on rational grounds are at least as much shaped by a major cultural distortion in the way the dominance and attachment motives are expressed. Our religious beliefs are perhaps more given to us by our culture than worked through by our individual reason.[7] To add a little more to the outline I have sketched so far, I want now to consider another culture-wide phenomenon that relates our religious beliefs to the motives described in part I.

The Eclipse of Conscience

A further effect of the outsized power of the dominance motive in Western societies is the way it sidelines the conscience motive.[8] This is not difficult to recognize: if dominance controls our thoughts and actions at the expense of other motives, then any elements of our psychology which hinder its expression will be pushed to one side, as it were. Now, like attachment, conscience is one of those elements, since it seeks to take account of the interests and needs of others when speaking its word to us. "You might want to do that (to achieve some success) but if you do so, it will hurt such-and-such—so do not do it!" Just as the dominance motive, when given too much freedom, suppresses the attachment motive, leading to an impersonal view of the world, so also the conscience motive, which is likewise inherently personal, is treated in the same way. In our culture, this sidelining takes the form of a transformation of the conscience into an impersonal force. As described in chapter 9, typically what occurs is that the conscience, as the personal address of God speaking to us in the depths of our being, is changed so that it now becomes the "gut feeling" we have that some course of action is not right and so we should not pursue it. The voice of God is replaced by an inner feeling. But this, of course, begs the question: if this feeling does not come from God, then what is its source, and, if it derives ultimately from our parents, why should it still be so authoritative for us?

The problem with reducing conscience—which, from its earliest development in the individual, is personal and relational—to an inner feeling is that it is much easier for someone to act against it. If we believe that no one will find out if we steal something, then it would be difficult

---

7. On the question as to why our culture should be the way it is, see chapter 11 of part I.

8. The effect on conscience might also be indirect, that is, through the weakening of the attachment motive.

for an impersonal conscience to argue against the urgings of an insistent dominance motive that tells us to go ahead and carry out the theft. Some will hold out against such promptings, and here we can think of people who want to project a public image as trustworthy, honest, and morally upright. They will aim to keep their inner and outer worlds aligned with each other. But we must keep in mind that our public image is the work of the dominance drive and as such it depends primarily on how we are *seen* by others, not so much on how we *actually* are. So, again, the temptation is always there to present a sober and moral outward appearance and to allow the inner reality to be less so. We call that "hypocrisy."

In Western culture, belief in God as our moral authority has historically been the normal outworking of the conscience motive.[9] In fact, without belief in God or at least some authority perceived to be absolute, there can be no moral sense as such, and the reason for this, as I have noted, is that conscience is necessarily interpersonal; it is the voice of Someone speaking to our inner being, and all the substitutes for this that people have proposed are at best poor approximations of genuine religious morality. Many have been persuaded by these substitutes. When they hear from proponents of utilitarianism that morality basically means following the rule that says you should act so that everyone's interests affected by your action should be taken into account, they think to themselves, "Yes, that sounds right. Why should we bring God into it?" What is not commonly recognized, however, is that such people are still relying upon hidden assumptions that are based not just on (impersonal) reason, but also on the moral training they received from their (personal) parents. For example, the above rule of conduct I mentioned assumes that all people should be treated equally, but this is a moral *assumption*, not one of observable *fact*, since the truth is that not all people are equal—they range from the most brilliant, morally upright person to the individual in a persistent vegetative state who has no awareness of their surroundings. We are left, then, with an unanswered question: Why *should* we treat all people equally? The fact that secular-minded people still cling to this conviction of equal treatment suggests that we humans

---

9. Other cultures have been much more open to accepting the moral authority of the state or of their community leaders. For example, it was the religion of ancient Rome operating at the service of that empire which caused the early Christians so much trouble. The "immorality" with which they were charged was their refusal to accept the religious-moral authority of the Roman state.

do not easily shed the ingrained—even though hidden—assumption of a *personal* conscience.

A common argument against the idea of a personal authority for conscience is the challenge: Why *should* we follow what God tells us to do? This was a difficult question to answer in former times when we did not take account of how conscience actually comes into existence. But when we realize that it emerges from within a relationship of *trust* in our parents and that a moral sense is hardwired into us before we can reason about the matter, then it is quite reasonable to accept the moral norms revealed to us by God if we trust in him and if we realize that no human can be the originating source of moral authority.

So far, I have argued that belief in God is strongly influenced by both distortions in the balance between dominance and attachment motives and in the suppression of conscience by an overly powerful drive for dominance. Let us now turn to a third, similar effect, this time on the social reciprocity motive.

Social Reciprocity as Justice

The third motive affected by an excessively powerful dominance is that of social reciprocity. Like conscience, it works by taking into account the interests of others as we do our own. Particularly in the way it aims to preserve justice, it bears on our question of belief in God. Again, within Western history, we see at work a very powerful idea of the divine judgment of humans after their death. To the secular mind—and I am thinking here of a mind in which the drive for dominance has marginalized other motives—this seems a naïve and unlikely idea. Why should any supposed deity bother about the absolutely insignificant doings of creatures who have existed during a miniscule period of history and who inhabit a tiny planet revolving around one of billions and billions of stars in the universe? A final judgment simply does not make sense according to this way of thinking.

Yet, if the deepest reality is (at least) personal—and it looks like we have been *made* to think that it is!—then if we value ourselves as personal creatures, we Westerners need to rethink the idea of ourselves as utterly insignificant in the whole scheme of things and to contemplate the possibility that we represent the very peak of a universe which—so far at least—appears to be otherwise impersonal. The center of the universe, from this new perspective, is no longer somewhere in space or in time but wherever and whenever personal beings exist.

Furthermore, if the Ground of reality is not only personal but interpersonal (as the Christian teaching about God as Trinity proposes), and the essence of being interpersonal is love (for how else are persons to exist and to flourish?), then *how* we humans, who are both personal and responsible, measure up to that love becomes crucially important. Why? Because God loves the other person as much as he loves you and me, and so any action of yours or mine that lacks love for the other is something that compromises or corrupts the love that is at the center of reality. God loves the other person and depends upon you and me to express his love for the other. When we fail, why should such a failure not be judged? Why should we not be held to account? Our deeply entrenched idea of the importance of justice sees many outrageous injustices inflicted on human beings (and on God's creation) which are not dealt with in this life. Is it any wonder that humans should long for a final accounting in the age to come? At the very least, we can reasonably suggest to one who is interested in these matters that the full flourishing of the motive of social reciprocity, especially as it shows itself in our desire to see justice done, accords well with a belief in God. But more than that, such belief is not simply a matter of arriving at an intellectual conviction; it seems also to have an element of anxious searching about it. That is, we are *made* to seek out such a God with the awareness that we are both morally "out of kilter" with him and his ways and in need of some kind of resolution to our dilemma. We long for peace with him. As St. Augustine expressed it, "O God, you have made us for yourself, and our hearts are restless until they find their rest in You."

Again, we find that dominance-driven individuals in Western culture cannot really grasp the significance of what I have just written because it requires of them that they conceive of a reality that is, at its very foundation, personal rather than impersonal. The dominance drive gravitates towards the perception of reality as impersonal. From its own perspective, it sees all that I have described as simply a hindrance to its own flourishing. It cannot countenance it even though *at some level* it might see its wisdom and the coherence that it brings to life.

On the other hand, in someone who has integrated the workings of their motives in a healthy manner, the attachment, conscience, social reciprocity motives along with dominance (in its competence form) motives each pull their weight in helping to shape how we think about the world and about ourselves. Religious faith, in that setting, emerges as something which *fits* with our makeup as human beings.

To conclude this discussion, I want to repeat my earlier warning to the reader not to think that religious belief is valuable simply because it aligns with our psychology, or that we should hold to religious belief because it is good for our mental health. That is certainly not my own understanding. Rather something like the reverse process is the case: belief in God is tailored to how we are constituted psychologically because the One who made us is a reality apart from ourselves. Belief in God is a true belief, as God's word teaches, and our makeup accords with that belief because that is the way God has made us. His will is that we seek him out, and we were created so that that should happen.

The Christian teaching and the experience of believers adds something further, and this is that God is not there sitting back, waiting for us to find him, but that, time and again, he reaches out to find us! As we have seen, there are all sorts of ways we humans can work to close our eyes to that reaching out on God's part, but many Christians can attest that God breaks into their lives in surprising ways. And he does so chiefly when we begin to set aside the barriers which we have placed in the way of our being discovered by him.

13

Meeting the Lord in Prayer: Distractions and Engagement

IN A LITURGICAL DIALOGUE commonly used in Christian churches during the Eucharist, the priest or minister invites us to give thanks to the Lord our God, to which we the people respond, "It is right and just."[1] This tells us that, as believers, the virtue of justice calls for us to give to God that which is his due: prayers of worship and thanksgiving. Here we see that the foundation of our faith rests on the healthy operation of the motive of social reciprocity. For, as the Lord God has blessed us, redeemed us, and promised us eternal life, so it is only right and just that we should respond with gratitude and love. Such a response begins and ends with prayer and extends beyond that to include active and faithful obedience. A life infused with prayer, then, is not an optional extra that we might offer to the Lord, but something that issues from the requirement that we reciprocate or respond to his generous kindness to us. In this chapter, I will examine only part of that relationship of prayer, specifically the aspect that has to do with the attitudes, feelings, and distractions we experience when we engage in prayer, whether that be the prayer we offer when "we go into our room and shut the door" or the prayer we participate in when we gather as a congregation with our brothers and sisters in the Lord. As I hope to make clear, it is this aspect of prayer that calls for us to take account of motives other than that of social reciprocity.

---

1. For example, *The Roman Missal*, 531.

In part I, I drew attention more than once to the fact that, while ideally our conscience guides or at least monitors all of our behavior, our normal, hour-by-hour consciousness is energized by other motives, especially that of competence/dominance. This means that when we come to the Lord in prayer, there is typically something of a mismatch between the mind oriented towards competence/dominance and that which is most suited to the activity of prayer. Thus, we find that our thoughts are oriented towards activity while what is called for is quiet and patience; our attitude is one of affirmation and protection of our self, whereas what we need in prayer is a willingness to see our faults and a vulnerability before God; finally, our focus tends towards our self and its interests, but prayer calls us to broaden our frame of mind to embrace the interests of others. No wonder we often find it quite difficult to settle into a prayerful attitude when all these barriers are there preventing it from happening. And it should therefore come as no surprise to us that prayer often provokes distracting thoughts in our mind. Let us consider these matters in light of the anthropology of part I. I will discuss private and public prayer in turn, but before I begin I want to briefly comment on the respective places of these two forms of prayer in the Christian life.

Within the Catholic tradition at least, public prayer has priority for the believer for it is the form of prayer into which we are born as believers. The Church is our mother, and we learn from her the ways of prayer. Other Christian traditions see the matter differently and give priority instead to private prayer, which they view as more intimate and better able to express the believer's true self before the Lord. In any case, it is probably fair to say that across Christian traditions both public and private prayer are necessary for growth in holiness and love of the brethren. Here I will first discuss private prayer, since this form of prayer is less complex in the way it is motivated than its public counterpart.

Private Prayer

To grasp the significance of our motives for how we pray, it is helpful to consider the place of distractions to prayer. It is our common experience as believers that when we enter into a time of prayer in God's presence, we experience distracting thoughts which are unrelated to our prayer. In the face of these distractions, we might say to ourselves, "Just turn aside from distracting thoughts, as you have read from those who are experienced in these matters." And that is what we do. Often, though, in time we decide that we are not getting anywhere in setting aside distractions, and we give up, or else we decide to follow one of the distracting thoughts and see where it goes, because it feels much better than repeatedly turning away from distractions.

Now, given that the primary motive of our everyday consciousness is that of dominance/competence, we can usually assume that the activity of resisting distractions removes oxygen, as it were, from the operation of that motive. On the other hand, when we do indulge these thoughts, we are providing our dominance motive with mental activities which allow it free rein. Either way, we become just that little bit less inclined to engage in focused and engaged prayer in the future.

Now, if we think through this situation again in the light of the anthropology of part I and understand where private informal prayer is actually heading, we will be able to approach it from a different perspective, one which allows us to arrive at a different outcome. The aim of this kind of prayer is to enter into deeper engagement with the Lord God, to really be present to him, to grasp at a more existential level his greatness, the need for us to praise him, to recognize our sinfulness before him, to offer our thanks to him, and perhaps to find a deeper peace in his presence. All of this is virtually impossible when our dominance motive is in the driver's seat of our mind. It can only occur when our conscience and attachment motives take its place. So the first task is to ease out dominance from control of our consciousness and make ourselves available to the attachment motive. Thereafter we will be able to connect more easily and fully with our conscience and with God. This is not to say that achieving *in its full form* such a movement in our prayer will necessarily be a common occurrence for us. It might arise only occasionally for most believers; for a few it might be their normal experience. But at least it is open to all.

How an Engaged Prayer of the Heart Might Be Experienced

What does this process look like in practice? It begins by treating distractions in the same way as I described above, but it requires *at the same time* that we feel our way into (a) the experience of psychological vulnerability (which dominance does not like!) and (b) also a sense of God's *personal* presence—a true *thou*. Here we are not asking the Lord for a miracle, since the process is a natural, psychological one with a predictable outcome. So, we say to ourselves during the difficult first few minutes that the resistance of our (dominance-driven) mind will soon subside as we slip into the mindset of vulnerability and awareness of God's presence.

In the early period of this transition process, it can be helpful to listen carefully to our mind's thoughts and to articulate them before the Lord. We tell him what we are thinking and feeling, whatever those thoughts and feelings are. We seek to be as honest as we can. And that means being honest about ourselves. We are not to defend ourselves before the Lord but rather to be willing to be critical of ourselves. Included in this conversation are expressions of our deeper uncertainties and the problems we face in living our life as a believer. All of this works towards opening up our heart to the Lord and experiencing our true self in his presence. It also serves to remove the dominance motive from control of our consciousness and allows the conscience and attachment motives to take over.

At some point during this activity, we will come to feel that we have nothing more to say to God and now our prayer will need to change. Instead of words as part of our relating to him, we will need to bring our feelings more into play, especially the feeling of yearning for the Lord. Some find repetition of a prayer like the Jesus Prayer, "Lord Jesus Christ, Son of God, have mercy on me, a sinner," helpful because it is a continual reminder to oneself of one's true condition before the Lord, and if it is expressed with genuine feeling, that is, with a keen sense that we are truly longing for the Lord's mercy, then this will move us towards a deeper, less distracted prayer. It is important that we not merely repeat a prayer such as the Jesus Prayer as an utterance, but that it is to be addressed *directly to the Lord who is present there with us* and it is done so with emotion because we are indeed sinners. Without the feeling as well as the words, our prayer will not be experienced as truly involving. On the other hand, by continual emotional repetition of words which express to God our vulnerability before him, and by frequently calling to mind his *actual* presence as the ineffably and inconceivably great God of the whole of reality, after a period of time, perhaps ten minutes, but sometimes up to forty minutes, we will experience a sense of being overwhelmed emotionally and tears will often appear at that point. This rush of feeling is our mind's reaction to giving up the pressure of living according to our dominance motive. Now, in its place, our attachment system will have been engaged.

At this time, we notice that we are thinking quite differently. We might even wonder why we ever allowed our dominance motive to run our lives and wish that we could always be controlled by our conscience and attachment motives. We typically feel at peace; our focus is no longer on thinking, and we find that we are more aware of our environment yet strangely also of God's presence with us. We do not sense any urge to grasp him more clearly for we are satisfied with what we have received.

However powerfully we experience something like this, though, it is important that we realize that it is not the end of the process of prayer but only its beginning phase. With our conscience and attachment systems engaged and our dominance set to one side, our prayer can be of the kind that the Lord desires for us. Now we are in a position better to see ourselves as truly who we are before the Lord, in deep need of his forgiveness, and vulnerable in an existential sense. In this frame of mind, we begin to sense the Lord in his greatness and indeed his utter reality, and also the importance of us praising him for all sorts of reasons, not least for saving us through the cross and providing us with a security that transcends that which the "world" can offer us. Now, too, we find that we can discern better those things for which we ought to make petition to the Lord, and it might dawn upon us just how often we are self-centered in the prayer requests we make of him when dominance controls our thoughts. Finally, the sense might surface that "It is good to be here!"

We might linger a while until all these thoughts and feelings subside, and on leaving the situation, we typically have the experience, in our social relationships, of being more relaxed with others, able to be more focused on them and less so on ourselves, because we have less anxiety about how others perceive us. Gradually these feelings dissipate, and dominance/competence takes over our consciousness unawares. But what we have undergone in that time of prayer will always stay in our memory. And when we understand how it happened in terms of motivation, we can recognize that it is open to us at any suitable time if we give ourselves to it. This is not to say that the Lord does not have anything to do with it; of course he does. But we must acknowledge that we cannot control the blessings of God's grace but only—with his help!—better dispose ourselves to receive them. Engaging our attachment and conscience motives is not the same as God's grace; it is a way of preparing ourselves to be its recipients. In fact, the very desire to enter into such an experience of prayer is the work of the Holy Spirit. So, while it might appear to us that we are initiators of the whole process, the deeper truth is that "*it is God who works in you, both to will and to work for his good pleasure"* (Phil 2:13).

Prayer of the Heart: An Account from the Spiritual Tradition

Spiritual writers through the centuries have often spoken of this form of private prayer, not, of course, in terms of fundamental motives, but nevertheless with a clear sense of its reality and the way that it requires of us to set aside our normal modes of thought. For example, St. Bonaventure (1221–74) wrote in this manner in his *Journey of the Mind to God*. Describing the believer's path towards deeper identification with Christ, he notes that "we must set aside all discursive operations of the intellect and turn the very apex of our soul to God to be entirely transformed in him. This is most mystical and secret. No one knows it but he who has received it. No one receives it but he who has desired it. No one desires it but he who is deeply penetrated by the fire of the Holy Spirit, the fire Christ sent on earth . . . If you want to understand how this happens, ask it of grace, not of learning; ask it of desire, not of understanding; ask it of earnest prayer, not of attentive reading; ask it of the betrothed, not of the teacher. Ask it of God, not of man; ask it of darkness, not of radiance."[2]

In reflecting upon these words, first, we note the necessity of setting aside "discursive operations of the intellect"; later references to "grace, not learning" and "desire, not understanding" echo this thought. Discursive thought is thinking about something, the kind of thought which dominates our daily consciousness. But sometimes we find that our minds set this aside and we experience what people call "being in the present." This is what St. Bonaventure has in mind. But we see immediately that he is not interested in *simply* refraining from thinking or just being aware of ourselves, for he then writes that we are to "turn the apex of our soul to God." This means that we are to direct our awareness to God, that is, the reality and the Person of God, without any "higher" part of our mind thinking about what we are doing. St. Bonaventure also emphasizes that this occurs not by understanding but rather by desire or a continuing emotional yearning for God. Our task is only to express this yearning in the presence of the Lord, and the eventual result—usually—is that we become open to being "entirely transformed in him." That is, that in time, our consciousness is changed to a readily discernible and clearly different

---

2. *Journey of the Mind to God*, VII, 4, 6, quoted in *The Divine Office* III, 113.

way of relating to God. "This is most mystical and secret": not mystical in the sense that the change in mind and emotion is unfathomable, but rather that what we feel is quite distinctive and different from what we normally experience in our daily lives. In ways which are hard to verbalize, we know that we are more open, more engaged with our God.

In the sort of prayer that St. Bonaventure wrote about we can see in a sometimes dramatic way the differences in consciousness that a change in controlling motives can create in us. But what about prayer as part of corporate worship—can something similar occur here as well?

Corporate Prayer

Certainly it is the case that experiences of prayer *like* that which I have just described—but of much less intensity—are possible in corporate prayer settings. However, we need to recognize the similarities *and* the differences between the two contexts. Similar to the time when we enter into private prayer, during the period following the commencement of corporate prayer, the well-entrenched dominance motive controls our thoughts in the same way as we have considered above. To begin with, having to sit still and being without the sensory stimuli of a computer or a mobile phone takes some adjustment on our part. Distracting thoughts can also be a problem; they might even stay with us for the whole of the liturgical celebration. And although we attempt to turn away from them and focus on what is happening at the front and around us, again, as in private prayer, we do not always succeed. It is not unusual for us to find ourselves with thoughts of irritation or annoyance: perhaps it is something the worship leader has said, the way he speaks, or the fact that the woman reading the Scriptures is difficult to understand, or the child in the pew in front of us is making a noise, or someone's phone has just rung. Amidst all or any of these things it is hard to imagine undergoing the experience I have described above in relation to private prayer. Dominance-provoked distractions abound; an attachment mindset seems unreachable.

The Modeling of Fervent Reverence in Worship

And yet, it need not routinely be like that. Most of us have experienced worship as it should be, in a way that fully engages us and nourishes our spirits. However, the sad truth is that much Christian worship conducted in Western nations today is led by people who do not communicate to worshippers that they (as leaders) are truly standing before, and addressing, the living God, praying on behalf of the people. Certainly, they might appear—superficially—to be speaking to the Lord, but so often our sense is that their main audience is us, the congregation. So, while their words are words of prayer to God, all the other elements of the communication, the various features of the voice and the attitude of body, indicate to us that they are wanting to communicate something about themselves to us who are their human audience.

In the Catholic tradition, especially in the Western Church, it has become the norm to discourage expressions of priestly devotion and reverence in the presence of the Almighty during the prayers of Mass, and this means that the congregation is not often led by a man who is consumed by God's presence and who is unashamed to let that heartfelt reverence to be seen by his fellow-worshippers. Modelling can have powerful effects on others, and to be in the presence of a reverent *and* vulnerable worship leader can often prompt our attachment motive into action even more easily than when we endeavor to do so during our private prayer. Furthermore, whatever the tradition of worship, for all believers, it is helpful in eliciting a genuine sense of openness to the Lord when they can see others in their congregation entering fully and humbly into the worship. When this happens, as worshippers, moving away from a dominance-controlled train of thought becomes easier for us.

The feelings we can experience when this occurs mirror those I have described in relation to private prayer—a sudden surge of emotion, sometimes accompanied by tears, and a warmth towards the Lord that sets our heart at peace and allows us to be more focused in our worship. Unlike in the setting of private prayer, when we gather in public, we are usually not free to allow ourselves to express that experience in our outward demeanor and so it is frequently not so immersive. Yet, the parallels between the two are clear.

The Role of Music and Other Elements of Worship

It is not only the worship leader and the other people in the congregation, of course, who help us to a deeper, heartfelt worship, but also the elements of the worship itself. Music plays a big part here, and we are assisted in this regard if it is of the kind that culturally engages the people who attend. While beauty is not the only consideration, it *must* figure in the selection of what is sung by the congregation and/or choir. For better or for worse, most pre-eighteenth-century church music is not beautiful to the contemporary ear, and while ancient musical traditions are to be nurtured and preserved, just as much care must be given to the fruit of their development and extension so that music is able to enhance worship rather than distract from it. There is much profound hymnody available to any worshipping church, and, if sung to attractive tunes, it can also touch the heart of a listener, that is, engage the attachment motive. The question of music in worship is a fraught one for many believers, but I think it fair to say that beauty in the music of worship—and not a beauty only discerned by the cultured few—is an essential element of worship life, for it honors God, protects the worship of his people, and opens them to a deeper engagement in prayer.

Beyond music, there are other elements of Catholic worship that help us to enter into a genuinely prayerful frame of mind. The prayers of confession prompt us to know our vulnerability before the Lord. This can occur if time is given when we are invited to call to mind our sins, and if the prayer is not rushed. Likewise, we can listen for a personal word for ourselves in the reading of the word of God, and thus we come to recognize Christ's actual presence in the gathering, equivalent to the first few words in the cry of the Jesus Prayer, "Lord Jesus Christ, Son of God!" A homily or sermon which draws upon the priest's deep spiritual experience with God; intercessory prayers that are directed to our loving Father rather than towards the people themselves; eucharistic liturgy prayed in a manner that does not conceal the sheer drama of what is being carried out; all this can push us in the right direction, away from dominance-driven thought and into an attachment frame of mind.

Sadly, many of us have become inured to worship which fails to engage our hearts, and we have come to imagine that such a reality does not in fact exist. That is the path to spiritual death. Seeking out places where corporate prayer is nourishing to the soul is a priority, but, for many believers, this clashes with their sense of commitment to their local church community. One of the themes I have sought to express in this book is that how we think about our faith depends not only on what we read and what we hear from others, but just as much upon the environments in which we place ourselves. Our mental efforts to counteract the corrosive effects of poor worship can only go so far. We need to be nurtured from outside of ourselves, and at least from time to time we require placing ourselves in settings where our heart is uplifted, where conscience and attachment both find at least temporary relief. Only thus can our corporate prayer be fed, grow, and bear fruit.

The notion that the dominance/competence motive controls most of our day-to-day consciousness is one which is not easy to understand because we are not used to thinking that way about ourselves. Likewise, developing an understanding of the workings of the attachment motive presents many challenges for us. However, it is in the experience of prayer, both private and corporate, that we can see—sometimes in dramatic ways—the manner in which these two motives can affect the outworking of our relationship with God. In fact, the context of prayer is one of the few circumstances of daily life in which, given the right circumstances, we can clearly see the influence of these two systems on our consciousness.

The form of prayer I have described in this chapter is part of the common heritage of the Christian faith. As long as we always view it from the perspective of orthodox Christian faith, we will interpret it as an aspect of our makeup as humans that can prepare us for a deeper bond with our Creator and Redeemer. As far as it serves this purpose rather than becoming an end in itself, it is something to be desired and sought after.

14

Seeking a More Real Hope of Eternal Life

The Problem of Death

THE BELIEF IN SOME kind of existence beyond that which we experience in our earthy lives is something that comes from deep within the heart of man. One could imagine a creature like ourselves who strives—as do other animals—to preserve its life as vigorously as do we humans but in addition to that is also adapted to an acceptance of the limits in length of life which nature imposes on all creatures. Such a creature, it seems, could have evolved in a natural manner. Indeed, one might wonder why it is that we humans have persisted with our horror of death throughout life in a way which extends well beyond a strong avoidance of death during our fertile and child-nurturing years. Surely, we might wonder, nature should have "worked" so as to ease significantly this existential fear as we grew older. (Of course, those who are past their reproductive years do not participate in the drama of natural selection to the same extent as younger humans, so in evolutionary terms survival would not be greatly helped by such easing).

Yet, to us something seems "not right" about the way we experience the fear of death and the way it impacts our life. We might hope that we could deal with it otherwise. As Joseph Ratzinger has remarked, "Death ought to be arranged as painlessly, if also as belatedly as possible, being perfectly normal and quite properly preceded by the maximum exploitation of life." He adds, however, that attempting to arrange things this way fails in practice. "This approach does not appear to work either. It is resisted by that quite primordial sensation which Nietzsche expressed in the words, 'All joy wills eternity, wills deep, deep eternity.' In human life, there are some moments that should never pass away. What is glimpsed in them should never end. That it *does* end, and even more, that it is only experienced momentarily anyway: this is the real sadness of human existence."[1]

Thus, we observe that right throughout life, we human beings resist with a powerful force the idea of our annihilation in death. Our self develops a life of its own, so it seems—one which is distinct from that of our bodies—and we cannot come to terms with the possibility that it expires after the demise of our body. The evidence from findings of very early instances of human burial as an intentional action, together with signs of a belief in the dead's continued existence in some spiritual realm, shows that these aspects of human experience have been with us from the earliest times.

The Age to Come: The Scriptural View

In the Old Testament, the kind of life after death that was envisaged was often vague and not necessarily of the sort to which those in this present life would have been much attracted. There we find sparse and enigmatic mentions of Sheol, the place of existence for the dead, where one's forebears dwelled but of which little else was spoken. Sheol lacked the positive elements of blessedness and happiness that we find in the Greek Elysium, which was thought to be the glorious place inhabited by dead heroes and those who were especially good. Theologians have suggested that the religion of the Old Testament, in which only one God was worshipped, was careful not to give any quarter to polytheistic notions which have typically arisen when too strong an emphasis is given to life in the age to come.

There is perhaps another reason for the limited role that heaven plays in the Old Testament Scriptures. In early times, ordinary people had identities that were largely based on the groups to which they belonged. Central to their view of themselves was that they were members of the Lord's people (unlike a Canaanite or a Moabite, for example); of

---

1. Ratzinger, *Eschatology*, 94.

the tribe of Benjamin, from the town of Ramah; of the family of Jacob the blacksmith, etc. Because these groups continued to exist after any of their members had died, individuals could think of their own identity (in its social aspect) as also being preserved beyond their own individual death. Although this by no means removed the elemental horror of death, it probably did have the effect of taking *some* of the edge off the fear of losing one's life, and thus there might have been slightly less urgency in contemplating life beyond the grave.

In later times, when God's people began to view themselves as not only members of groups but as individuals in their own right (cf. Jer 31:29–30: *"Everyone shall die for his own sin"*; also Ezek 18), the anxieties surrounding personal death become more acute. The book of Ecclesiastes expresses this clearly with its depressive laments about the emptiness or vanity of life (though we need to keep in mind that this developing mindset would have been present mainly among the cultural elite rather than the average Jewish man or woman). Furthermore, with the focus more fully on the individual, the traditional idea that the universe is ordered so that God rewards the just and punishes the evil came in for serious questioning. It was argued that a just outcome might apply to groups— someone else in my group can receive the reward for my good deed and that is okay—but it does not seem that life works that way for individuals. Thus, we find the challenges to this traditional idea of rewards and punishment that we meet in the book of Job. A righteous man, Job, is afflicted with painful sores, and his friends have difficulty in explaining how this should be the case. At the same time as these questionings, there is also a growing awareness that if the God of Israel is truly Lord of the Universe and the One who cares for his people, then his dominion must extend to every aspect of reality, including even that which is beyond our earthly experience. All of this pushed the Jewish people towards a deeper understanding of the matter, and by the time of the New Testament, we find a broad opening up to other ideas that responded to that disturbing quandary which is death.

In Jesus' teaching we notice his sure conviction of a judgment and an age to come. We can even say that this is a core assumption of the good news he proclaimed. Without it, such preaching would have made little sense. From the point of view of his audience, it seems that they too shared this conviction, that is, apart from the Sadducees *"who say there is no resurrection"* (Matt 22:23). If that were not the case, one would be hard pressed to understand the powerful impact Jesus' preaching made on his hearers.

And yet, there is no doubt that it is with Christ's own resurrection from the dead that the problem is broken open in a remarkable and, indeed, unprecedented way. In hindsight, it is certainly the case that we can recognize pointers to this in Jesus' ministry. It is also true, nonetheless, that there is an essential contrast between the event of Christ's resurrection and his earthly teaching about the end of the age. The Gospels describe an urgent message about an impending crisis point in history, and, as Jesus taught so insistently, life in the age to come was to depend directly on the moral quality of one's earthly actions. But with the resurrection, this framework was overtaken by an actual, concrete reality. The element of apocalypse or dramatic ending to history had itself been engulfed, though not dissolved, by the new age of the Risen Lord. The Prototype of eternal life, beyond history, stood before his followers.

In an important respect, however, the character of the resurrection event was closely in line with God's ways in the Old Testament. We read that the risen Christ appeared only to his disciples, and in this way the resurrection could not become something that could be objectively or scientifically analyzed and critiqued by outsiders. By being limited in this manner, it preserved the "way" of God which, throughout salvation history, has been to rely upon the authenticity of witnesses, rather than on rational "proofs," in commending and communicating his word to his people. Thus, just as with the revelation given through Moses and the prophets, so, too, the resurrection is above all God speaking—through witnesses—to us as individuals, confronting us and, at the same time, loving us, rather than simply telling us that something is abstractly the case. Put another way, God's message about eternal life is, in an all-consuming manner, *personally engaging*. It appears very much to be the case that he wants us to give a response to it.

In sum, then, we might say that Jesus' teaching about the age to come aligned with how his listeners viewed that matter, yet his resurrection also represented an extraordinary step forward in God's plan of salvation by demonstrating the possibilities of resurrected life. Apart from its existence or reality, however, what more do we learn about its nature?

The Age to Come: Some Few Precious Insights

The Gospel accounts give us a limited insight into what the age to come will actually be like. Still, what we do glean from them is something very precious. Until it happened in Christ, all we had was human speculation; now some truth about it is offered to us, though the whole thing is still mostly veiled. What we can say is that Christ's resurrected body and mind are the same as before but now transformed in a kind of "spiritual" manner. He can still relate to earthly people, but he seems not to be limited by the laws of nature that constrain the rest of us (e.g., John 20:26: "*Although the doors were locked, Jesus came and stood among them*"). It appears that the spirit has full control of the body. For this reason, we might say that the body, and thus the world as we know it, is not the be-all-and-end-all of things. It is reasonable, then, to think that the age to come will truly transform and transcend this world so that we can speak of "*new heavens and a new earth*" (2 Pet 3:15, cf. Isa 65:17). This will not, however, remove the continuities between now and then about which Paul wrote in Romans 8:21: "*The creation itself will be set free from its bondage to corruption and obtain the freedom of the glory of the children of God.*"

Still, that is about as far as we can go in drawing implications from Christ's resurrection concerning what God has in store for us. "*Beloved, we are God's children now, and what we will be has not yet appeared*" (1 John 3:2). Besides, thinking too much about that future reality—rather than contemplating the face of the One who will one day *consume* our "consciousness"—is, I suspect, rarely a healthy spiritual activity in which to engage.

There is, however, one other feature of the resurrection of Christ that speaks to our present situation. Having risen from the dead, Christ's focus now becomes oriented primarily towards his heavenly Father. He is going; soon the disciples would no longer see his face, for he is to ascend to the Father. Yet what we have here is not a focus upon his own future with the Father, an attitude that might lead him to consider as secondary the earthly life of his disciples. In fact, all his post-resurrection words look towards the prospect of others sharing his experience. When he speaks to his followers, he has in mind the work of nurturing and expanding—even on a global scale—those who, as with the first witnesses, will likewise come to see *their* life—just like his own—as, above all, directed towards the Father. The result is that for those who receive his message, from now on, this earthly life will no longer be quite so important, no longer quite so all-consuming of their energies, nor death quite so disturbing. *"O death, where is your victory? O death, where is your sting?"* (1 Cor 15:55).

The Response of Believers

When we trace the path mapped out through the Scriptures, we can see that, over the centuries, God has gradually unveiled before his chosen people a reality—made most real and compelling in Jesus—in which he invites all peoples to share. And yet, this reality is not to take up our attention in a way that leads us to neglect this earthly life we have been given. The latter, too, is a gift from God, given to each of us to make use of. How to achieve a balance between the two has been difficult for Christ's followers, and we would have to admit that we believers have failed badly at times, whether by neglecting this present life and ignoring the cries of Christ who suffers in the poor and wretched or by treating the age to come as if it were not a reality at all, even though we might pay lip service to the idea.

It is undeniable that Western Christians today have erred mainly in the latter direction. By and large we no longer live life with a resurrection mindset. At least for those of us who are better off, life in this world is too exciting, too engaging, full of too many possibilities, for us to see it as essentially a pathway or journey towards the age to come. Certainly, we Christians mouth the words of the Nicene Creed, "[I believe] . . . in the resurrection of the dead and the life of the world to come," but, it seems, the less we have to do with that aspect of our faith, the better! If this loss of hope among ordinary believers is a reason for us to be disturbed, even more unsettling is the fact that it appears to have reached even to such a traditionally reliable source of Christian teaching as the Catholic magisterium. A recent survey of papal documents on the mission of the Church issued over the past century has found that the more recent the document the less likely it is to mention salvation to eternal life and similar themes in its account of the reasons for mission.[2] This is disturbing because it suggests that the forces pushing a loss of Christian hope run very deep indeed and are probably touching believers and others at a level that is far more influential than any of the arguments we might hear which support such a hope. Today most people *feel* that there is no age to come. The way we see it, people in past centuries either kept up religious

---

2. Patterson, "What Has Eschatology," 285–99.

appearances around the Christian hope but did not really buy it in their heart of hearts, or else they did actually accept it but for reasons that would no longer withstand close scrutiny.

Yet, as we have had reason to observe with the question of belief in God, here too we must be wary of not placing more reliance on so-called rational arguments and on feelings than they truly warrant. Yes, using our reason to think through these matters is important, but equally required is the effort to discover where our ideas *and feelings* come from, so that we might evaluate them for their validity.

The Social Motives and Hope

How are we to understand Christian teaching about the last things as it has been handed down to us within the community of faith? Or perhaps, we first need to ask: What is happening to make the truth of such teaching so difficult to accept in our time? Can our considerations concerning the major social motives throw some light on the matter? Let us look a little more closely at these questions.

As an initial observation, we might note that our culture, with its appreciation for scientific knowledge, views death as a biological process in which both the body and the self, as organized and active forces, are permanently lost. And however much we might balk at the idea, death looks like the complete end for us. Yes, it is true that we still talk about people going to heaven when they die, but there is always a kind of a "wink, wink, nudge, nudge" sense about such talk. The message is: "We know it's not true, but it's better to keep up appearances with such myths than to upset others or continually to stare reality squarely in the face." Such attitudes have infected believers as well as unbelievers. We can see this in the social taboo that excludes talk of the age to come from conversation even among the faithful, as well as in the awkwardness that its mention creates in us.

In some ways, the practice of many church leaders can be seen as conceding the truth of this conviction about life after death. During the ongoing pandemic in Australia, there was little protest from church authorities over the government regulations putting barriers in the way of ministry to believers who were approaching death. Traditionally, this time would have been used by the believer to make preparation for their death and the final judgment and to strengthen their hope in eternal life with Christ, yet in acquiescing to the decision by the state that such clergy-assisted preparation was "non-essential," church leaders effectively signaled to their people that such ministry was not really very important.

So, we can see that this is a serious problem for believers, one which is rarely discussed, even though most believers, no doubt, give considerable thought to it in the privacy of their own hearts. In addressing the matter, the first thing to note is that convictions about the age to come are not based solely on rational considerations but have deeper roots which are arguably more important. I use the word "solely" because reason does come into play. The traditional Catholic notion of the soul which is immortal but also has the faculties of intellect and will—a notion which the faith, in part, took over from Greek philosophy—is increasingly struggling to be of much use in giving an alternative account of death in the face of the convincing description offered by modern rational thought. Thus, Christian theology has much work to do to shape a theological anthropology, or a theology of man, which can ring true for contemporary Western believers. This is not the place to consider that problem, but it is worth noting that there are other or complementary possibilities for such a theology; we are not bound to descriptions of mankind (in terms of body and soul, etc.) when they arise from sources other than revelation.[3]

The Priority of Motivation in Relation to Reason

In terms of the deeper roots of our thoughts which I have pointed to, we recall the principle set forth above, that rationality is only the servant of more profound motives. And this is the case in the matter of convictions about eternal life. We Westerners are, of course, immersed in the ways of thought of our secular culture, but more than that we have become quite attached to them. This worldview is a kind of attachment figure because it represents the wisdom of the cleverest people in society, *and* it is shared by the vast majority of the people of the culture. Recall, in our discussion of belief in God, that these two influences were powerful in shaping our convictions. In the emerging phase of an idea, we are strongly influenced by its high-status promoters, but when that idea begins to take off within a culture, the more important influence becomes the support that a majority give to it. So too these processes have affected our beliefs about the age to come. In this matter, both these elements (high-status support and

---

3. For one attempt in this direction, see my book *Chalcedonian Personalism*.

majority viewpoint) have worked to convince the Western individual that the culture's beliefs, which now reject any element of transcendence and thus life in the age to come, really are the truth about the matter.

Key to grasping the point being made here is the recognition that our culture's convictions on this matter are primarily driven by the attachment motive, not reasonableness as such. We look to our elites as possessing insights upon which we can rely. But the question remains: Does it make sense to be attached in this way to a "parent figure," in this case, our culture, given that, if the high-status leaders of that culture were quizzed carefully about their beliefs, it would be found either (a) that they possessed "a tin ear" for the absolute mystery of reality, that is, their minds are closed to deeper existential questions, or else (b) they would acknowledge their own existential perplexity and insecurity in the face of the mystery of reality? In either case, these people *as individuals* cannot serve as sources of security in the way that the vast majority of less influential participants in the culture think they can. So, the question that the man or woman within Western culture must face is: Why should I have confidence in these views about the age to come when the core "authorities" of my culture, those upon whom I rely for guidance and direction, display either an unconvincing confidence or no confidence at all in this matter? That is, does it make sense to be psychologically dependent on a cultural "attachment figure" which, as it turns out, has no capacity to provide the confidence we seek after? Viewed in those terms, the answer would clearly have to be no.

Turning now to the Christian situation, we can say that, for the believer, although an understanding of the age to come cannot afford to be *irrational*, in fact, a fully understood reasonableness on this matter is simply not possible. No human being *as* a human being can provide that for us. What *is* helpful to us is trust in the person of Christ whose teaching and resurrection give some assurance of our sharing in eternal life. (In passing, we note that this trust issues not merely from a weighing up of the objective evidence but rather from the trustworthiness of the witnesses both to Jesus' teaching and his resurrection. As noted above, such more generally is the way of God, it seems.) But, *within Western culture*, this trust of the believer—*as an individual*—in Christ is insufficient in providing him or her with genuine convictions about the matter.

Recall how attachment to the secular understanding relied upon the presumed authority of influencers and experts in this area *and* the example of other members of the culture as the basis for trusting in those secular beliefs which reject the idea of transcendence. For the Christian, too, the same two elements, authority *and* convincing exemplars, are required for genuine conviction. This means, above all, spending extended periods of time interacting with believers who show, through their actions and words, both their trust in Christ and true convictions about the age to come. Put another way, we can say that for the faithful to discover a lively hope in the age to come, they must find their place in a *Christian sub-culture*, one which displays a compelling faith and which allows those convictions to grow from within into the virtue of hope. Without such an immersion, it is doubtful that the individual Christian in the West can do much to resist the corrosive influences of the dominant culture.

A Hope-Nurturing Christian Community

Perhaps I should spell out a little more the nature of a hope-generating Christian sub-culture. Such a setting would require the presence of leaders or other gifted/charismatic individuals who are and are seen to be truly holy and deeply connected to Christ. These persons would be considered by members of the community as in the same mold, in the same *style*, as those of the past who have been made saints. We would have to admit that such individuals are a rarity today given the general shallowness of character which marks the cultural ideal of the West. Yet, the Lord does raise up such people, and when they are found, they must be sought out and valued.

Immersing ourselves in a community or sub-culture that I have in mind requires a level of contact and engagement similar to that of which we read in Paul's letters. This is unusual within our broader culture, but it is nonetheless necessary for the growth of hope. The required depth of fellowship or community is such that a group member will no longer automatically and simply trust his or her own judgment, for it is likely the case that this has probably been infected by distortions they have been exposed to in the past. Rather they will consider their own default position to be that of the tradition of faith rather than their own thinking. Yet to do so would represent a significant change in mindset for most Western believers!

A third component of this kind of Christian community would be its willingness to face head on both death itself and the human vulnerability we experience in the face of death. Its members would need to be exposed to those who are dying as well as to death itself. This is one reason the presence of older members is of such importance to the life of the community I speak of. Unlike our wider culture, which protects us from being directly exposed to actual death as much as possible, a Christian sub-culture will encourage its members to face up to the reality of death *and simultaneously* to the ways, available to the Christian faith, of thinking and acting in the face of death.

Considering, then, the three elements I have mentioned, authority, community modelling, and dealing with death, we find their succinct encapsulation expressed in the second-century letter of Barnabas in its advice to believers: "Cherish as the apple of your eye anyone who expounds the word of the Lord to you. Day and night keep the day of judgment in mind. Seek the company of God's people every day."[4] Such, at the very least, is what is necessary for the reemergence of the virtue of hope.[5]

Implicit here is the idea that full participation in the community of faith I have described will require a withdrawal from the wider, secular culture, not so much through removing ourselves from work situations or even from friendships but rather from time spent in the culture and especially via exposure to its dominant means of communication, mainstream media, social media, etc. Of course, some will protest that this seems like urging a ghetto mentality. Yet the church communities Paul founded and ministered to were not ghettos, even though, as we can see clearly from his letters, they were truly the core social communities in the lives of their participants. Their non-ghetto-like character is evident from the fact that they grew! They were open to the wider community, but that very openness was expressed primarily through the striking message they communicated: "Repent and believe in the Good News!" My sense is that concerns about becoming a ghetto are expressed mostly by those of us who have excessively deep attachments to secular culture.

What can a believer do if the sort of community of faith I have described is not yet available to him or her? Less effective but at least of some help can be a deep exposure to the lives and teachings of the saintly believers who have lived through the ages who in this situation would stand in for experiencing face-to-face contact with holy leaders. And as

---

4. Louth, *Early Christian Writings*, 180.

5. Another factor not mentioned here is briefly discussed in a footnote in chapter 11. There I suggest that our attitudes to convenience and pleasure lead us to become too attached to this life and thus less attracted to the age to come. We can learn much from the spiritual tradition on this matter if we are open to its wisdom.

a substitute for the full immersion in a community of faith, the frequent reading of the Scriptures, especially the New Testament, can provide contact with the way of thinking that will engender hope. By themselves, however, over lengthy periods of time, these are usually less than sufficient measures. More is needed.

Embracing the Age to Come

Something of the thinking behind what I have written can be found in Paul's First Letter to the Corinthians: The apostle writes about his time among the Corinthian believers: *"My speech and my message were not in plausible words of wisdom, but in demonstration of the Spirit and of power that your faith might not rest in the wisdom of men but in the power of God."* But he goes on to observe that *"among the mature we do impart wisdom, although it is not a wisdom of this age or of the rulers of this age, who are doomed to pass away. But we impart a secret and hidden wisdom of God, which God decreed before the ages for our glory. None of the rulers of this age understood this, for if they had, they would not have crucified the Lord of glory. But, as it is written, 'What no eye has seen, nor ear heard, nor the heart of man imagined, what God has prepared for those who love him—these things God has revealed to us through the Spirit'"* (1 Cor 2:4–5, 6–10). The wisdom that Paul points to is not based primarily on rational considerations—although the requirements of reason must always be met—but rather comes from the action of the Spirit through the tradition of faith working in actual Christian communities, especially those which, by the lives of their members, show that they no longer rely so strongly on their own insight and cleverness.

Note here that when such a community is in place, our mind's thinking changes so as to align with the Christian faith. In that case, our existential attachments are altered. It is not that we come to that position by thinking the whole question through, but that the faith and the hope it engenders come to *feel* right. This might appear to be a problem, since a person will want to base their beliefs on solid foundations rather than on what *feels* true. But recall that there is no place where a human can stand that will give him or her an all-embracing view of the whole of reality, and since our convictions about the age to come are based on *some* worldview to which we are *psychologically attached*, it is best to choose the one which both makes sense in its own right *and* provides a foundation for living our life to the full. That option is the Christian faith.

Failure to take full account of the utter mystery of existence in shaping one's worldview and life direction is one of the signature characteristics of our age. Certainly, crossing the threshold to an "eyes-wide-open" view of one's situation in the face of the enigma of life and death presents great difficulties for many Westerners, and yet, once faced and addressed, the possibility arises of a remarkable and life-changing engagement with Christ. To meet him is to find true hope. For he is the only one who has seen the "other side" of death and has shown us something of the resurrection life. Thus, he urged his disciples, "Be not afraid!"

15

Why Do I Struggle with Belief in Hell?

WE HAVE ALREADY NOTED how people in Western societies, believers and nonbelievers alike, tend to avoid thinking about the so-called last things, things to do with Christ's judgment, heaven, and hell. Of these there is a special resistance to the thought of hell. Most Christian denominations sidestep the mention of it as a matter of faith, but this means that the numerous New Testament passages which refer to it are a continuing source of awkwardness. Among the unspoken thoughts of many Christians is the idea that eternal punishment simply does not fit in with the rest of the faith, with the idea of God's love, with Christ's sacrificial death for our sake, and with the mercy which believers are called to show towards others, including those who consider us their enemies.

When we moderns ponder how it could be that our Christian brethren of former centuries could so easily accept the doctrine of hell, we struggle to find answers. How could they be so hard-hearted? How could they lack the capacity to imagine themselves in the place of those supposedly condemned to eternal punishments? Such deficiencies in imagination push us to one of three positions: either we decide that we cannot accept the kind of faith they held to and as a result we must forge something better—this commonly leads eventually to a liberal or unorthodox option—or we accept the truth of hell as taught by our forefathers in the faith and in doing so affirm that in any case we trust in the goodness and justice of God; or finally, we continue to affirm the whole Christian faith but quarantine the notion of hell in a place where it might safely exist without intruding on the rest of our faith life! Looked at in this way, we would have to admit that none of these alternatives looks very attractive, and so we might ask, "Is there not a better way?"

I believe that we can be helped to understand this matter a little more by drawing on what we have discussed so far about human motives, particularly as they relate to groups. From that material, we might then gain a more accurate understanding of the biblical teaching on hell, and even find a way to actually embrace that teaching as an important part of our faith.

Social Motives Shape Our Beliefs about Hell

Social Reciprocity

Central to the Old Testament way of thinking is the idea that we humans are responsible to God for obeying his law and we are thus liable to God's punishment in case of infractions of that law. This, of course, is not particular to Israelite religion, since it is found across many cultures and is simply the application, to the domain of religion, of the basic principle of the social reciprocity motive: that there are to be negative consequences for infringement of moral rules, just as a positive action, for example, the giving of a gift, warrants a like positive response. This motive lies at the very foundation of our view of society and of ourselves as individuals who are responsible for the way we act in relation to other members of society. When it comes to our interactions with God, we see that we must apply the same kind of thinking to them: to get off the ground, as it were, those interactions require that we consider ourselves as responsible before him because if that were not the case, if we bore no responsibility for how we acted, we would be engaging in what would be, in effect, a sham relationship with him; we would be at the mercy of our biological and psychological natures, and any "interaction" with God would be merely manipulation rather than genuine mutually responsive conversation and engagement.

For almost all of the Old Testament period, the due punishment for disobedience was thought to be enacted in this life, since there was no clear idea of an age to come as the place where humans were to be held to account, either by reward or punishment. By the time of Christ, when the resurrection of the dead was a common belief among influential Jewish groups, human accountability before God was seen to apply not necessarily in this life but, following the death of an individual, at the point when they stood before God's judgment throne. This did not mean that the matter of judgment related solely to the individual since it was still held that, in some respects, the social groups to which individuals belonged, could be held accountable before God. So, for example, individual Samaritans, by virtue of being members of the Samaritan cult, were viewed as bearing responsibility for their wayward beliefs. But increasingly, the individuals themselves, aside from their membership in social, religious, or political groups, were more fully treated as responsible before God.

The Contributions of the Dominance and Attachment Motives

Now complicating the convictions about hell among Christian believers is the impact of the motives of group attachment and group dominance. Before we consider their effects, let us quickly review the main outlines of how they work.

In general, both these forces push members of any reasonably strong social group to draw clear contrasts between in-group and out-group status so that in-groups are viewed positively while out-groups are seen in negative terms. In relation to attachment, we hold fast—psychologically, that is—to our group (family, tribe, nation, culture, etc.)—and especially to those key members who can be most relied upon—and this provides us with a sense of security. At the same time, we jealously guard against group outsiders who might insinuate their way into our group and seek the preferential favor of its leaders. As an example of this, we can think of the young child who vigorously intervenes when his mother cuddles another child who is not part of his family, or of the wife who expresses annoyance driven by jealousy if her husband becomes too friendly with another female. Similar processes operate at the group level. According to this way of thinking, if God has singled out for salvation us who believe—especially those who follow his law—then the out-group made up of nonbelievers, those who are outside the scope of God's protection, do not deserve to be the recipients of his kindness. We know that this is not a Christian view of things, but that does not prevent the force which prompts it from influencing our thinking. If God is *our* God, it is all too easy to believe that he is *not* also the God of those outside the fold.

With group dominance, we find a similar negative view of out-groups. This dynamic operates mainly in countries which are largely and traditionally Christian and where the populations have little contact with people of non-Christian beliefs. Heathen nations, from this perspective, are commonly considered as not only other but also of lesser value in God's eyes than Christians. On the status ladders of moral virtue or spiritual knowledge they are viewed as benighted, ignorant, and immoral, and that makes it relatively easy to imagine that, at the last judgment, God will have good reason to consign them to outer darkness. Again, this is not a Christian viewpoint, since as believers we owe any holiness and goodness that we possess to God's grace rather than to our own strengths and endowments. But that does not stop group dominance from flavoring our thinking.

A complication arises here, however. Although, in this context, the workings of both group attachment and dominance are dangerous to Christian faith, there is an element of truth lurking behind them. For truly there is a difference approved by God between those in Christ's community of faith and those outside it. As the Scriptures express it, we believers in Christ are *"a chosen people, a royal priesthood . . . called out of darkness into the wonderful light of Christ"* (1 Pet 2:9). This is not to be denied or downplayed even though we know that among the people of God are both wheat and tares, those who are genuinely of the kingdom and others who only appear to be so, and any simple drawing of the boundary line is to be rejected.

Still, without that distinction, we compromise the basic Christian belief that—all things being equal—it is much better both here and in the age to come to have received the grace of faith than to have never heard the good news or, worse, to have rejected it. But we must immediately add that any "us-versus-them" attitude is far from God's way; he is not limited by our human psychology and can never wish that any of his creation should exist as a "them" rather than an "us." When the Scriptures teach us that *"God . . . desires all people to be saved"* (1 Tim 2:4), we must not imagine that there is any hint of an "us-and-them" thought in the divine mind hiding behind that word "all." The Lord desires and actively works towards the salvation of all people, though, of course, many turn away from him either directly or through their sin. As followers of the Christ of God, we are to model that same divine attitude, particularly in the way we direct our activities outward so as to invite all those who currently live as the "them" of God to become one of "us." We are to be *"ambassadors of Christ, God making his appeal through us"* (2 Cor 5:20).

Hell: Some Theological Principles

Keeping in mind what we have discussed about reciprocity, dominance, and attachment so far, let us now set out some principles for a meaningful understanding of the place of hell in Christian theology.

First, we recognize a responsibility which we possess before God, one which can never be taken away from us without destroying our dignity as humans made in God's image. Any conversation between two persons assumes that each bears responsibility for what they say and how they respond to the words of the other. So, too, with our relationship with God, we assume the same thing, not only that the Lord God has the freedom to engage with us, but we also have a similar capacity for free action. For this to happen there has to be the effective working of the dominance motive in its form as competence ("I am someone who acts") and that of conscience ("I am responsible for my acts"), and without these there can be no personal relationship with God. Those who would deny the possibility of the "place" of hell, that is, the status of a human who has finally rejected a relationship with God, are by that very denial also rejecting the *necessary* conditions for a personal relationship between man and God.

Secondly, we hold to a doctrine of grace which works to soften some of the hard edges of the attachment and dominance motives, that is, those elements which push us to believe too easily that certain people will end up in hell. Several of Jesus' parables make clear the priority of grace: think of those of the prodigal son, the workers in the vineyard, and the unforgiving servant—each of these parables shows the surprising depth of God's grace which exceeds our sense of fairness, but also the expectation that Jesus' listeners should imitate such generosity. In doing so, they will work against the instinctive push of their group attachment and dominance motives but also against that limited sense of fairness that our social reciprocity motive demands. God's generosity exceeds fairness; so too must ours.

Finally, and following on from this point, we must also affirm that God's purposes for the salvation of all are so fundamental to the way he engages with his creation that even the justice that the social reciprocity motive establishes as a necessary element of all our social relationships has been, to some extent, subverted by a strange action whereby God the Father sends his Son to repair all the offences against justice on our behalf. God has taken upon himself that punishment which was our due.

Tensions between These Principles

We can recognize the tensions that exist between these three elements of faith and imagine that one or other of them might easily be overemphasized at the expense of the others. So, we might center our faith so tightly around the principle of human responsibility that the other two elements are neglected. Or we might hold that the desire and grace of God are so powerful as to override our human responsibility. To see how the church has sought to deal with these tensions, let me mention two insights, prominent among Catholic and Orthodox believers, which have helped them deepen their understanding of the way of Christ as it relates to the teaching on hell.

Cyprian, a North African bishop of the third century, in wrestling with the problem of how to treat believers who, during a time of persecution, lapsed when pressured to renounce the faith, sought to avoid a strong "us-versus-them" way of thinking. His reflections led him along the path towards the idea that even those lapsed believers, after death, might be prayed for and helped to reach a full vision of God. Thereby the way was opened to a more nuanced understanding of how the Lord exercises his power of judgment. While the stark contrast between the saved and the lost is still maintained, also introduced into the picture is a third "category" of soul whose members, not yet ready to face the full glory of God, are being purified in order to bring them to that place. They are assisted along that pathway by the prayers of living believers who seek their salvation. Cyprian's insight led to a gradual weakening of the "anti-other" perspective that the group attachment and group dominance motives encourage in us. In its place, it proposed a death-transcending communion or fellowship among believers, holy and fallen, which could work for the final salvation even of those whom we might otherwise have considered lost. Through the prayers of the faithful, those who had lapsed by failing to defend the faith under pressure of persecution could also receive the blessings of eternal life. "Them," through love, could become "us."[1]

At a much later time in the church's history, the sixteenth-century mystic St. John of the Cross, and following him the Carmelite spiritual

---

1. Other Christian writers followed Cyprian's lead. Ambrosiaster distinguished between the truly wicked who warranted eternal torment and Christians who had fallen into sin who might receive punishment of only temporary duration. Ambrose and Jerome follow a similar line. However, others held to a sterner teaching, and among them was Augustine, who nevertheless made some slight concessions for specific groups of sinners. For a brief summary, see Kelly, *Early Christian Doctrines*, 484–85.

tradition to which he belonged, came to an understanding of Jesus' descent into hell as a sign that the Lord was even willing to show solidarity, and indeed profoundly sacrificial love, to those who had rejected him. In this way, it was thought, there might be hope that they could turn away from their no to God and through receiving his love be reconciled to him. This understanding continues to acknowledge the freedom which each person has in their power to truly and finally reject God, and thus it affirms the importance of the notion of hell—so the traditional teaching is preserved fully intact—yet it also gives full weight to the fundamental truth of revelation that God moves beyond the constraints which the human psychology of attachment and dominance places on our thoughts. When we have dark thoughts about how someone who has inflicted a heinous evil on others should be consigned to the eternal torments of hell, it is likely that it is the unhelpful aspects of the attachment, dominance, and/or social reciprocity motives which are working on our thoughts, and we need to be reminded that the Lord would have us move beyond those limited perspectives to embrace his boundless love not only for us but also for others. The conscience sensitive to God's word must always win out in the end.[2]

Concluding Comments

Returning to the original question about the place of the doctrine of hell in the life of a believer, we can conclude that it must be preserved as a "call to the responsibility incumbent upon man to make use of his freedom in view of his eternal destiny."[3] At the same time, it is also the case that God does not wish *"that any should perish, but that all should reach repentance"* (2 Pet 3:9), a truth demonstrated by Christ's descent even to the depths of hell. Our modern sensitivity to the dilemmas raised by the doctrine of hell is at least partly the result of the diminished importance, in our time, of group identifications, whether they be attachment- or dominance-related; our preference is more for understanding individuals as just that, individuals with their own particular qualities, ideas, and attitudes. For that reason, we are not so prone to being affected by the harmful aspects of dominance and attachment motives in their group forms. However, in our individualism, with all its intellectual and emotional self-reliance,

2. For a fuller treatment of this topic, see Ratzinger, *Eschatology*.
3. *Catechism of the Catholic Church*, sec. 1036.

we are much less open to the Lord's call to trusting obedience, and to participation in the community of faith. Our gain in sensitivity in one aspect of belief is counterbalanced by a loss of an overall faith-sensitivity in another respect. For this reason, we ought to be careful not to look down on believers of past eras who adopted stricter understandings of hell than our own, for it is likely that those same people knew a humility and faithfulness that largely eludes us contemporary Western Christians.

16

Marriage: "Love and Truth Walk Together"

IN WESTERN NATIONS, MALE-FEMALE relations have undergone major changes which have brought about a reduction in the differences between the sexes. Many have observed that males have become less masculine and females have become less feminine.[1] In the past, biological maleness and cultural masculinity matched quite well with each other (and culture sometimes even exaggerated nature). Now, for the sake of "equality," cultural pressure has pushed males in the direction of gender neutrality or even femininity. We know that males on average are still significantly taller, stronger, and more driven by the dominance/competence and mating drives. They are better suited to large-scale cooperative ventures, more interested in things mathematical/scientific/mechanical, and more prone to physical violence. However, many of these features no longer play such an important role in how males relate to females and more generally how they live in society. Females, too, have moved in a complementary direction. They are physically weaker than men, they are still the ones to bear and nurture children, and thus are, for a time, more in need of support. They still display superior language skills as well as relationship- and community-binding capacities and greater interest in social activities. But as with their male counterparts, today some of their own distinctively feminine qualities play a lesser role in how they live out their lives.

1. For a recent example of work in this area, see Hsu et al., "Gender, 'Masculinity,' and 'Femininity,'" 987–1011.

This softening of differences has occurred over a period of decades and has been so insistently urged upon us as the way to true progress that now it all seems so obvious to us. We might wonder how we could have ever thought that gender differences had to be so important. And yet there are perhaps moments when we might have second thoughts about the direction we have taken. Possibly, when we view older movies, we are caught off-guard by something attractive about how the sexes behaved towards each other. The masculinity of a Cary Grant or the femininity of an Audrey Hepburn are so palpable, so striking. While we might respond by inwardly reminding ourselves of how much better things are in our own days, I suspect that at a deeper level we experience a sense of unease or even regret about what has been lost. Perhaps we see in the movie characters a respect for and an interest in the womanly and the manly and the ease with which these elements allowed the sexes to relate to one another. Or maybe we are touched by the female openness to being cared for and the male willingness to do so. Such thoughts might even prompt us to wonder whether or not we have taken a few wrong turns along the way this past fifty years or more. For the most part, however, I suspect that such thoughts do not linger long in our consciousness. Well, then, what is the effect on marriages of these changes in relationships between the sexes? How, as believers, might we respond to them, in the light of the Scriptures and in view of the framework I have offered in part I? These are the issues I want to address in this chapter. My focus will be upon three key questions: (a) What part do gender differences play in marriage? (b) How are believing couples to deal with the question of authority? And (c) How can husbands and wives take full account of the place of attachment in their relationship? I hope to show that these three are all related to each other, and finding the right answers to them, though difficult, is an important step in establishing a healthy marriage.

Gender Differences at the Heart of Marriage

One of the key observations of this book is that Western societies have by and large invested heavily in the dominance motive (at the expense of those of attachment and conscience) and have favored the individual form of dominance over that of its group expression. This means that, when it comes to gender, our identity as male or as female (group membership) is no longer as central to our sense of self as it was in former times. Now, we wish to be known primarily for what we *as individuals* have accomplished, how well we have advanced in some area of endeavour, how much attention we have received from others for our achievements. It is certainly the case, especially for women, that they still identify with their gender and show this by taking care about their appearance *as women* in public. But perhaps their deeper motivation in doing this has less to do with the (mating) drive to find a life partner and have children and more about gaining attention *as individuals* from others, as much from their own sex as from males. In other words, their purposes are likely driven more by dominance (in its individual form) and less by mating and the attachment that is an essential part of that drive.

All this means that while there is necessarily some element of these last two motives operating in any marriage, it is also the case that for many couples these driving forces do not figure in a serious way in shaping the marriage relationship. In fact, many modern marriages can be described better as parallel (rather than as complementary) relationships. What I mean by "parallel" is that such marriages involve two individuals, essentially *the same*—apart from what they do in sexual intercourse—who have developed a friendship and a way of supporting each other so that the separate life goals of each might be more easily pursued. (This is different from "complementary," which means that they see themselves as different and as complementing each other in important ways.) The presence of young children often complicates the "parallel" arrangement, since only a woman can get pregnant and give birth to a baby, but this, it is thought, need only be a brief interruption to the deeper goals associated with the dominance motive. To assist the process, society has provided the means and the justifications for dealing with this issue.

Yet however much these changes in marriage might allow the achievement of the desires of both men and women for a fulfilling life, the problems within the institution of marriage seem to be mounting up and touching us at a deeper level. We know that about half of couples in long-term relations, that is, those who are bound to each other with powerful attachment bonds, will suffer the devastation of a relationship breakdown.[2] As we have already seen, this is an event from which couples rarely fully recover. Also, marriage as a legal relationship is losing favor, and many couples today prefer instead the greater flexibility of cohabitation. This is likely an indicator that younger generations are giving up

---

2. CDC, "Marriage and Divorce."

on the possibility of discovering the experience of a lifelong and life-enhancing bond of (male-female) attachment that marks the marriage relationship at its best. It looks as though people are losing depth of soul. For all their efforts towards the goals of happiness, a sense of life as a truly meaningful existence often eludes them. Perhaps, then, there is a need to think again about that primary bond that stands at the beginning and foundation of human society—the mating pair.

A mating pair, of course, begins its life through the operation of the mating motive, which we have considered in chapters 7 and 8. It is important to note that, although we discussed it last among the "biological" motives, in an important sense it is the primary social motive upon which all the others build. First, nature requires that reproducing pairs come together, and once that process is in place the effectiveness of the mating motive itself can be enhanced and refined through dominance (improved mate selection) and attachment (better quality nurture). Also, the stability of larger social groups, helped along by the social reciprocity motive, can play a role in enhancing success in the business of reproduction. This means that, at the level of biology, the fundamental limits set by the mating motive will determine how much leeway the other motives can have before they start to undermine the whole process of reproduction and survival. This same principle applies also to the cultural changes that are such a key part of human societies. Offending the basic biological "rules" which have evolved in the development of the mating motive will diminish the long-term survival of a culture. Societies that break those rules will not survive long since evolution is generally much "wiser" than our best cultural ideas! Let us see how this works out in relation to contemporary husband-wife relations.

Like so many other mammals, humans have evolved, as we have seen, so that mating pairs are actively initiated, that is, by approach, on the part of the male. Females might initiate but only by a more passive display. Such a difference in operation sets the scene for a developing relationship culminating in sexual intercourse, which has the same (male) approach—(female) reception quality. But it does not end there. In the event of the birth of a child, the active work of providing for the basic needs of the new mating unit as a whole falls to the male, while the female must devote herself more specifically to the nurture of her infant, less so to her own survival and even much less so to that of her male partner. If this arrangement is to succeed, an element of overall oversight for the good of the family must have applied to the male-female relationship, especially when matters of survival were at play. If the male, who is normally more adept than the female at protecting the unit as a whole, was to carry out that function, he would have needed to have exercised a form of authority, and that authority the female would willingly accept.

On the other hand, it is likely that in evolutionary terms the human female has evolved to be suited to her own form of responsibility. Recall that she is more attuned to the movements of the attachment motive, for it is the attachment-linked hormone, oxytocin, which is associated with the birthing process, breastfeeding, and relationships of trust (as well as the climax of the sexual act). This suggests that she might well find herself taking greater—though not exclusive—responsibility for ensuring that the emotional bond between herself and her male partner remains healthy.

Finally, thinking about a couple as part of a clan or a tribe, we note that the fundamental group rule of reciprocity which applies to all relationships between equals would have also operated within a mating unit. Neither the man nor the woman would have thought it appropriate that either one should bear an excessive amount of the burden or costs nor share disproportionately in any benefits. Certainly, at times a female might have depended on the relationship more than her partner, but serious imbalances in this respect would not have become entrenched in our biology. For in this case they would have resulted in the breakup of mating units and therefore would have worked to defeat the whole purpose of pair bonds as an effective way of increasing the odds of survival of offspring.

In describing how gender differences have affected the male-female mating relationship viewed in evolutionary terms, we must keep in mind that in the cultures which had the most influence in shaping modern Western societies—the Semitic, Greek, Roman, and Germanic—there was much less scope for some of the evolved arrangements to show themselves. This was because, for the most part, partner choice was the prerogative of the parents rather than the individuals involved. A father and mother might have applied the criteria of reproductive success in making decisions about the sort of woman their son should have as his wife. However, they could also take account of the value of marrying into a certain respected (i.e., dominant) family, or they might even think in terms of purely financial benefits. Today, at least in Westernized cultures, such practices are much less common. This means that, strangely enough, those mating strategies which evolved at the dawn of the emergence of our species, that is, well before the arrival of settled cultures with their complex behavioral norms, now come into prominence again and contribute significantly to shaping the way men and women engage in the process of mating.

In our times and culture, there are many reasons, not least of which is the availability of easy-to-use contraception, why the arrangement of an actively initiating male and receptivity-signaling female might be set aside. In the past women possessed a greater wariness than men before entering into a sexual relationship, and this was central to how things evolved between the sexes. But with her ability reliably to avoid getting pregnant or, if need be, to abort an embryo or fetus, this caution no longer serves its original purpose. Both men and women now have the possibility of engaging in short-term relations aside from any intention to form mating units and have children. Thus, the practice of male initiation would appear no longer to have strong reasons to sustain it.

However, it is not clear that this newly won freedom among females to approach potential male sexual partners is working out as many might have hoped. Rather than an increase in frequency of sexual intercourse, as one might have expected, there is evidence that across the age spectrum men and women are actually engaging less in sexual activity.[3] Recall, too, that the short-term female sexual strategy described in chapter 7 required a payoff in the form of resources from a potential sexual partner for her to enter such a relationship. This accords with survey data which indicate that women gain less enjoyment than men from casual sexual contact considered in itself.[4] Thus, it is likely that the psychological makeup of females, apart from any rational cost-benefit considerations, discourages them from fleeting sexual encounters; such encounters seem to require some kind of offsetting compensation. Moreover, there might well be something in males which pushes them to discount the attractiveness of those females who initiate sexual contact. A female who enters a sexual relationship too easily might signal to the male her unsuitability as a long-term partner since she might not be trusted to remain faithful to him throughout marriage.

All of this converges towards the conclusion that there is continuing value in taking account of the evolution of gender differences when it

---

3. Wellings et al., "Changes," I1525; Ueda et al., "Trends in Frequency," e203833–e203833.

4. This is especially the case for women in long-term relationships. See Wongsomboon et al., "Women's Orgasm and Sexual Satisfaction," 285–95.

comes to how we moderns approach the task of finding a mating partner. For the man to approach a woman, to actively initiate fuller social contact, for the woman to give her attention to the display of her suitability as a potential wife, and to respond to a man according to how she evaluates him as a potential husband, this process would appear to provide the best opportunity for allowing the whole mating system to operate smoothly.

Conscience, Authority, and Marriage

As was discussed in chapter 10, conscience and the various forms of authority that rely upon it draw on several elements found in human dominance. The dominant features of parents (physical size, experience, knowledge, voice, etc.) help them to exercise authority in families and to form working consciences in children. In other social groups similar signs of dominance are used by leaders to make it easier for them to carry out their duties as authorities. Importantly, we have noted that these signs of dominance are *not* to be used to achieve the fundamental purpose of the dominance motive, that is, to demonstrate superiority, but rather to help parents and other leaders in the task of pursuing the good of all, whether it be the family or some other group. Now, in order for this to happen, a parent/leader, as authority, needs an effective conscience, that is, they must make use of the only motive which ultimately takes account not only of their own good but also the good of others. Without this, they cannot accomplish the common good over longer periods of time.

The other key element linked to conscience and authority is trust. In social or political groups, trust in the leader is normally a condition for their successful operation. When it is lost, a leader either must rely upon his or her coercive powers or else renounce the leadership role. In families, too, we have remarked on a similar process. The emergence of a conscience in a child—a condition for healthy family life—requires a "good enough" attachment bond between parent and child. In thinking about these processes, we must ask the question: To what extent do they apply to the marriage relationship among believers?

It has been well documented that woman prefer mates who are older and taller than themselves and who demonstrate an income-earning capacity and willingness to provide for a family.[5] With age commonly

---

5. The largest scale cross-cultural study of sexual preferences is still that of Buss, "Sex Differences," 1–49.

comes greater life experience, while earning potential often calls for competence either within a specific field or more generally. On account of both characteristics, a woman might reasonably respect or "look up" to a prospective partner; in some respects, then, she might recognize in him features which her subconscious mind associates with authority.

Another quality already noted is the biologically and culturally evolved tendency for the male to approach the female in mating. So entrenched is this that even in our hyper-egalitarian society males are still socialized to take the initiative in seeking a partner in marriage. Today it remains exceptional that a woman formally requests the hand of her boyfriend in marriage; almost always it is the man who does so. Within marriage, too, the initiative in engaging in sexual activity more often than not rests with the husband. Here it is of interest to note that the willingness to take the initiative is also a characteristic of the exercise of authority in any situation—marital or non-marital. So, a husband's general disposition towards initiation, beginning with the more specific practices in mating, can also signal to his wife a quality linked to the exercise of authority even if she is not consciously aware of it. Apart from these authority-signaling qualities, we might also note masculine voice and facial and other features which support the picture I have painted of the mating/marriage relationship.

So, the overall idea we gain in taking account of the evolutionary development of the mating relationship is that some element of authority is going to be helpful in its operation. But how might it show itself today in marriages between believers? If we assume that they are committed to complementary roles for husbands and wives (rather than a fully parallel relationship), and also a willingness to be generous in having children, perhaps a sound case for it might run along the following lines:

Generally, it makes sense that there be a willingness and indeed a commitment on the part of both a husband and a wife to the man's responsibility for the *overall* well-being of the family. This would show itself less in any claim of his that he has exclusive decision-making about, for example, where to live, or what sort of dwelling to choose, than in his acceptance of his role in taking the initiative in such matters, to see it as primarily his responsibility to address them. The reason for this is that such decisions have much to do with the kind of work in which the husband is employed and the weighing up of risks associated with that work. "How far is it feasible for me to travel to and from my place of work? What is the possibility of me losing my position and so affecting my ability to repay our housing loan?"—these and similar matters fall mainly within the responsibility of husbands if they accept the task of being the primary (though not necessarily the only) provider for the family. In acknowledging this fact, a wife will be willing to defer to her husband when such issues arise. We might say that the trust she placed in him when she accepted his proposal to enter into a marriage with him should continue when it comes to decisions touching upon the overall good of the family.

At this point, and with all the above in mind, we can begin to make sense of biblical teaching about how couples are to relate within marriage. The clearest New Testament witness to the matter is found in the Letter to the Ephesians, chapter 5, where we read the wives are to *"submit to [their] husbands as to the Lord"*; husbands are to *"love [their] wives as Christ loved the church and gave himself up for her."* Similar teaching occurs in Colossians (Col 3:18–19) and in the First Letter of Peter (1 Pet 3:1–7).

For Catholic Christians, there are the further clarifications of the scriptural text which have been provided by papal teaching. Thus we find in Pope Pius XI's encyclical letter *Casti connubii* (1930) the following: "[The order of love] includes both the primacy of the husband with regard to the wife and children and the ready subjection of the wife and her willing obedience."[6] More recently, St. John Paul II's document entitled *Mulieris dignitatem* sought to soften some of what were perceived as the "hard edges" of earlier teaching, both scriptural and magisterial, but perhaps at the expense of clarity and practical usefulness. One particular part of that document, however, speaks directly to the question of dominance, responsibility, initiative, and authority and how they are related. The pope writes: "When the author of the Letter to the Ephesians calls Christ 'the bridegroom' and the Church 'the Bride,' he indirectly confirms through this analogy the truth about woman as bride. The Bridegroom is the one who loves. The Bride is loved: it is she who receives love, in order to love in return."[7] Here we see the differing roles of husbands and wives with respect to the question of initiative: the husband initiates in love; the wife responds to that initiative with her own love. As a statement of the foundational dimension of the relationship of marriage, in line with earlier teaching, it speaks the truth. Having made the approach to initiate a relationship with a potential life partner, as a married man he continues

---

6. Pius XI, *Casti connubii*, 26.

7. John Paul II, *Mulieris dignitatem*, 2.

to display that same initiative, now in loving his wife, and part of that love is to take primary responsibility for the overall well-being of the couple.

And yet there is more to magisterial teaching than this general principle of husbandly initiation and responsibility. In the above-mentioned encyclical of Pius XI, we note that he is careful to add some qualifications to it in order to discourage any notion of a domineering mentality on the part of husbands.

> This subjection, however, does not deny or take away the liberty that fully belongs to the woman both in view of her dignity as a human person and in view of her most noble office as wife and mother and companion; nor does it bid her obey her husband's every request if not in harmony with right reason or with the dignity due to the wife; nor, [finally], does it imply that the wife should be put on a level with those persons who in law are called minors, to whom it is not customary to allow free exercise of their rights on account of their lack of mature judgment or of their ignorance of human affairs.[8]

With this warning for husbands to take full account of their wife's responsibility and capacity for initiation, which mirrors the tenor of the Ephesians 5 text, we can begin to fill out the picture of day-to-day married life. If the taking of initiative is the marker of responsibility and therefore authority, we can see that over the range of tasks that make up married life, there is a patchwork of "authorities." Thus, much conflict is avoided by the simple expedient of deciding who, in a couple, is *primarily* responsible for each of the various areas of life together. Responsibilities for the cooking, the washing, the cleaning of the house or apartment, for the work of maintenance and repair, the finances, the supervision of the children (here the age of the children is important), the maintenance of relationships with the wider family and with friends—all these and more can be negotiated and agreed upon. On the other hand, when couples, in interests of "equality," attempt to share equally all the domestic tasks, without either of them designated as principally responsible for particular ones, this is much more likely to lead to conflict over the longer term.

In establishing agreed-upon areas of responsibility, it is also helpful for couples to take account of their individual capacities and skills, as well as cultural expectations (as long as these are consistent with Christian values). While some men are better cooks than their wives, and some

---

8. Pius XI, *Casti connubii*, 27.

women excel their husbands in handyman skills, for the most part there are gender differences in skills called for in the areas of responsibility I have listed above. This is the result of both cultural and biological evolution, and again, for a couple to work against these developments is to make things more difficult for themselves. On the other hand, to accept equality in dignity rather than equal in the sense of being the same is to acknowledge that there is no necessary difference in value in the cooking efforts of a wife who is "barefoot in the kitchen" and the husband who is a master chef!

At this point, we need to return to the text of *Casti connubii* for a further clarification of what we have described so far.

> But [the earlier statement about the freedom of the wife] forbids that exaggerated liberty which cares not for the good of the family; it forbids that in this body which is the family the heart be separated from the head to the great detriment of the whole body and the proximate danger of ruin. For the man is the head, the woman is the heart, and as he occupies the chief place in ruling, so she may and ought to claim for herself the chief place in love.[9]

Again, we can recognize in this comment some resonances with what was discussed earlier concerning the evolved differences between men and women. Although we might not be comfortable with the former pope's way of expressing the matter, in the idea that the man is the head while the woman is the heart of a family, the key point is to highlight the value of different or complementary functions within a marriage for the sake of its unity, which effectively means in the interests of its *stability and well-being*. Couples without children might not be convinced of this point, and even those with a single child might wonder about the necessity of complementary roles for the health of their marriage, especially if each party is intent on pursuing their own careers and they are willing to entrust the daytime care of their young son or daughter to paid workers. However, if it is decided that a wife will continue the maternal pathway set by nature in the form of pregnancy and early care of an infant and herself carry out the task of looking after her young child, then there will normally be a need to adjust the arrangement of responsibilities more strongly in favor of mutually distinct functions. Almost necessarily, to the husband will fall the task of providing most of the financial resources

---

9. Pius XI, *Casti connubii*, 27.

for his family while, at the same time, the home will be the primary place where the wife exercises her responsibilities. With further children, this specialization will be even more in evidence; more mouths to feed means heavier obligations on the father to meet the financial needs of the family, and likewise a more home-focused theater of operations for the mother. In fact, one might well view the presence of more than one child as an aid to the well-being of a marriage!

Of course, the ideal I have described is strongly resisted by influential groups within Western societies. It is a resistance that manifests itself mainly in the form of almost frenetic efforts to involve more women in full-time careers—with the harmful (and unacknowledged) consequence of limiting their involvement in their families. For women who do wish to have children, there are increasingly powerful "encouragements" (social disapproval of remaining "at home" to care for young children and financial incentives to return to work as soon as possible after giving birth) to avoid damage to their careers. Also in line with this antagonism to the marriage ideal I have described is the move to have fathers share the burden of looking after infants by providing strong incentives for them to take the same amount of maternity/paternity leave as their wife following the birth of a child. This opposition to a Christian understanding of marriage can be at least partly put down to the fact that the number of children women are bearing in virtually every Western nation is now well below replacement level. For most men and women, the approach of the faith is simply too threatening to the control which the dominance motive exercises over their lives.

Beyond these headwinds, another problem faced by women who opt for home care of their own children is the lack of structures for social interaction available to them and also the difficulty in finding outlets for their abilities and interests which accommodate their parenting responsibilities. The demise of daytime women's community groups over recent decades now leaves many mothers who are looking after children isolated, lonely, and undervalued. This means that even women who, for whatever reason, are committed to caring for their own children at least until an age when they attend preschool still experience discouragement and perhaps wonder about the benefits of such an arrangement.

With such a contentious matter as I have addressed here, there is much more that might be added. However, the fact that many, if not most, couples in Western societies face great difficulties in developing and preserving a stable and mutually beneficial marriage relationship strongly suggests that the whole complex of attitudes and beliefs about marriage which has emerged within Western culture over the past generation or more must be treated with great caution. What to many now seems obviously—almost instinctively—right is, according to a Christian understanding, probably harmful to marital health. The approach I have taken here has argued that the difference or specialization in the responsibilities between husbands and wives, a complementarity grounded in our biological and cultural history, can be drawn upon to assist couples to achieve a more harmonious and life-enhancing bond. But this can only happen if both husbands and wives take seriously the scriptural teaching on marriage. Given the stresses faced by marriages today, without the resources that the faith is able to provide, the sustaining joys and blessings are largely closed to those who would engage in the noble enterprise of mating.

Gender Differences in the Attachment Relationship within Marriage

Awareness of how men and women differ in the way they deal with marriage as an attachment relationship can be of great benefit to couples in understanding each other and preserving and developing the marital bond. The primary difference between the sexes in this motive shows itself in a greater willingness (and capacity?) of women to open themselves up emotionally to their partner. Their upbringing—and also, likely, their genetic makeup—attunes them to both the emotion of fear and to the expression of warmth which eases fear. Such characteristics allow them to take better account of the feelings and experiences of others, and within the context of marriage the wife is commonly more willing to communicate psychological vulnerability to her husband than he is to her. In each of these areas, men typically demonstrate more limited skills: they often deal with their emotions awkwardly, are less ready to empathize, and are often resistant to "opening up" (that is, vulnerably) to their wives.[10] We can draw the conclusion from this that, as a generaliza-

---

10. This might sound like men are poorly suited for intimate relationships, but it must be remembered that their deficiencies in that domain are compensated for by capacities in other areas. For example, the wider society typically benefits greatly from masculine energy insofar as it is directed towards socially valuable goals. *Large-scale* group action (e.g., defense forces, large businesses and other organizations, religions) in which an end can only be achieved by the subordination of self-expression and

tion, the attachment motive is more easily elicited—at least within social relationships—in women than in men. On the other hand, the nurturing role, that is, providing the support to one who is emotionally or physically vulnerable, is something that husbands—when they are raised well!—are well capable of fulfilling.

Many couples will have observed that sexual interest in wives usually surfaces *after* the attachment motive has already been triggered and fed. In practice this means that in order to help a wife into a receptive frame of mind for sexual contact, some or all of the following are needed: a setting of privacy and peacefulness; the putting aside of dominance/competence/activist thinking; psychological intimacy in the form of sharing of inner thoughts; physical contact, holding, caressing, and non-sexual stroking of skin. All of these nurturing activities are aids to prompting the attachment motive and, especially for the wife, they allow for a more satisfying sexual relation.

For husbands, the process is no different in the basics, but it differs in emphasis in a way that has important consequences. He is more open to direct sexual engagement with his wife and does not generally require the prior attachment-responsive interaction which is so helpful to her. For him, triggering the attachment motive and the feelings that accompany it normally comes into play during intercourse and more strongly at the point of orgasm. Even for men who are seemingly quite closed emotionally in their day-to-day life, the time during and following sexual intercourse can render them uncharacteristically willing to share their inner selves in a sincere and vulnerable manner. This reminds us of the commonly remarked observation that women require love before sex and men sex before love. Although there is much wrong with this saying, it does nevertheless contain an important element of truth: that husbands and wives differ in the ease with which the attachment motive is aroused, and this has its impact on their sexual relations.

Outside of the bedroom, we can also note that attachment-related behaviors (touching, holding hands, hugging, etc.) and particular ways of communicating between spouses (talking together about matters of deep significance to each other) can help sustain emotional well-being, ease stress when this becomes a problem, and strengthen the relationship overall. This aspect of marriages is the one which is frequently ignored

---

the coordination of many individuals is something that men are better suited to, and the skills it calls for are probably those which render them less adept within intimate one-on-one relationships.

or neglected, and when that happens it can be the trigger for other seemingly unrelated difficulties within a relationship. For this reason, its careful nurture should be a priority for couples and for those, such as counsellors, who assist them. As an example of the dangers of neglecting attachment matters in marriage, let us consider a sequence of events which many couples experience to their great distress.

A Toxic Mechanism in Marriage

As most couples know, their sexual relations fluctuate in intensity and satisfaction for many reasons, but the usual pattern is that, in general terms, this aspect of their relationship centers around an equilibrium that both parties are either happy with or are willing to tolerate. To say this, however, is not to deny the well-documented decline in quality of sex life in a marriage over time. This decline occurs over a period of years and decades, yet it is most noticeable in the initial years of the relationship and generally settles down after that. Also, it can be impacted for better or worse by such factors as the presence of children in the family, work pressures/work-life balance, the health of the spouses, and children growing up and leaving home.

However, when the sexual relationship is affected in such a way as to lead to limited opportunities or willingness for intercourse, a destructive feedback loop can become entrenched and bring serious stress to the marriage. The process can be described as follows:

The husband is typically the first to experience the lack of sexual contact and will seek to engage in intercourse with his wife. But because he is missing not only sex but also probably the nurturing of his attachment drive, he will be impaired (that is, discouraged and expecting failure) in his ability to engage in the emotional intimacy that his wife generally requires before she is open to sexual contact. His attempts will therefore be deficient or seemingly half-hearted, and this will have the effect of "turning off" his wife from having intercourse. "All he wants me for is sex" will be how she experiences the situation.

He, for his part, will become even more discouraged and angry with his wife. "Why is she cold towards me? Why is she turned off by the prospect of lovemaking?" This will lead to increased irritability on his part and more marital arguments both about sex and likely also about other unrelated matters. She in turn will become more emotionally sensitive to slights and criticisms because she is not receiving the attachment nurturing that she needs from him.

Thus, the relationship spirals in the direction of less warmth, greater conflict, and, for both parties, thoughts about the long-term prospects of the marriage. Encouraging the husband to woo his wife, or her to just to have sex with him, does not typically help the situation, since this is asking too much of the *emotional* capacities of either party. Neither of them has the emotional reserves to accomplish this.

What sort of circuit-breaker is needed? Two things are necessary in this situation. First, both spouses must become aware that the problem is not to do with sex only but rather sex *and attachment*. The husband is missing sex, but at a deeper level he is missing the opportunity to open himself up to the attachment drive and the experience of his wife's love which normally occurs during and following sexual intercourse. The wife, on the other hand, is not actually turned off from sex, but just sex which does not issue from the experience of a nurtured attachment drive. So, first what is required is an awareness of the deeper problem.

The second requirement is that one of the parties move beyond the display of anger towards the other so as to communicate hurt and vulnerability at the situation in which they find themselves. Such an exchange has the effect of doing what emotional intimacy would normally do before intercourse: it exposes what is happening inside the mind and heart of one of the spouses even though it might also be accompanied by angry feelings. The result will be that this vulnerability typically triggers feelings of care and sympathy in the other. If it is the husband who is the one who shows his vulnerability, his wife will see that it is not simply sex that he is missing but the expression of the attachment bond that they share. If, on the other hand, it is the wife who initiates this process, her husband will more readily be able to offer the nurturing that she needs in order for her to open up to him sexually. Only in this way—dealing with the attachment motive—can this toxic mechanism I have described be tackled and overcome.

This chapter has aimed to demonstrate some of the ways that an awareness of basic human motives can illuminate the core social relationship of marriage, especially as it is lived out by believers. Behind all that has been written here is the assumption of a living faith and a healthy conscience on the part of husbands and wives. Without these, much of what I have said will seem "old fashioned," "traditional," or otherwise unsuited to today's world. Yet, as believers we are not to be conformed to this world, nor are we to hold on to the past as the past, but rather to steer a path that is guided by our Leader and Lord, Jesus Christ. On that foundation, believing spouses can open themselves up to the blessings which can attend marriage because they will be receptive to the word of God, the truth that surpasses all understanding.

17

Is There a Distinctively Christian Approach to Politics?

Though the title of this chapter indicates that it is about politics, in it I wish to address only one major topic: How is a Christian to think about the left-right dimension of politics? Are we bound to such a way of thinking? So I will not be writing directly about matters such as how we are to understand the state as a political entity, how a people should be represented by its political leaders, what the qualities most suited to the role of politician are, or how believers should decide for whom to vote. Each of these is an important question in its own right. But I have chosen to consider the key political dimension and its increasing polarization because this process is one which is leading to growing anxiety—and, we would have to admit, distorted thinking—among many today, including Christians. As in previous chapters, I will attempt to connect the issue with the main principles I have set out in part I. How might we think about the two main sides of politics in terms of the core human motives? What are some of the dynamics involved? And in light of answers to these questions, how might Christian believers shape their own political views in response to current circumstances?

Conservative-Progressive: A Brief Description

The realm of politics is a remarkably complex business and doubtless involves a host of specific matters which I have no competence to address. Yet, in Western nations in our time, many of those matters can be related to broader considerations that come down to the distinction between conservative and progressive worldviews, and it is at this point that they connect with faith and theological reflection. These worldviews might be treated as very general intellectual and emotional frameworks which are often thought of as a single *dimension* with "reactionary" and "radical" positions placed at either end of the spectrum. "Conservative" and "progressive" would fall somewhere in between, but each closer to different extremes.[1] One of the common observations about the political spectrum is that, over the past generation or two, there seems to have been a steady movement in the direction of greater polarization, so that fewer people occupy the center, while greater numbers identify with positions further away from that center. Several lines of research appear to confirm that perception.[2] To gain a better sense of the lay of the land, as it were, let us first think about what we mean by "conservative" and "progressive" political mindsets.

Conservatives are typically committed to many of the traditional ways in which their society and its political system have operated, and the label of "traditionalist" is frequently applied to them, especially—but not solely—by opponents who see that tendency as a hindrance to progress. In line with this instinct for tradition, a common theme among conservatives is the rule of precedent: "What has been well established in the past is to be preferred over novel ideas." Perhaps because Western societies have, in times past, given greater value to the common good (and because of that also to larger-scale institutions and social structures), conservatives usually emphasize society-wide social and economic values over those of smaller sectional interests or minority groups. Thus, the death

---

1. According to an alternative understanding, "conservative" and "progressive" might be treated as political *types*, relatively discrete in relation to each other and to other types such as libertarianism and socialism, and relating them to each other would not be possible through representation on only one or two dimensions. In this view, people falling in the middle between conservative and progressive, for example, would be understood as not yet having thought through their positions to the point where they are intellectually consistent. Affirming simultaneously the need for higher taxes and a reduction in unemployment benefits would, according to this scheme, be an instance of such incoherence of overall political viewpoint. My comments do not generally call for a judgment between these alternative approaches, although the way I characterize "conservative" and "progressive" in the following section could be altered in the light of, for example, the emerging differences among the left between liberalism and socialism.

2. Hare and Poole, "The Polarization," 411–29; Doherty, "7 Things to Know,"; McCoy et al., "Polarization," 16–42.

penalty, marriage only between a man and woman, lower payments for those who are unemployed or receive social welfare benefits, increased defense spending, and priority to law-and-order matters are more readily accepted among conservatives than progressives. For the sake of the wider society and for that which is traditional, and at times to preserve a stable order in society even though that means tolerating some injustices, often the conservative will appear to lack empathy for those who face hardships and misfortunes.[3]

Progressives, on the other hand, tend to align their values to those of the Enlightenment and primarily to its commitment to the possibility, if not the inevitability, of progress across all domains of human endeavor. The purest form of progressiveness rejects religious beliefs as belonging to less enlightened times and displays a marked aversion to beliefs which affirm the reality and importance of the age to come. One result of this is that the freedom—and possibility—to invest fully in this life is considered paramount as a social and political value; constraints of tradition and custom on persons are to be accepted only as far as they serve to advance the (this-worldly) interests of individual citizens. The preservation of the social order or the status quo more broadly is therefore less valued. In this respect, however, progressivism can accept significant limitations of individual freedom, as, for example, in Scandinavian countries, if broad state intervention has proved itself able to enhance the lives of individual citizens. With less interest in the need to maintain traditional social ordering, progressives are more attuned to empathic concern for those who fall victim to that ordering. Gay rights, more generous welfare funding, feminist ideals, the availability of abortion, and more careful scrutiny of the corporate world are all argued for by appeal to the need to champion various groups in society which are viewed as victims of an often destructive economic, social, and political order.

If the reader has broadly followed me in the way I have characterized the left and right poles of the political spectrum, let us now consider what are the motivational drivers of each.

---

3. This description of the conservative mindset reminds us that a single dimension captures only a part of the range of political viewpoints. Libertarian positions which emphasize the place of the individual in society do not readily fit in with a conservative framework even though there are some shared elements. A similar comment about libertarianism could also be made in relation to the progressive side of politics.

Conservatives and Progressives: What Motives Drive Them?

For conservatives it seems that they are especially attuned to the attachment motive in that they are sensitive to threats to that form of security resulting from a settled political and social order. One's nation, social customs, family, the constitution that grounds a political order, the predictability of the law, traditional religion—for the conservative, all these serve as (impersonal) attachment figures to which one can cleave and in which one can find one's security. Thus, in their political thinking, conservatives are on the lookout for any threats which might undermine settled order. Threats external to the nation must be dealt with through a strong defense force and a focus on alliances with like-minded powers; changes to a national constitution will typically be opposed by the conservative, as will laws which move society in the direction of greater diversity and less order; threats to the traditional functioning of families are a particular concern for the conservative.

Yet, often the attachment of the conservative is of the insecure-anxious kind. This means that the challenges to their security, particularly by those who would disrupt the status quo, and also the often-limited power of political and social "attachment figures" to defend against such threats, lead to anxiety in the conservative mind, pushing it towards "clinginess" and an excessive focus on guarding and preserving the established order. This has significant consequences: the first is the development of a mindset which is overly resistant even to changes that are clearly adaptive and valuable, such as, in historical times, universal adult voting rights, or, in our own times, the move towards renewable forms of energy. Another result of this insecurity is a tendency to neglect the value of justice in its empathic dimension ("a fair deal for all") as an important force in politics and to overemphasize justice as the maintenance of order ("law and order"). Conservatives often have difficulty in recognizing the full dignity of citizens who have few financial resources, little education, limited support from their family, or who suffer from various forms of addiction. They commonly hold that such people in some sense deserve their situation and that the level of welfare support should recognize and take account of this moral failure. Similarly, this mindset is attracted to the idea of a penal system that inflicts punishment on criminals in a way which mirrors the suffering which their crime caused to others. "An eye for an eye and a tooth for a tooth" well represents this way of thinking, mainly because it serves as a deterrent to social disorder.

Conservatives also demonstrate a rather weak appreciation of the value of equality which, as we have seen, is an expression of the social reciprocity motive. Rather, it is rank ordering within society that is more highly valued, and on this account there is typically little awareness of how a sense of solidarity might call for a softening of that ordering. Thus, they are more likely to take social class into consideration, to favor those who attended expensive private schools or came from wealthy suburbs, and to minimize the value of bringing into fuller participation in society those groups which are marginal or have traditionally been viewed as outsiders. Such might be some of the drivers of a conservative mindset. What about that of the progressive?

Progressives, by contrast, appear to possess an insensitivity for the attachment motive, and as a consequence they orient their political thinking mainly towards dominance/competence and social reciprocity. For them, there is little pleasure in the traditional, the established, the ordered, and much more interest in the possibilities of progress, the breaking free from the restraints of tradition, and the pursuit of the truly new that can emerge from creative chaos. In the conservative's secure society, the progressive sees a deadening numbness, but, more insidiously, injustice and oppression, which need to be opposed and removed. In pursuing these goals, the progressive is provided with a way of gaining meaning in his/her life. And because Western culture has been moving in fits and starts in the progressive direction for the past two centuries or more, the person with that mindset has great confidence that, though difficult and often beset with defeats, these goals and the life meaning they afford can be achieved. Here we can think of the goal of obtaining "equality for women," or that of justice for LGBTQ people, black, and native peoples, a better treatment of the natural environment, or the repair of historical injustices. On the surface, engagement with these and similar causes might appear to be essentially the outworking of the social reciprocity motive, since they have to do with the righting of injustices. However, dominance/competence is also powerfully at work in the progressive mind, both in the individual and group forms of the motive. As individuals, progressives seek to move beyond social structures (e.g., the family) from which they are personally alienated or which they perceive as unjust (e.g., the complementary relations between men and women). Transcending such limitations gives them a sense of accomplishment but also of superiority. In addition, and in some ways as an alternative, progressives can view themselves as members of groups which are created around beliefs such as the acceptance of the notion of fluid sexuality, or a pro-choice conviction, or that associated with climate change. These morally defined groups become increasingly cohesive when their members demonstrate hostility towards "out-groups," that is, those who are transphobic, who are "anti-choice," or who are "climate change deniers." As with the individual form of dominance, the task of groups is to compete with and to defeat their opponents.

In the mind of the progressive individual, the attachment drive, while often pushed beneath the surface, is nevertheless not silenced—for that is not possible in such a powerful motive. Rather, it takes the form of avoidant insecurity. Recall that this form of attachment shows itself as a tendency to deny the existence of attachments because, in the past, security figures were not equal to the task; they failed to provide the care and dependability that was needed in times of physical or emotional vulnerability. So, for the progressive, subliminally there is a yearning for the security of a fulfilled attachment drive, but at the level of awareness, this is denied. In a sense, the excessive focus on dominance/competence motive is a compensation for this unsatisfied attachment drive.

When it comes to politics, the progressive worldview therefore has no "safe havens" in this world or in the world to come because what is on offer in this regard they view as defective, unworthy of trust, or simply unavailable. Yet these are the very things their unconscious mind longs for. The effect of this is that, while denying their *own* vulnerability in the domain of attachment, they recognize vulnerability among *others* who are abandoned in the world, people they describe as marginalized, or those who are oppressed or otherwise unjustly treated by society. It is their concern for these people—at least notionally or in principle, but often also in practice—that gives meaning to their lives, and they are frequently willing to invest all their energies in the work. The downside of this is that in following this path, that is, in overemphasizing particular groups in society, they tend also to lose sight of the value of a healthy society taken as a whole and the long-term considerations that are necessary for its maintenance.

This brief survey of how some of the major motives are connected to, and influence, the two major poles of political orientation of conservativism and progressivism has highlighted a few of the tensions that are inherent in them. Clearly there are problems with both forms of thought.

Let us think a bit more about them, but from the point of view of Christian faith.

Christian Faith and the Political Spectrum

How is the believer to view the conservative-progressive dimension? What approach should we adopt to avoid the limitations of both orientations while retaining each of their strengths?

When it comes to engaging with these worldviews, the Western believer with a biblical faith is powerfully tempted to throw in their lot with conservative political ideology for, in many ways, its values overlap with those of the faith. This is the case not least because Christianity has so greatly influenced our culture, though it is an influence that is admittedly waning. It is understandable that our instinct should be to seek to preserve that influence as much as possible. Traditionally, laws against divorce, euthanasia, abortion, same-sex marriage, Sunday trading, and similar social ills have found their basis in the Christian faith, and the cultural trend in the direction of setting them aside is something that believers usually find disturbing. No wonder, then, that they wish to oppose that trend.

But adopting a conservative outlook as side salad to the faith, as it were, often means that, for the believer, it becomes the main meal. When this happens, the faith itself comes to be shaped by the ideology rather than the other way round. Aspects of the faith that urge us to take seriously the injustices in our society lose their power, and we can even find ourselves joining causes such as support for capital punishment, unconstrained capitalism, or opposition to gun control measures, each of which is questionable from a Christian point of view.

The temptation to progressivism for the believer is usually less pressing since, as a worldview, it is typically less sympathetic to Christian belief. What genuine believer would buy the argument that an unborn baby's life can be sacrificed for the sake of its mother's interests? Or that one must not publicly express the view that sexual activity among those with same-sex attraction is sinful? The faith makes no provision for these ways of thinking. Neither does the faith sit well with progressive causes such as those of feminism and gender ideology more generally, the marginalization of the family, secular education, and many other matters sponsored by progressives.

And yet, there is much in this political ideology which aligns with Christian sensibilities. This is because the Old Testament teaching in defense of the poor and oppressed in society has never been abrogated; it provides an irremovable foundation on which Christians are to shape a broader evangelical mission to society. Even the apostle Paul, whose Christ-appointed task was to preach the gospel, in response to the urging of the other apostles in Jerusalem, responded: *"Only, they asked us to remember the poor, the very thing I was eager to do"* (Gal 2:10). Viewing the matter in a clear-eyed way, we will observe that progressive compassion for those who struggle in our society typically springs from less-than-wholesome motives (as does that of the conservative, but for different reasons). Yet its goal of improving their lot must resonate with lay Christians who are serious about the mission with which Christ has entrusted them in the world.

Thus, two problems arise for believers settling into either of the conservative or progressive modes of thought. The first is that, by doing so, they lose sight of key elements of the Christian mission and therefore neglect them. As a result, they give an impoverished witness to those nonbelievers who belong to the opposite viewpoint. How harmful are conservative believers in modelling the faith to progressive nonbelievers when they show insensitivity to the needs of the marginal people within a society! A similar though less frequent impairment of witness is given by progressive believers who scandalize both believing and non-believing conservatives with their promotion of policies which offend God's law.

The second problem goes deeper and is more difficult to discern. It has to do with the character of "idolatry" that marks Christian commitment to either conservative or progressive ideology. Idolatry in the Old Testament refers to commitments to gods other than the true God. In those times, idolatrous allegiances were to fictions, non-existent beings, but they were nevertheless "personal" in a way that mirrored personal faith in the God of Israel. Thus, the presence or otherwise of idol worship was obvious. The equivalent reality exists in the New Testament among lists of vices (e.g., 1 Cor 5:10–11, 6:9; Gal 5:20; Eph 5:5; Col 3:5; 1 Pet 4:3; Rev 21:8) but precisely similar kinds of concerns found in the Old Testament are not really present among early Christians. Mostly it had to do with eating foods which had been blessed in the name of pagan gods. Yet, the letter to the Ephesians extends the idea of idolatry by including in its meaning a commitment to those worldly powers which are not subordinated to Christ, powers seen as being tied to the darker forces of evil. *"For we do not wrestle against flesh and blood, but against the rulers, against the authorities, against the cosmic powers over this present darkness, against the spiritual forces of evil in the heavenly places*" (Eph 5:12). Here, unlike Romans 13:1–7, where the state serves the purposes of God in ordering society, the exercise of political power is seen at least potentially as being linked to that evil which is at the core of the worship of alien gods. Such power can thus be in opposition to the worship of the true God. In this light, when both conservative and progressive political beliefs become commitments which are greater than those to the faith, they must be seen by the believer for what they are—alternatives to the honor and respect owned to God alone. Such political commitments are ideologies, but they are also idols.

Returning now to our consideration of the motives underlying political commitments, we can see that only when our allegiances are well ordered can we avoid the damage inflicted by the insecure attachments that undergird both conservative and progressive political philosophies. Anxious insecurity in the conservative and avoidant insecurity in the progressive both lead to the growth of unhealthy division in the political realm. Progressives are viewed as existential threats to the conservative world, while conservatives are seen by progressives as malicious defenders of an unjust order.

Similarly, believers need to be wary of the over-importance of the dominance/competence motive among progressives which leads them to neglect the value of what exists for the sake of their desire to have an impact on their world either as individuals or as a member of a group. At the same time, Christians will give wide berth to conservatives' weak empathy and their failure to take full account of the equality and fairness that are the expression of the social reciprocity motive (and, one might add, of the Christian notion of solidarity with our fellow citizens).

In their efforts to take account of these limitations, believers will also be mindful of the need to be actively guided in their political thinking by their faith. They will thus need to align their thinking to those positive social values which emerge from a life lived continually in the light of the gospel. Let us consider ways in which this might be accomplished.

Believers Should Avoid the Labels "Conservative" or "Progressive"

Some have argued that our openness to conservative or progressive ways of thinking is partly influenced by our genetic makeup and by the way we have been brought up.[4] If this is the case—and it certainly seems to make sense—we will want to take account of our tendency to favor one side of the political spectrum more than the other so that it does not unduly distort our understanding of political matters. But more than that, the increasing polarization in our society and the idolatrous character of right and left political orientations should prompt us to avoid altogether any identification with conservative and progressive stances. As idolatries, they give priority to political values rather than to God. As idolatries, they necessarily contain elements of evil, primarily in their social divisiveness and in the way they engender hatred or at least disregard of others. Rather, our position as believers is to be that of one who draws political values from faith in Jesus Christ. "Jesus is Lord" is our conviction; we are not conservative—though many of our political beliefs will coincide with those of conservatives—and we are not progressives—though, again, there will be much overlap. A Christian perspective will not, of course, be monochrome, for there will be much diversity in the way believers see reality, that is, in how they understand the way the world works, or how humans think and act, or what are the best ways to achieve agreed-upon goals. But they will strive to avoid thinking of those who differ politically from them as outsiders or as enemies who are to be despised or hated. At least in some respects, a Christian political outlook will find common cause with virtually every political stance but will also distance itself from some aspects of every position that does not seriously attempt to conform to the Christian faith.

A Christian Politics: Not a Mixture of Views but a Distinctive Understanding

How believers think politically is founded upon and is greatly helped by a healthy balance in how they take account of their key social motives, that is, dominance, attachment, reciprocity, and mating, via an openness to the word of God and a well-attuned conscience. We saw earlier that the

---

4. See, for example, Friesen and Ksiazkiewicz, "Do Political Attitudes," 791–818.

dominance system tends towards competition and social division unless we carefully limit its social comparison aspect ("I'm better at this than you") and instead express it in the form of competence ("I gain satisfaction in doing something well"). Yet it is difficult to be convinced of this without the clear teaching of Christ. That is, dominance will become disordered and thus twist our political thinking without our conscience calling us to follow the way of Christ in this matter.

So, not only the four "biological" motives but also conscience itself must be well formed in order for us to be in a position to develop a distinctively Christian political framework. As a key ingredient of such a conscience, our capacity for empathy is to be cultivated such that we have the ability and willingness to feel ourselves into the situation even of those with whom it is difficult to empathize. At the same time, being able to feel for the suffering of others will not lead us to view them as lacking the dignity of personal responsibility. In almost every situation, even the most afflicted and bereft of individuals is able to carry *some* responsibility for him- or herself. Often our failure to recognize and act upon this fact points to the presence in us of a kind of savior complex, or, more deeply, an anger at God for allowing the suffering we observe in others. Thus, a deformed sense of empathy is characteristic of both conservative and progressive mindsets, the former through deficiency of compassion, the latter from a failure to recognize personal responsibility. As a result, in both cases, it is likely that there is a general weakening of conscience.

With the foundation of a well-ordered set of motives in place, where then do we go to find a set of basic political values that might inform our Christian stance? Christians have reflected on this question over the centuries and, at least within the Catholic tradition with which I have some familiarity, a number of key principles have been developed and articulated. Major principles relate to such notions as authority, the common good, participation and personal responsibility, respect for the human person, equality and difference among men, human solidarity, and subsidiarity.[5] Each of these—understood in general terms—can be appropriately applied so as to support many policies now in force in Western societies. However, if we define them more carefully, we find that they push us towards applications that, in fact, diverge from several commonly accepted convictions of both conservatives and progressives. I

---

5. Here I have simply listed these principles. Their explanation can be found in the *Catechism of the Catholic Church*, part III, chapter 2.

will propose here several examples, each of which deserves a much fuller explanation, but in this context, I can do little more than enumerate them.

1. A basic moral commitment grounded in the New Testament (e.g., Rom 6:1) is that both the means and the ends we pursue must be morally legitimate. Even if we have an end which is good and urgent, we cannot use an evil means to achieve it. "The end never justifies the means" is how this principle is commonly expressed. So, for example, the good end of avoiding a death of great suffering cannot make right the intentional killing of the sufferer. Or, to take another example, in recent times, we have observed quite draconian laws operating for months on end as a result of a pandemic which prevented Christians and others from fulfilling their duty to gather for worship. The end, that is, the health of the community, was sought through means which were so extreme as to be immoral.[6] Certainly, we can recognize that there has been general agreement in Western nations that the "ends don't justify the means" norm of action I have described is one worth preserving, at least considered in general terms, but more and more it is being breached mainly because it is difficult to defend on non-Christian intellectual grounds.

2. Respect for the human person, within a Christian framework, implies the refusal to intentionally harm others ("*'Vengeance is mine, I will repay,' says the Lord*," Rom 12:19), and, as I argued in chapter 6, we might reasonably derive from this a view of criminal justice which renounces vengeance while focussing instead upon restoration and repair. Imprisonment, within this latter perspective, no longer serves to inflict suffering on the guilty person. Certainly, it aims to protect society from further harm, but its key purpose is to provide him or her with the opportunity to compensate both the victims and the wider society for the disorder created by the crime. This is a profound change from the normal way of thinking and practice. In fact, we can see just how much conservatism has become an idolatry by the powerful instinctive resistance that many Christian believers have to the idea of justice as restoration.

---

6. There is more to the matter than I have mentioned here, but it fair to say that many Christians would consider corporate worship and access to the sacraments as essential as food and drink, cf., "*Man shall not live by bread alone . . .*" (Matt 4: 4). This does not nullify the necessity, driven by love, to restrict public contact with others for the sake of their health.

3. The principle of subsidiarity holds that "a community of a higher order [e.g., national government] should not interfere in the internal life of a community of a lower order [e.g., regional government], depriving the latter of its functions, but rather should support it in case of need and help to coordinate its activity with the activities of the rest of society, always with a view to the common good."[7] The higher- and lower-order communities might also be, for example, the state or regional government in relation to local governments, or any level of government in relation to community organizations. At the core of the principle of subsidiarity are two convictions: that we are more responsible for those who are closer to us either physically or emotionally, and that personal relations are more important than impersonal ones. Wealthy nations typically operate with large bureaucracies, and these are generally committed to the value of efficiency at the expense of the local and the personal. A Christian political order would prioritize lower orders as well as the personal dimension in ways quite different from how things commonly operate at present.

4. The Christian conviction is that Jesus is to be Lord not only of individuals but also of relationships and of social and political structures. This means that the actions of a Christian government on the international stage must be driven by the morality of faith, that is, by love rather than merely by self-interest. It is common to hear political leaders justifying in terms of the national interest their aid to poor nations or their support of a people oppressed by its government. We are told, "We're doing this because it's actually good in the long term for *our* nation." There seems to be a rule in international relationships that the best outcomes are achieved if all nations operated this way, but so often this way of thinking covers up genuine compassion and the pursuit of justice, or, alternatively, it is employed to explain what is actually *a lack* of care for the peoples of other nations ("It is not in our national interests to help nation A in this situation"). A Christian government would set aside such language and both act and explain its actions as driven by the prudent and just exercise of love.

---

7. *Catechism of the Catholic Church*, sec. 1883. What I have quoted from the Catechism is sourced from John Paul II's encyclical *Centisimus Annus*, 48, no. 4.

5. The "equality and difference among men" principle that Christians might propose to society acknowledges the enormous efforts that Western societies have made in bringing about its first part—equality. We need think here only of the long-term reductions in income inequality in many advanced economies to see that this has been a significant achievement. However, the second part, "difference," especially in the form of the male/female distinction, has typically been actively opposed in ways that I have already spelled out in other chapters. A Christian approach to politics would acknowledge and rejoice in gender differences and order society so that the strengths specific to each of the sexes are accommodated and encouraged. Again, most progressives and even conservatives would balk at such an idea.

6. How a government raises revenue through taxation varies greatly across nations. Some have a history of taking a sizeable percentage of their citizens' income in different forms of taxation; other nations seek to limit the imposition of taxes on their population and leave individuals with as much disposable income as possible. The reasons given often make superficial good sense, but ultimately they depend primarily on practical judgments as to what an electorate will tolerate. Of course, a Christ-led government will take account of the expectations of its people, but it will also have at hand a basic view of society and human nature, derived from the reflection on God's word, which it can use to articulate a distinctively Christian understanding of how governments ought to tax their citizens. Central to this are the ideas of the common good and solidarity, the principle of subsidiarity mentioned above, and that of the dignity of individuals and families. Drawing on these, the notion of taxation becomes, in this case, a truly moral rather than simply a pragmatic one, and a less conflicted and exploitative relation between state and citizens becomes possible.

7. The above ideas are, strictly speaking, not particular to a Christian perspective, although they are well aligned to it. The final idea I wish to propose is certainly one which only believers could justifiably affirm, and it underlies all the preceding ones. It expresses the fundamental conviction about where the final authority in a nation should reside. The Christian can and ought to say, "among all the possible 'lords' that society might honor, we know that 'Jesus

is Lord' alone. His lordship is what we endeavor to bring about for our nation." Following on from that, the believer might then take the next step, one quite radical for Westerners, of asserting that there is *no such thing as a religiously neutral position* from which one might view society and determine how it is to be organized. Every such viewpoint is religious, and as such it follows some "lord" or fundamental conviction about reality. According to a Christian framework that claims Christ as Lord, government and the arms and agencies of government would come under his lordship and would conduct themselves according to his ways. The state would acknowledge the Christian faith as its foundation and there would be no such thing as government departments operating from a position of religious neutrality. The Treasury Department, the Public Works Department, all government bureaucracies would be guided in their core purposes by the truth that Jesus Christ is Lord. There would, however, be limits to this, so that institutions commonly funded either fully or partly by government such as schools, universities, hospitals, aged care facilities, and welfare agencies would be sponsored or run by any *non-government* community groups, religious or non-religious, that sought to do so.

Now, for many of you reading that last paragraph, there would have come to mind the idea of a state church, or the enmeshment of church and state as it occurred in past centuries in the West and still exists in some nations today. However, this is far from what I am suggesting. Mixing up church and state almost always leads to the serious weakening of the Christian mission and is therefore not something to be desired. To allow Jesus to be Lord even of politics certainly does not mean that the church itself, that is, as an institution, should be a political lord. Indeed, there needs to be a strict separation of church and state in the sense that Christian *churches* and their clergy should be kept at arm's length in relation to the actions of the state; they should not be involved at all in political processes except in a few rare situations.[8] Thus, in what I am suggesting, the government would be guided in its basic values by Christian beliefs, but it would also be known for its commitment to full religious freedom and its avoidance of relationships with church leaders whose

---

8. See the *Catechism of the Catholic Church*, sec. 2245, 2246. I have discussed some of these matters in "A Constructive Approach," 123–35.

own responsibilities, it must be said, are of a higher order than that of earthly politics.⁹

Of course, within such a Christian state, much that we appreciate about our current forms of government would be the same, since common sense, reason, and a commitment to effectiveness and usefulness are not the exclusive preserve of any worldview, religious or secular. Yet, from the little I have described here, it would be clear that the fundamental values of a Christian government would be quite different from anything we in our time have ever experienced or, I suspect, from anything in the church's long history. The most widely accepted forms of progressivism and conservativism hold to the idea of a religiously neutral state, and this is another reason, among many, why believers are advised to distinguish themselves from such ideologies. Yet extracting ourselves from this idea of neutrality will require great commitment and effort and is unlikely to happen unless we followers of Christ work to avoid the pathologies of motivation that mark both ends of the spectrum of political belief.

I hope that the above examples are sufficient at least to open the reader to the possibility of a distinctively Christian approach to politics. Much more, of course, needs to be added to make a more persuasive case. But my deeper point is to suggest that distortions in the way the key social motives operate in our lives both as individuals and as communities make it difficult for us to actually *imagine*, let alone appreciate, the power of the Christian faith to shape a way of thinking about politics that

---

9. It must be admitted that there are difficulties with the traditional Catholic way of articulating the purpose of the state as being that which pursues the overall common good of its people. Its approach derives largely from the thought of Aristotle. Perhaps the chief problem is that it does not contain a strong enough principle that would preclude authoritarian regimes, and here we can think of examples of these in past centuries which were sanctioned by both the Church authorities and Catholic theology. The common good, according to Catholic thought, is to be shaped by the natural law, that moral law which God has given to all peoples, but the Church claims the right to authoritatively determine what that law is. According to this way of thinking, a Christian state would have to proscribe the use of contraception or IVF, for example, unless it was deemed prudent in any given circumstances not to do so. Perhaps a better foundation for a community's discernment of the natural law as it applied to a particular matter would be to take seriously the different understandings of that law among the various religious perspectives and upon that basis, rather than the Church's authority, reach a common view. This might mean that some laws would be less restrictive than a Christian understanding would support but it would probably demonstrate more clearly a genuine hospitality on the part of Christians towards those of other faiths.

is truly different from the ideologies that currently dominate Western democracies.

Conclusion

The pull of these ideologies of left and right, of progressivism and conservativism, is so great that many if not most of us believers have unwittingly distorted our faith by openly or more subtly identifying ourselves with one or other of the two poles on the political spectrum. Most of us who seek to be faithful to the word of God would think of ourselves as Christian conservatives. We usually reason that, for all the faults of conservative political parties, they at least stand for many of the things that we believers are committed to, while the parties of the left tend in the opposite direction. However, if we think of political positions in their current versions as idolatrous, such a line of reasoning looks suspiciously like preferring Baal to Asherah among the pagan gods of the Old Testament because the former—Baal worshippers—are more like the worshippers of the one, true God than the latter! We Christians must have greater confidence than we currently display in the lordship of Christ and in the power of his people—especially laypeople—to influence the manner in which governments are run. For God's will surely includes the redemption from sin not only of ourselves as individuals but also of the relations which go to make up our social and political life.

18

"Love One Another with Brotherly Affection"

AN OFT-QUOTED PASSAGE FROM the Vatican II document *Lumen gentium* states that the eucharistic sacrifice "is the source and summit of the whole Christian life."[1] This statement is, of course, profoundly true, since it expresses the fundamentally *graced* character of the life of a believer (Eucharist as source) as well as the fact that worship of the Lord God is the highest human act (Eucharist as summit). However, this is not the whole story, for, while the Eucharist is indeed these two things, there is a large part of the Christian life—the bit in the middle between source and summit—that must also be acknowledged and nurtured. It is this element, the middle part—or at least one essential dimension of that part—that I want to consider in this chapter. I am referring here to the activity of fellowship, or what one might call the necessary training of Christians in a parish in how to *live out* their participation in the Eucharist. Such is its importance that we might even consider it as the other half of church life—and certainly the half that has often been neglected.

First, I want to draw attention to a striking mismatch between the way churches in the apostle Paul's time expressed fellowship, on the one hand, and our experience of church in Western societies, on the other. Then I will reflect on fellowship in light of the theory of part I, with a focus on attachment, dominance/competence, and social reciprocity motives as they manifest themselves in group participation. I hope to show that thinking about church fellowship in these terms can provide

---

1. Second Vatican Council, *Lumen gentium*, 11.

a framework for us more clearly to see its crucial place within the life of faith and might also offer us at least some ideas about how we can retrieve this essential quality of church life.

Koinonia

Koinonia or fellowship is a common theological concept. We find it first named and described in Paul's letters, as the life in common that believers in the different church communities experienced, but after his time it has had a rather fluctuating and chequered history. In the early period of the church's history, it came to refer to the communion between large groupings of believers, for example among patriarchal sees such as Rome, Alexandria, Antioch, and Constantinople. In more recent times Protestant churches have sought to recapture its biblical use by emphasizing the fellowship of individual believers within a single local church community, or even in the deeper form which is found in small groups of the faithful—typically between seven to twelve persons—meeting for Bible study and mutual spiritual encouragement. But for many Western believers, especially us Catholics, who study Paul's letters to the churches, we have a sense of mismatch between the poverty of fellowship in our own experience of church life and that which we discover in the biblical text. When we read Paul's encouragement to the Philippian congregation: "*Complete my joy by being of the same mind, having the same love, being in full accord and of one mind. Do nothing from selfishness or conceit, but in humility count others better than yourselves. Let each of you look not only to his own interests, but also to the interests of others*" (Phil 2:2–4), we know that the apostle is writing to a close-knit fellowship of faith, and most of us would confess that in our own experience, such a reality is mostly absent.

What is more, as we saw in chapter 3, the individualistic lens through which we in our time interpret many of Paul's moral exhortations means that we do not naturally see the fellowship he assumes and is writing about. When Paul tells the Roman believers, "*Let your love be genuine*" (Rom 12:9), we read such an injunction as being addressed to individual believers in Rome who were each called to exercise this love generally in their daily lives. In applying that to ourselves, we modern believers understand that we are called to do the same in our own situations. However, this is not primarily what the apostle has in mind. Rather, his concern was that this love should express itself within an *actual* fellowship of believers, not simply among those with whom we might chance to come in contact in our day-to-day lives. He assumed that these specific groups or fellowships each had a sustained, deep life together in which members could nurture and live out the life of faith, hope, and love within its midst. Just as Jesus taught his disciples to "love one another," and as John in his first letter affirmed to his readers—not individuals, but congregations gathered together to hear what was written—"*We know that we have passed out of death into life, because we love the brethren*" (1 John 3:14)—so, too, Paul simply assumes that Christian love is put into practice *first and foremost* within small communities of faith.

Occasionally in Paul's letters we find mention of churches meeting in houses. When he includes Aquila and Priscilla in the greetings chapter at the conclusion of his letter to the Romans, he writes: "*Greet also the church in their house*" (Rom 16:5; also 1 Cor 16:19). To the Colossians, Paul requests that greetings be conveyed "*to Nympha and the church in her house*" (Col 4:15). The New Testament scholar Robert Jewett, in his commentary on Paul's Letter to the Romans, has studied the function and operation of these centers of fellowship and provides evidence that fellowship groups in Rome met both in houses (for the better-off), and in tenements (for the poorer believers). He writes: "These details point to a movement that had grown to several thousand adherents [in Rome] by the summer of 64 CE. With membership in early congregations ordinarily estimated between twenty and forty persons, there would have been dozens of groups at the time that Paul wrote his letter some seven years before the fateful fire [in the year 64]."[2] Jewett further fills out this assessment by suggesting that house churches contained typically thirty to forty members, while tenement gatherings, due to space limitations, probably contained ten to twenty people.

The Importance of Group Size

Of relevance here is some recent work by the British social psychologist Robin Dunbar and his fellow researchers who have explored the various sizes of gatherings formed by humans and have found that there are typical group sizes for different social functions.[3] These specific sizes, it is

2. Jewett, *Romans*, 62.
3. Dunbar's team has been prolific in its publications. For an accessible overview of

argued, reflect something about the human brain; the theory is called the "social brain hypothesis" and it proposes that primate brains evolved to be larger, relative to body size, in order to be able to handle complex social networks. One striking finding is that humans have a limit of about 150 friends; beyond that number, some friendships will be dropped because we humans do not have the mental capacity to sustain any larger number of relationships, that is, as friendships rather than as acquaintances. In general, we have circles of social contacts whose size depends on the level of intimacy of the relationships they contain. We share with our spouse in our most intimate and engaging relationship, a group size of two; we have a family circle, perhaps limited to about twelve or fifteen members, again, because the level of closeness required of family-level relationships consumes much of our energies and thus larger groupings would discourage such intimacy. Further up the range of friendship circles are those with people whom we have quite frequent contact but are not as familiar to us as are the members of our family; this group together with our family circle numbers about fifty. Finally, those with whom we can sustain genuine friendship, even though contact might be infrequent, is limited to a total of 150.

Now it is the first three of these groups which are of interest in the present context: fifty people with whom we can maintain relationships ranging from very intimate to solid friendship. Set aside the spousal bond and close family circles of between twelve and fifteen, and we are left with about thirty-five others. This number falls within the twenty to forty number for the typical house church size mentioned by Jewett. So, it would seem that these house churches served the kind of relationships that were close and well-maintained, and which allowed for particular forms of relating to flourish—agape love, sincere care for one another, etc.—that we read about in the New Testament.

Now, given the particular features of groups of this size, and their value in maintaining and growing fellowship in the New Testament church, how might we understand them in terms of human motives?

---

this work, see Dunbar, "The Social Brain Hypothesis," 562–72.

Koinonia and the Social Motives

Group Forms of Attachment and Dominance

As we discussed in chapters 2, 3, and 4 of part I, the attachment and dominance motives express themselves when we think of ourselves not only as individuals but also as members of groups. I can be attached—as an individual—to my wife, but also—to a lesser extent—as a member of a group, say, to my close-knit friendship group. Likewise, my motivation for dominance can work in my (individual) desire to be noticed by others for my achievements (individual), but it can also show itself in my pleasure when my football team wins the premiership (group). Applying this to life in the church, we can see that the group forms of attachment and dominance can serve as motives for how we participate in church life, especially if we are seriously committed to the faith.

Considering the Church as a universal reality, group-level motives can make me pleased when I read of some success or something good that has happened in the Church and disheartened when Catholics, wherever they might live, cause shame or scandal to those who follow Christ. Thus, during the pontificate of Pope John Paul II, among orthodox Catholic believers there were widespread feelings of confidence and expectation as he conducted his ministry, building up the faith, strengthening communities, and defending the Church against external and internal attacks. On the other hand, there was profound embarrassment among Catholics in several Western nations when we learned of serious and widespread sexual abuse of children by clergy. The "wins" of some in the Church become the "wins" of us all, while the "defeats" of some are experienced as the "defeat" of all of us. As the apostle Paul writes to the Corinthians, *"And, apart from other things, there is the daily pressure on me of my anxiety for all the churches. Who is weak, and I am not weak? Who is made to fall, and I am not indignant?"* (2 Cor 11:8–29).

What I have just described refers primarily to the dominance motive, especially in its form as competence. That is, we are not so much buoyed by the church's superiority over other groups in society, but by a sense of competence on the part of the church (guided and strengthened by grace) in its life and mission. But, as we know, the motive of attachment is also to be discerned when we analyze our relationship to the whole church. Many of us who came to the Catholic faith as adults were deeply moved by the sense of security we experienced when we entered fully into the life and culture of the Church. Some of us have talked in terms of finding a true home, of being supported in our faith and encouraged by the hope in eternal life which still features prominently in Catholic teaching and liturgy. By contrast, the anger and despair experienced in recent years among faithful Catholics at the undermining of orthodox faith by many Church leaders is an expression of the shaking of the attachment bond they have with the Church as a whole. Many have expressed some form of the following question: "Can I truly rely upon the magisterial teaching office of the Church to remain faithful to the truth entrusted to the apostles, or is this security I have known in my faith slowly being taken away from me?" Both these responses, then, are the manifestation of a believer's working attachment drive as it relates the individual to the Church as a whole.

Yet, as we have noted above, this is not the only level of group-identification by which Christians are connected to others of the faith. I have made the argument that linking oneself to a group of believers of size between thirty and forty for the purposes of *koinonia* or fellowship is an element of the Christian life that has been neglected in our time but which, if rediscovered, could feed our attachment needs in a way that is mostly unavailable to us in other areas of our lives. For example, if we think of the single believer, whether they be someone who is unmarried or whose spouse has died or left them, in many cases the opportunities they have for establishing lasting individual attachment relationships with others are limited. Such people are commonly "attachment needy." And it is also the case that even a close-knit believing family, in which deep attachments exist among its members, can often find itself isolated socially, a single Christian family among many non-believing families in the local community. So, we might expect that they, like their single fellow-believer, might hanker for a social group to which they as a family might be supported and cared for. Both these groups of people, isolated individuals and families, could discover in a fellowship group that which their impoverished attachment needs are seeking.

It appears, too, that loneliness is a particular mark of Western societies today. One recent US study showed that a remarkable 76 percent of the sample of survey participants reported moderate to high levels of loneliness.[4] Clearly there are many nonbelievers who are lonely and

---

4. Lee et al., "High Prevalence," 1–16.

would be attracted to life in the church if they were to experience firsthand the workings of fellowship groups.

In relation to the dominance/competence motive, we can imagine that a fellowship group might serve as a vehicle for the expression of that motive through the opportunities each group member would have to exercise his or her spiritual and other gifts. Socially skilled persons can feel competent in their efforts to support more reserved members and bring them into contact with others in the group. Those gifted with spiritual wisdom, with group leadership skills, for prayer ministry, or for hospitality, if encouraged to use these gifts for the good of the whole group, can gain a sense of competence as they see themselves assisted by the working of grace in their lives.

Furthermore, individual members of a fellowship group might also gain a sense of group competence in observing the power of its working in bringing others, and especially outsiders, into a deeper life in Christ and in the church. Thus, they might remark, "See how the Lord is working through our group and through its individual members!" The cautions that Paul mentions in his first Corinthian letter must, of course, be observed. *"The eye cannot say to the hand, 'I have no need of you,' nor again the head to the feet, 'I have no need of you'"* (1 Cor 12:21). There must be no evaluative comparisons between the gifts that members possess. Competence must not turn into competitive dominance.

Group expressions of attachment and dominance/competence are not the only social dynamics that we need to consider here. It is also the case that, in the history of the church, the social reciprocity motive has been suppressed in ways which have weakened church life, and we can better understand the deeper processes that work in fellowship groups if we think about them in the light of this motive.

Social Reciprocity and the Church

We need not look very far for evidence within the church's history that fellowship among believers in church communities has often been weak. Yet this does not mean that it has been entirely absent in church life. For there is a "natural" instinct among believers to desire some form of fellowship. Through the ages fraternities, sodalities, funeral societies, and other such groupings of Christians have often given expression to this desire. Above all, within the older church traditions, the religious life—Benedictine and Orthodox monasteries and mendicant orders such as the Franciscans and Dominicans—have catered to this need for Christian community. However, at any given time, those benefitting from these forms have been rarely more than a small portion of the total number of the faithful. What existed in the early church—the form of communion expressed in groups of twenty to forty participants, the level of the "service of love"—disappeared over time from the experience of most believers, and all that was left in church life was (a) the local preaching and sacramental ministry, i.e., the parish; (b) the city or regional level of church organization, i.e., the diocese; (c) the wider levels of communion such as existed within a nation or a language group; and (d) that highest, international levels of communion served by mutual fellowship within the Orthodox churches or by the Bishop of Rome among Catholics. It is the oddest thing to reflect on the fact that all these higher levels of ministry have been well established during the time of the church, and yet the very activity that they were "designed" to serve, that is, *agape love at the local level*, has largely been ignored!

Perhaps the most damaging consequence of the failure of fellowship is the widespread loss of opportunities for ordinary believers to exercise their spiritual gifts. Whereas the New Testament model for church life was for leaders such as apostles and elders to support and guide the fellowship that existed within churches, over time, where fellowship died off, the leadership began to fulfill ministry with a more limited scope, that is as teacher, leader of worship, and dispenser of the sacraments. The exercise of the spiritual gifts bestowed upon every believer, which characterized the life of New Testament fellowship groups (cf. 1 Cor 12), no longer found outlets and the laity fell into a kind of "charismatic" passivity which has persisted to this day. Unfortunately, although there have been efforts to provide opportunities for laypeople to use their gifts in parish life, mostly this has meant them carrying out "clerical" functions, such as assisting at the altar, reading the Scriptures and prayers of the faithful during Mass, and serving as extraordinary ministers of the Eucharist. But however valuable these ministries, they have failed to address the problem of a lack of outlet for the expression of the lay rather than clerical spiritual gifts.

When we view the distortions to church life which I have described in terms of the theory of part I, what stands out for us is the failure of that life to accommodate the social reciprocity needs of believers especially of laypeople but also of the clergy. This has meant that the interactions between lay people and the clergy, as well as among the various levels of clergy themselves, have been virtually taken over by the dominance motive. What I mean by this is that we lost sight of the core Christian conviction that all believers are fundamentally equal before the Lord, from the most honored church leader down to the lowliest layperson (Gal 3:27–28). This idea comes out in Paul's notion of the *mutual* sharing of gifts (1 Cor 12:7; Rom 12:4–8) and, especially in the ancient churches, we would have to admit that it has largely been lost. What we are left with in its place is a ranking of believers where those belonging to the upper ranks are considered superior to lower-ranked members, and thus the sense of fundamental equality finds little place. This means that it is not usually considered appropriate that the clergy open themselves up to receive the benefit of the spiritual gifts of the laypeople; the flow of spiritual goods is not mutual but is rather in one direction only. Social reciprocity is thus absent, and this harms the ministry especially of laypeople but more generally of the whole church.

Conclusion

Thinking about fellowship in terms of human motives, the contrast between church life in our time and what we read of in the Pauline Epistles can be understood as a disorder in how the motives of attachment, dominance, and social reciprocity work together. From this perspective, too, we can see how fellowship groups of the appropriate size might be able to contribute to the correction of this disorder. In writing this, however, I am not suggesting simply that Christians, like other human beings, have attachment, dominance/competence, and social reciprocity needs which are met through participation in groups and therefore that parishes should establish such groups in order to fulfil those needs. Rather, my thinking is that the contrast we recognize between the fellowship frequently described in the New Testament and the lack of it within churches of our time is firstly a problem of faithful listening and obedience to the Lord, and, given an openness to the word of God, a way forward might take account of our understanding of the way human groups work and what motives are involved. Considered as a servant rather than master, such knowledge, nevertheless, has much to offer.

19

Contemporary Christian Mission: Its Failures and Possibilities

The Call to Mission

IN THE PREVIOUS CHAPTER, I noted that thinking about church life in terms of human motives can help shed some light on the problems we face in making concrete the agape love which is to mark our life as believers. A similar kind of reflection, I believe, can illuminate another group of problems that we as Western believers face at present and which is leading to great discouragement and loss of energy among us; I am referring to the difficulties we are having in communicating the good news to nonbelievers.

"*All authority in heaven and on earth has been given to me. Go therefore and make disciples of all nations*" (Matt 28:18–19). This is the promise and the command which our Lord gave to the church just before he ascended into heaven. Since "*Christ Jesus came into the world to save sinners*" (1 Tim 1:15) we know that the way people respond to the gospel has a connection to their eternal destiny, although we do not know exactly *how* the Lord God will work things out. What we can be quite certain of, though, is that we as believers in advanced Western nations are called to be Christ's coworkers in the daunting task of bringing his light into what is a fairly dark and godless part of the world.

Certainly, we would have to say that we are not doing too well either. Thin congregations are composed of mostly grey-haired faithful; parishes suffer amalgamations; there are insufficient numbers of clergy; very small percentages of students completing their secondary education at faith-based schools become regular church attenders in adulthood; and for the most part Christians are barely distinguishable from their secular counterparts in terms of moral beliefs. In fact, if there was such a thing as a "gospel" of secularism, you would have to say that it was doing remarkably well! In wealthy Christian nations it is gaining many thousands of formerly Christian followers to its cause each year. We might call this process "reverse mission!" Sadly, many of us have made our peace with the situation and decided that all we can do is to hang on to our own faith and continue to show, by how we live, something of the Christian way. Deep down, we know that the situation looks grim.

Although this is the context in which most Western Christians now find themselves, the gospel imperative remains valid; it is there in black and white. Somehow, we need to regain our confidence in the good news of Jesus Christ and find ways of more effectively communicating it within our own local setting. In offering my own limited contribution to tackling what is, in truth, a multi-faceted issue, I will begin by asking the question: How do those outside the faith think about us as believers and about the message we bear? In doing so, I hope to be able to highlight two ways that we Christians might retrieve a more biblical view of ourselves and thereby open up some new possibilities for mission.

Nonbelievers' Views of Christians

How do secular-minded people think of us Christians? How do they evaluate us and what we stand for? My sense is that we often loom large in the minds of nonbelievers. This seems to be the case because they usually have an opinion—and often quite a strong one—about the Christian faith. In this we see that they have made some kind of response to the information they have received about us from various sources (if they have had no personal experience themselves), and they have fitted all of this into that wider cluster of beliefs and opinions that go to make up their worldview. "I don't believe in God so the Christian faith is irrelevant to me"; "Who could believe in their religion after what has emerged about clergy sex abuse?"; "With their hang-ups about issues such as homosexuality, abortion, and euthanasia, they really ought to move out of the Dark Ages and into the modern era"; or "Perhaps it is the case that Christianity does some good in society, but going to church is not something that really attracts me."

In the eyes of most secularists, we Christians have unsupportable beliefs, and, while many of us might be nice people, there seems—to them—to be a rotten or at least a hypocritical core at the heart of the whole Christian endeavor. Maybe, so they might say, if we believers took a little more care to follow Jesus, our professed Lord, we might do a bit better! After all, he never said anything about abortion, about homosexuality, or any of those sorts of things!

I would like to suggest that underlying these attitudes there is a common assumption which helps partly to explain why secular people are so closed to the message we want them to hear. In short, *those with a secular mindset believe that we worship a weak god.* To them, the Christian God does not seem to be able to do much, certainly much less than is claimed for him. It is true, many secularists hold, that Christians make a contribution to our society in terms of caring for others, but why, they wonder, do you need to be a Christian to do that? Many people care for their neighbors and for those in need without any expectation of reward in the hereafter. These considerations lead many secularists to view Christians as mostly inoffensive but sometimes annoying do-gooders. And, they might add, look at how they are losing influence and numbers. Before long they will be an insignificant remnant bypassed by the rapid progress our society is achieving. That is certainly not a sign that Christians worship a strong god!

Considered in terms of human motives, we can see that the perspective with which secularists are viewing believers is primarily from within the workings of the dominance motive, specifically in its group expression. According to this perspective, there exists a range of worldviews in society—and that includes religions—and these vary in their impact on individuals and on society at large. In this hierarchy, the Christian faith has come to be seen as something of a loser. While it was highly influential in past times, increasingly it is shedding power. In sum, the god that Christians worship is a weak deity, the secularist will affirm. Sadly, if we Christians are honest, we would have to concede that much of this understanding is true. It is easy to call to mind several instances in recent decades of political contests over moral questions in which our "team" has lost.

Now, the notion of a strong or weak god (or worldview more generally) is a vague one. We need to break it down a little more to see better what it looks like.

In the eyes of human observers, a god can be strong through powerful signs such as miracles. The word "miracle" means a small marvel or wonder. When Jesus healed a blind man, the onlookers were amazed, they marveled. Here was someone who had the power of God available to him. And in the rest of the New Testament, we read of miracles and other supernatural signs indicating that the God of Jesus Christ is a powerful God.

But this is not the only way a deity is recognized as strong. If a god's followers are powerfully influenced by their religion, if they live in ways which are strikingly different from the surrounding culture, if they act fearlessly for the sake of their religion, this, too, shows that their god is strong, whether their beliefs are attractive or not. Thus, many secularists might despise Islamic beliefs or those of Jehovah's Witnesses or Amish Christians, yet there is still frequently a measure of respect for these groups on account of the power of their faith to influence their actions.

So, then, if we Christians are seen to worship a weak god, what are the major defects in our way of life which give that impression to secular people? Let us consider two such deficiencies: first, our desire for social acceptance, and secondly, our unacknowledged idolatrous attitudes towards the state.

Worshippers of a "Weak God"

Our Desire for Social Acceptance

As we saw in chapter 2 of part I, the desire for social acceptance belongs primarily to the dominance motive. While we can gain social standing if we are accepted into groups consisting of individuals who possess higher status than ourselves (status enhancement), mostly we find ourselves belonging to groups of people who are of roughly similar status to ourselves (status maintenance) but containing members whose acceptance we value above that of others. Approval by them means that we are able to maintain an adequate level of status. If, however, we were to experience rejection by them, this would be a very heavy blow to bear. For this reason, while we are typically on the lookout for opportunities to raise our status within our own group or, if possible, even join higher-status groups, more important to most of us is that we do not *lose* status through being rejected by our existing social groups. Thus, we are willing to do all manner of things to avoid that happening, since we have a sense of how profound is the negative impact that arises from social rejection.

Many Christians give the impression to their secular friends that they are especially fearful of being socially rejected. They are often seen to be rather lax in adhering to the rules of their religion; they do not tend to object too strongly when laws allowing moral evils are approved, and, in comparison with their large numbers in society, they have a fairly weak effect on public opinion. Of most of them, a secularist would say, you would not even know they were Christians. All of this looks, in the eyes of the non-believing observer, to be a case of fear of social rejection.

In fact, this is probably not the full story, because many believers have been raised and formed to show sacrificial love to others, and this can easily come across as being overly compliant when that is not necessarily the case. But even this can easily morph into an actual fear of being rejected for their faith. Perhaps a Christian's group of non-believing friends is organizing a get-together and the time that suits most of them is Sunday morning when the believer normally attends church. Often, instead of resisting pressure to forgo worship, the believer falls in with the arrangements. "God won't mind, since I'm showing love to my friends" is how they might justify their actions. But the hidden dynamic is more likely to be related to the warped workings of their dominance motive.

Some Christians respond to this charge of fear of social rejection by noting that they are not interested in "shoving their faith down other people's throats" and that their approach is gently and humbly to present a Christian witness in the hope that over time they will influence their non-believing friends towards a greater openness to the faith. However, by and large this way of proceeding is ineffective since, as we have noted, the nonbeliever tends to see it as a fear of social rejection and a further demonstration, for them, that Christians worship a weak god.

Rodney Stark, among other sociologists of religion, has argued that religions and Christian denominations which are able to move beyond a fear of social rejection are more likely to grow. He cites the example of the Mormons, who, over a period of decades, have achieved significant growth in numbers and a cohesive organizational structure not least due to their willingness to hold firm to their beliefs in the face of a somewhat hostile secular society.[1]

Over-sensitivity to rejection, then, is the first "evidence" for the secular person that the God of the Christians is weak. But there is another sign, a deeper and more hidden pointer of this truth, which has to do with how we Christians relate to the state, a matter we have already come across in chapter 17.

Our Attitudes towards the State

In accord with scriptural injunctions to be obedient citizens (e.g., Rom 13:1–7), and with the encouragement of our leaders, over the centuries we Christians have been quite compliant when it comes to the laws of our governments. This is no doubt partly due to our conviction that this earthly life is not all there is and that means that we do not need to over-invest in it. Thus, we have been reluctant to pursue earthly utopias and are content, rather, to fit in with the laws of the land in which the Lord has placed us.

Another reason for Christian obedience to the state seems to have something to do with a darker side of church history. I refer here to what, since Emperor Constantine's time in the early fourth century AD, became a widespread "gentleman's agreement" between church leaders and rulers whereby bishops and other prelates would receive acknowledgment and high status from kings and princes as long as they urged upon the faithful their compliance with the laws of the state, thus helping to foster stability in a nation. Church and state were often in close partnership, in fact so much so that it became virtually impossible for pastors to give priority to the responsibility they bore for their sheep since they had become addicted to the benefits they received from their secular rulers.

This situation has not always been in play, of course, and we can think of the early church (pre-Constantine) in which for much of its existence, it was outside the law of the Roman empire. In that case, Christians were willing to endure martyrdom in the interests of affirming that their obedience to the Lord God prevailed over that to Caesar when the two came into conflict. In such circumstances, believers might well have been scorned and reviled by the ordinary Roman citizen for not "fitting in" or

---

1. Stark, *The Rise of Mormonism*.

for undermining the unity of the empire, yet no one would have thought for one moment that Christians of those times worshipped a weak god!

Here we can see at work the dynamics of the attachment motive. For the early Christian, refusing to cast a pinch of incense into the fire as a sign of their acceptance of the imperial gods, the unconscious attachment (in the form of a sense of security) to the state had been replaced by a much more powerful attachment to Jesus Christ as Savior and as Lord. With him and with his community of faith, believers had thrown in their lot. This meant that, rather than relying upon the state, they put their trust in the One who, while he did not assure them of earthly well-being, could nevertheless give them that deeper security which comes from a sense of his presence and the hope of heaven.

By contrast, as I discussed in earlier chapters, we can see that contemporary Christians have unwittingly invested much trust in all those things that modern life can offer: a healthy and long life aided by modern medicine, opportunities to get ahead in life through access to education and to a range of career paths, entertainment to provide them with pleasure, and underneath all of that the rule of law and an effective social security system that the state provides them. No wonder we feel secure! But we do so—even we Christians—because we live as "good" citizens in a secular society with a secular government. Certainly, as believers, our hearts cry out for more, since all that which society and the state offer us touches only upon this life and its experiences, and the fact is, *"we desire a better country, that is, a heavenly one"* (Heb 11:16). Yet, it is sadly the reality we live with at present that when we are tested in a "state-versus-the-Lord Jesus Christ" contest, our instinct is to argue our way to compliance with the state rather than to risk faithful obedience to our Lord.

We have only to observe, in recent times, how easily believers have given up on face-to-face worship and participation in the sacraments in compliance with state-authorized pandemic regulations to see that this unfortunately is the case. The justifications for such attitudes seem so obvious to us until, that is, we compare our need for heavenly food with that for earthly sustenance and we recall how ready we are to risk infection for the sake of obtaining bodily nourishment. In this regard, we might also call to mind how easily Christians have acquiesced to the growing number of laws introduced across many Western countries which call for believers to act against their conscience: legal requirements for employers to provide employee health insurance cover for morally objectionable services; laws which do not recognize the seal of the confessional;

criminal sanctions for nurses who are unwilling to participate in abortion procedures; regulations compelling the use of false forms of address for transgender persons are a few examples of such laws. We hear of those brave believers who refuse to comply, but there are, for each one such person, thousands of others who wilt under the pressure.

A profound distortion of attachments among Christians is thus apparent in our respective attitudes to the state and to Jesus Christ. And since in this respect we are no different from our secular neighbors, those outside the faith are well justified in concluding that Christian believers do indeed worship a weak god.

Retrieving Mission

In considering how Christians might free themselves for a more effective missionary effort, we must take account of the different motives that control each of these deficiencies of faith I have described: fear of social rejection and an idolatrous attachment to the state.

The essential first step is to listen with one's conscience to the word of God. With an open heart and mind, it is not difficult to find teaching which relates directly to the challenges I have described. The injunction *"Do not love the world or the things in the world. If anyone loves the world, the love of the Father is not in him"* (1 John 2:15) provides general advice for the believer caught up in the social networks of nonbelievers, while Paul's comments when he was faced with rejection by the Galatian Christians provide us with more specific guidance as to the appropriate attitude of the believer. In reproaching the believers of that church, he asks, *"Am I now seeking the approval of man, or of God? Or am I trying to please man?"* He continues, *"If I were still trying to please man, I would not be a servant of Christ"* (Gal 1:10).

Likewise, we can find New Testament teaching that affirms the priority of obedience to God over that of the state. Thus, Jesus urges us to give to God that which belongs to him, and to Caesar what is left over! The apostles Peter and John, when hauled before the Jewish authorities, acted in accordance with a similar principle; and in the First Letter of Peter, the readers are exhorted to *"fear God, and honour the emperor"* (1 Pet 2:17), a clear sign of the prior obedience owed to the former.

Yet, as we have noted in part I, conscience operates not as a replacement for other motives but in concert with them, so more than simply a strong and obedient conscience is called for. In relation to social acceptance, believers, while being ready to speak their Christian convictions before their non-believing friends and ensuring that, as followers of Christ, they do not dishonor God as they participate in their social circles, will also need to rely upon the support and acceptance of groups of *believing* friends. When working at their best, such groups can serve group attachment and group competence needs. Thus, a member of a group of believing friends might remark that "it is good to spend time with my Christian friends because I can speak honestly and openly with them and not feel judged, and as a group we are able to support each other in living out our faith in the world." With this kind of support behind a member, he or she might find more manageable the challenge of relating to nonbelievers in ways which are not controlled by the desire for social acceptance. Again, we can see the principle at work that our thinking and actions can be powerfully shaped by the social environment in which *we place ourselves*.

The courage and energy needed to address the idolatrous attachment to the state is perhaps greater than for the matter of social acceptance. It is sometimes said that those who control a society's taboos also control the culture at large. And one of the strongest taboos in Western culture is that which prevents us from affirming that Jesus Christ is Lord, and the implication we must draw from that confession is that there is no such thing as a neutral state, a state which stands apart from all religious or non-religious beliefs. And it is not only the government that claims to be neutral; the claim or assumptions holds for virtually all the communication we have with the outside world. Apart from an hour or so on Sunday, almost all the contact we have with the outside world, i.e., work, friends, TV and radio, internet and social media, our participation in education and other public institutions, the advertisements we watch, etc., occurs in ways that are meant to signal that they are religiously neutral. In fact, they are atheistic, since those we engage with consistently present themselves to us as nonbelievers and avoid looking at the world from the point of view of a believer. In other words, all this contact pushes believers to follow the taboo preventing them from acknowledging that Jesus is Lord—and here I mean the One who is not just *our* Lord, but *the* Lord of all.

But if we believe that Jesus is truly *the* Lord, then in the end people and institutions can only be either for him or against him. There is no neutral, unattached position, because *all of us* seek group (existential) attachments for ourselves, and these are either of a religious or religion-like nature. Our desire as Christians is that *"every knee should bow . . . and every tongue confess that Jesus Christ is Lord"* (Phil 2:10, 11). We have no option as followers of Christ but to live and act in a way that looks towards that wonderful day. In fact, my sense is that mission will never really take hold among Western nations unless the taboo against affirming that Jesus is Lord is loudly and persistently broken. As was suggested with efforts to deal with social acceptance, so too facing this challenge will demand strong social support among believers. It cannot be done effectively by lone individuals.

Will Dealing with Social Acceptance and State Idolatries Really Help Our Mission?

When we first examine this matter, we can easily wonder whether simply addressing these idolatries could make much of a difference to the power of Christian mission in our community. One thing that such efforts would certainly do would be to *put many people in our societies off-side*. Those who benefit most from the way things are at present will instinctively reject and oppose believers who involve themselves in the kind of proclamation I have suggested. People who belong to what are termed "cultural elites," that is, academics, political leaders, those in the media, the professions, and corporate leaders, have been educated in a system that has been able to suppress religious ideas both socially and in the political sphere, and this leaves these same people with little capacity to conceive of, let alone accept, a world in which Jesus Christ is Lord of all aspects of life. So, in the face of a bold witness to the Lordship of Christ, such people might begin to reevaluate the Christian faith as being "stronger" than they previously thought, but this will not of itself open them up to the truth of the gospel. In fact, they will more strongly resist it.

However, there will be parts of society, especially those who have not been as "successful"—and I am thinking here of those who have less education, who have lower-paid jobs, or have no job, in short, those who do not see themselves as very competent—who would be more open to the gospel message. This openness will happen when they observe, first, the power it exercises in the lives of courageous believers, and, secondly, the nurture and support that are available in Christian groups. These are precisely the sort of people who attended the house churches in Corinth in Paul's time. *"For consider your calling, brothers: not many of you were wise according to worldly standards, not many were powerful, not many were of noble birth. But God chose what is foolish in the world to shame the wise; God chose what is weak in the world to shame the strong"* (1 Cor 1:26–27). We remember, too, that passing comment in Mark's Gospel, where he writes that, in contrast with the scribes' response to Jesus' teaching, *"the great throng heard him gladly"* (Mark 12:37). Individuals who are lower on the social pecking order are not only more commonly "poor in spirit" but are also poor in relation to the attachment and dominance/competence motives. They are a mature crop, ripe for harvesting, but this will require believers to ready themselves for the work.

Concluding Comment

The aim of this chapter has been to describe how thinking about social motives and group identity might shed light on the question of the church's missionary witness. What I have offered is, of course, only an initial effort to sketch an understanding of the situation. My main point has been to highlight the disturbances in group attachments among Western believers which have led to an excessive desire for acceptance and an idolatrous dependence upon the security offered by the state. The work of evangelization has therefore greatly suffered. In addition to the brief suggestions which I have made about how believers might respond, here I would again highlight the necessity that they participate in Christian support groups so that they might nurture the spiritual and emotional strength required for a renewal of mission. How all of this might be made concrete is, of course, another matter altogether. Still, with progress in addressing these issues, who knows what impact there might be in the outworking of Christ's Great Commission?

Conclusion

WELL, DEAR READER, if you have reached this point in the book, you will have covered much material and been presented with many ideas, some of which I trust will have been unfamiliar to you. My hope is that, from time to time, you will have paused for a moment or two to reflect on a point that I was making and that those reflections might have prompted you to recognize their practical relevance for you in a new way.

I have first sought to keep in mind the needs and interests of the believer who day by day seeks to grow in holiness and in love. There are many such people today who, I believe, could be helped in their efforts if they could understand a little more of how they work as human beings, what pushes them to have the thoughts they do, where their attitudes come from, and why some things stir their feelings and others do not. Grasping some of the processes involved in driving and shaping these elements of our lives can allow us insight into ways by which we might deepen our trust in the Lord and more generally grow in conformity to Jesus Christ. As a way of helping you review the path we have taken, here are a selection from among the points I have made in part I:

Some Key Points

1. Most human thinking, feeling, and action can be understood as arising from a handful of social motives. I have described dominance/competence and attachment (in both their individual and group forms), social reciprocity, and mating as the major human drives which we also share with other animals. Keeping these in mind and seeing how they manifest themselves in ourselves as well as the actions of others can be of great benefit in daily life both in

our relating to others and in helping us to sympathize with their weaknesses.

2. Overseeing and guiding the operation of these "biological" motives is that of conscience, a mechanism which is distinctively human. It is this motive which allows us genuine freedom and makes us both responsible and accountable for what we do. I highlighted the fact that an authentic conscience requires that we have God as our moral authority and that we can obey our conscience best when we are psychologically attached to God.

3. I returned several times to the notion that the dominance motive, if not very carefully monitored and trained, leads to division between people and tempts us to think more highly of ourselves than the truth warrants. Jesus' teaching about this is commonly overlooked by believers. On the other hand, the drive for competence, that is, the non-competitive part of the dominance motive, is to be nurtured as a major source of our sense of psychological well-being.

4. One of the difficult-to-digest ideas I proposed in my discussion of dominance was that it is the primary driver of our everyday thoughts (though not the only one, since the other motives also play their part), and it needs continuous oversight by one's conscience to prevent it from leading us from the way of Jesus.

5. Attachment is primarily a subconscious motive which is much more powerful in its influence on our behavior than we usually recognize. It must be treated with great care and, as we have seen, it provides a means for effectively toning down the excesses of the dominance motive. To see the true nature of the attachment motive is an eye-opening and life-changing experience, so it is worth spending time thinking about it and reading further about it.

6. In adult life, for many of us, our lives are profoundly shaped by our attachment relationship with our spouse. The health or otherwise of that relationship is one of the most important determinants of our experience of daily life. Those who are single can draw upon other relationships to provide them with a basic sense of emotional security.

7. I highlighted how important it is for the believer to develop a form of attachment relationship with God and, in another form, with the church and with other believers. This provides a sense of existential

security and shows itself in a confident faith and an openness to others. It can also serve as a support, especially in times when one's primary family attachments, e.g., with one's parents or one's spouse, which are normally much stronger than other attachment relations, are for some reason impaired or severed.

8. Although in many traditional cultures, social reciprocity predominates in shaping social interactions, for most Western peoples, it mainly shows itself as a keen interest in questions of justice. In this guise, it has pushed many nations towards ever greater efforts to achieve equality and fairness for all their citizens, and this is surely a good thing. The danger arises, however, when it is exalted to the exclusion of the other motives. Mating, for example, has its own ways of ordering relationships between men and women, and these must not be undermined by a single-minded focus on the reciprocity motive. Furthermore, from a Christian perspective, we know that God's grace and our cultivation of the virtues of generosity and forgiveness are part of a fuller picture that sees beyond the limitations of justice.

9. In the discussion of the motive to form mating relationships, I emphasized the fact that we moderns carry around with us unconscious psychological mechanisms which evolved many thousands of years ago in vastly different circumstances to those of today. This creates great challenges for those of us who seek to find a spouse and raise a family, but the key to dealing with these difficulties is not to suppress the operation of those ancient mechanisms but rather to work within them, softening them in situations in which they directly clash with Christian values. In doing this, however, we must be prepared to live in a countercultural manner.

10. In my treatment of conscience, I wanted to get across the idea that this motive emerges from within our relationship with our parents; it does not arise from "nowhere." On the basis of trust in our parents, we come to take over their values, and they become our first moral authorities. Conscience, then, works like an inner conversation, initially with the voice of our parents in our minds but as we mature it takes on the form of a prayerful conversation with the Lord God. This way of thinking about conscience is quite different from some very popular contemporary understandings.

11. Another idea that I suggested in discussing conscience is that it is when we are most fully and deeply in touch with our conscience and thus with the Lord that we find our real self. This is the place where we most truly know ourselves as we really are and where we receive the freedom to be able to manage and to bring together in a harmonious way our other motives. Without that freedom, we are at the mercy of those "biological" motives, and sin inevitably takes over even though we may not always be fully conscious of it.

12. Throughout part I, I tried to avoid giving the impression that an understanding of motives by itself was sufficient for interpreting our and other's actions. The truth is that motives are always shaped by the culture in which we find ourselves. Still, the motives I have described are foundational for all humans and therefore show themselves across all cultures. For this reason, an understanding of how motives work can help us to stand back from our own Western culture and see not only how it adapts appropriately to our human nature but also how at times it distorts, overvalues, and neglects them and what we might do as Christians to counteract any harmful effects. I have frequently drawn attention to the overemphasis upon dominance in Western culture and the attendant failure to take full account of both attachment and conscience motives. Reintegrating these key drives must form an important part of the believer's growth in holiness.

If you have come this far, I hope that, in reviewing these twelve points, you will be helped to consolidate in your own mind the overall framework of the social motives. Moving beyond this understanding so as to make the framework something of practical value, in part II I sought to demonstrate its fruitfulness in addressing questions of faith and life. The issues I considered are, of course, only a sample of the possible areas of application; there are many other matters great and small that would lend themselves to a similar analysis.

Beyond what I have already described, there were two other purposes I had for this book which I trust are worth rehearsing briefly.

Science and Faith

In relating the findings of psychological science to the faith, a central issue that must be addressed and resolved is the way that the two spheres of knowledge relate to each other. It is still the case today that many believers have a vague and unsettling anxiety about some aspects of modern science. They wonder whether perhaps our growing knowledge about humans and about the world is leading to the realization that there are scientific truths which contradict those of the faith. They imagine, perhaps, that their beliefs will not be able to withstand such challenges. And so they steer clear of such matters. Among the purposes of this book has been that of giving examples of how evolutionary understandings can be related to orthodox Christian faith in a way which might be both illuminating and helpful. As we have seen, in the practical outworking of the faith, the believer must make careful judgments when it comes to drawing implications for faith from knowledge of how the social motives have evolved. That of dominance calls for great care in getting the best out of the motive and so, too, elements of the attachment, reciprocity, and mating motives have to be controlled by the values and wisdom of the faith. The pride that attends an unfettered dominance drive, the willingness to give priority to earthy attachments, or the profligate casting abroad of our genes through multiple sexual relationships are not part of the life of the follower of Christ. Yet, this requirement of restraint should not cause us any concerns, since we know that the best lives are lived with a degree of tension, and besides, such "rough edges" that we observe in our human nature are a reminder that this earthly form is not the final version! It is the temptation of sin and the ever-present reality of the effects of the fall, and not so much our still incomplete nature, which call for careful vigilance on our part.

Nods in the Direction of Theologians

As I mentioned in chapter 1, in writing this book, I also had in mind those theologians whose interest is in the area of theological anthropology, the study of the nature of mankind in relation to God. For centuries, especially among Catholic theologians, the standard anthropology has drawn upon the psychological theories of Aristotle and Thomas Aquinas. These have served theology well in the absence of better contemporary psychological explorations, but they would appear to require extensive correction and extension if they are to be of continuing service to the work of reflecting on the faith. As will be noticed, my model of human motivation, with its distinction between the conscience and the other motives, mirrors that of Aquinas's framework of the intellectual and non-intellectual inclinations.[1] Without such an understanding, an anthropology could scarcely be Christian. Yet, within that basic understanding, the theologian will notice that I have described in rather different terms the parts on either side of the divide. I have moved away from the notion of an independent inclination towards the true/good and have suggested a kind of moving center of consciousness whose core depends on the leading motive at any point in time yet ideally always guided and overseen by the conscience. Also, in my treatment of conscience, I have hinted at the problem of how God can be a true moral authority in the face of Kant's trenchant criticism of the idea by suggesting that the absolute moral authority of God "piggybacks," as it were, on the developmentally original form of conscience which emerges in a child's relationship with his or her parents and in emphasizing that a "good-enough" attachment relationship between parent and child is necessary for that early form to be established.[2] Taken together, these proposals are the fruit of the engagement of contemporary psychological science with the understanding of human nature which we are able to discern within the pages of the Scriptures. They rely on the idea that theological anthropology is partly based upon a *scientific* investigation of us humans, and for that reason it is open to further developments in our understanding.

I am acutely aware that what I have offered here is merely a rough sketch of part of the terrain of theological anthropology. There is much that I have not included in the interests of readability and conciseness. There is much, too, that might have helped the account I have provided but of which I am unaware. Part of the difficulty is that the matter of this book—that is, in its breadth of scope—has not much been addressed from the perspective of faith or indeed within the broader field of psychology. Being the work of a single author, it will no doubt reveal many blind spots.

Yet, the work that it seeks to advance must continue. In our time, science, with its great successes and, yes, also with its failures, represents the most powerful story in the Western world, and the Christian faith must engage with it in all seriousness. The growth in faith among individual believers, the liveliness and faithfulness of Christian communities, and the effectiveness of the mission entrusted to the whole church by

---

1. See, for example, Aquinas, *Summa Theologica* II/I, q.94, a.2.

2. For further thoughts on the matters raised here, see Patterson, *Chalcedonian Personalism*.

Christ himself; all this depends on it. Fortunately for us in our weakness and sinfulness, however, such a work is not ultimately up to us—for we live under the grace and providence of God. Thus, we joyfully acclaim: Jesus Christ is Lord!

Bibliography

Aquinas, Thomas. *Summa Theologica*. Translated by the Fathers of the English Dominican Province. London: Burns, Oates & Washbourne, 1941.
Barkan, Steven E. "Religiosity and Premarital Sex in Adulthood." *Journal for the Scientific Study of Religion* 45.3 (2006) 407–17.
Benedict XVI, Pope. "Homily." August 24, 2005. https://www.vatican.va/content/benedict-xvi/en/homilies/2005/documents/hf_ben-xvi_hom_20050424_inizio-pontificato.html.
Birnbaum, Gurit E., et al. "When Sex Is More than Just Sex: Attachment Orientations, Sexual Experience, and Relationship Quality." *Journal of Personality and Social Psychology* 91.5 (2006) 929–43.
Birot, Antoine. "'God in Christ, Reconciled the World to Himself': Redemption in Balthasar." *Communio* 24 (1997) 259–85.
Bonhoeffer, Dietrich. *Letters and Papers from Prison*. New York: Touchstone, 1997.
Bowlby, John. *The Making and Breaking of Affectional Bonds*. London: Tavistock/Routledge, 1979.
Bugental, Daphne Blunt. "Acquisition of the Algorithms of Social Life: A Domain-Based Approach." *Psychological Bulletin* 126.2 (2000) 187–219.
Buss, David M. "Sex Differences in Human Mate Preferences: Evolutionary Hypotheses Tested in 37 Cultures." *Behavioral and Brain Sciences* 12 (1989) 1–49.
Buss, David M., and David P. Schmitt. "Sexual Strategies Theory: an Evolutionary Perspective on Human Mating." *Psychological Review* 100.2 (1993) 204–32.
Butzer, Bethany, and Lorne Campbell. "Adult Attachment, Sexual Satisfaction, and Relationship Satisfaction: A Study of Married Couples." *Personal Relationships* 15.1 (2008) 141–54.
Cassidy, Jude, and Phillip R. Shaver, eds. *Handbook of Attachment: Theory, Research, and Clinical Applications*. 3rd ed. New York: Guilford, 2016.
Catechism of the Catholic Church. Homebush, NSW: St. Paul Publications, 1997.
CDC. "Marriage and Divorce." https://www.cdc.gov/nchs/fastats/marriage-divorce.htm.
Clark, Russell D., and Elaine Hatfield. "Gender Differences in Receptivity to Sexual Offers." *Journal of Psychology & Human Sexuality* 2.1 (1989) 39–55.
Conley, Terri D. "Perceived Proposer Personality Characteristics and Gender Differences in Acceptance of Casual Sex Offers." *Journal of Personality and Social Psychology* 100.2 (2011) 309–29.

De Dreu, Carsten K., et al. "The Neuropeptide Oxytocin Regulates Parochial Altruism in Intergroup Conflict among Humans." *Science* 328.5984 (2010) 1408–11.

De Waal, Frans B. M. "The Chimpanzee's Sense of Social Regularity and Its Relation to the Human Sense of Justice." In *The Sense of Justice: Biological Foundation to Law*, edited by R. D. Masters and M. Gruter, 241–55. Newbury Park, CA: Sage, 1992.

De Waal, Frans B. M., and L. M. Luttrell. "Mechanisms of Social Reciprocity in Three Primate Species: Symmetrical Relationship Characteristics or Cognition?" *Ethology and Sociobiology* 9 (1988) 101–18.

The Divine Office III. London: Collins, 2015.

Doherty, Carroll. "7 Things to Know about Polarization in America." *Pew Research Center* June 12, 2014. https://www.pewresearch.org/fact-tank/2014/06/12/7-things-to-know-about-polarization-in-america/.

Drugli, May Britt, et al. "Elevated Cortisol Levels in Norwegian Toddlers in Childcare." *Early Child Development and Care* 188.12 (2018) 1684–95.

Dunbar, Robin I. M. "The Social Brain Hypothesis and Its Implications for Social Evolution." *Annals of Human Biology* 36.5 (2009) 562–72.

Falkenström, Fredrik, Fredrik Granström, and Rolf Holmqvist. "Therapeutic Alliance Predicts Symptomatic Improvement Session by Session." *Journal of Counseling Psychology* 60.3 (2013) 317–28.

Feeney, B. C., and J. K. Monin. "An Attachment-Theoretical Perspective on Divorce." In *Handbook of Attachment: Theory, Research, and Clinical Applications*, edited by Jude Cassidy and Phil Shaver, 934–57. 2nd ed. New York: Guilford, 2008.

Feeney, Judith A. "Adult Romantic Attachment: Developments in the Study of Couple Relationships." In *Handbook of Attachment: Theory, Research, and Clinical Applications*, edited by Jude Cassidy and Phillip R. Shaver, 456–481. 2nd ed. New York: Guilford, 2008.

Fehr, Ernst, Urs Fischbacher, and Simon Gächter. "Strong Reciprocity, Human Cooperation, and the Enforcement of Social Norms." *Human Nature* 13.1 (2002) 1–25.

Feynman, Richard, and Ralph Leighton. *Surely You're Joking, Mr. Feynman! Richard Feynman: Adventures of a Curious Character*. New York: Bantam, 1985.

Fisher, Anthony. "Lefebvrism—Jansenism Revisited?" *New Blackfriars* 71 (1990) 274–86.

Fiske, Alan P. "The Four Elementary Forms of Sociality: Framework for a Unified Theory of Social Relations." *Psychological Review* 99.4 (1992) 689–723.

Foa, Edna B., and Uriel G. Foa. "Resource Theory of Social Exchange." In *Handbook of Social Resource Theory*, edited by Kjell Törnblom and Ali Kazemi, 15–32. New York: Springer, 2012.

Friesen, Amanda, and Aleksander Ksiazkiewicz. "Do Political Attitudes and Religiosity Share a Genetic Path?" *Political Behavior* 37.4 (2015) 791–818.

Gallagher, James. "Fertility Rate: 'Jaw-dropping' global crash in children being born." *BBC* July 15, 2020. https://www.bbc.com/news/health-53409521.

Gangestad, Steven W., Randy Thornhill, and Christine E. Garver. "Changes in Women's Sexual Interests and Their Partner's Mate-Retention Tactics across the Menstrual Cycle: Evidence for Shifting Conflicts of Interest." *Proceedings of the Royal Society of London B: Biological Sciences* 269.1494 (2002) 975–82.

Gintis, Herbert, et al. "Strong Reciprocity and the Roots of Human Morality." *Social Justice Research* 21.2 (2008) 241–53.

Government of Hungary. "Population Census 2011: National Data: Population by Religion, Denomination, and Sex." https://www.ksh.hu/nepszamlalas/tables_regional_00.

Gregory, Pope. *Morals on the Book of Job*. Translated by J. H. Parker. 3 volumes. London: J. G. F and J. Rivington, 1844-45. http://www.lectionarycentral.com/GregoryMoraliaIndex.html.

Groeneveld, Marleen G., et al. "Children's Well-being and Cortisol Levels in Home-Based and Center-Based Childcare." *Early Childhood Research Quarterly* 25.4 (2010) 502-14.

Hare, Christopher, and Keith T. Poole. "The Polarization of Contemporary American Politics." *Polity* 46.3 (2014) 411-29.

Harlow, Harry F. "The Nature of Love." *American Psychologist* 13.12 (1958) 673-85.

Hawley, Patricia H. "Ontogeny and Social Dominance: A Developmental View of Human Power Patterns." *Evolutionary Psychology* 12.2 (2014) 318-42.

Henrich, Joseph. "Cultural Transmission and the Diffusion of Innovations: Adoption Dynamics Indicate That Biased Cultural Transmission Is the Predominate Force in Behavioral Change." *American Anthropologist* 103 (2001) 992-1013.

———. *The Weirdest People in the World: How the West Became Psychologically Peculiar and Particularly Prosperous*. London: Allen Lane, 2020.

Hsu, Ning, et al. "Gender, 'Masculinity,' and 'Femininity': A Meta-Analytic Review of Gender Differences in Agency and Communion." *Psychological Bulletin* 147.10 (2021) 987-1011.

Hudson, Nathan W., et al. "Coregulation in Romantic Partners' Attachment Styles: A Longitudinal Investigation." *Personality and Social Psychology Bulletin* 40.7 (2014) 845-57.

Inglehart, Ronald. *Religion's Sudden Decline: What's Causing It, and What Comes Next?* New York: Oxford University Press, 2021.

Jeremias, Joachim. *Jerusalem in the Time of Jesus*. London: SCM, 1969.

Jewett, Robert. *Romans: A Commentary*. Minneapolis: Fortress, 2006.

John Paul II, Pope. *Centesimus Annus*. https://www.vatican.va/content/john-paul-ii/en/encyclicals/documents/hf_jp-ii_enc_01051991_centesimus-annus.html.

———. *Mulieris dignitatem*. https://www.vatican.va/content/john-paul-ii/en/apost_letters/1988/documents/hf_jp-ii_apl_19880815_mulieris-dignitatem.html.

Kelly, J. N. D. *Early Christian Doctrines*. 5th ed. London: A. & C. Black, 1977.

Kochanska, Grazyna, and Nazan Aksan. "Conscience in Childhood: Past, Present, and Future." *Merrill-Palmer Quarterly* 50.3 (2004) 299-310.

Konrath, Sara H., et al. "Changes in Adult Attachment Styles in American College Students over Time: A Meta-Analysis." *Personality and Social Psychology Review* 18.4 (2014) 326-48.

Lambert, Nathaniel M., et al. "To Belong Is to Matter: Sense of Belonging Enhances Meaning in Life." *Personality and Social Psychology Bulletin* 39.11 (2013) 1418-27.

Lee, Ellen E., et al. "High Prevalence and Adverse Health Effects of Loneliness in Community-Dwelling Adults across the Lifespan: Role of Wisdom as a Protective Factor." *International Psychogeriatrics* 30 (2018) 1-16.

Louth, Andrew, ed. *Early Christian Writings*. Translated by Maxwell Staniforth. London: Penguin, 1987.

MacCrimmon, K. R., and D. M. Messick. "A Framework for Social Motives." *Behavioral Science* 21.2 (1976) 86-100.

Marshall, Roger. "Variances in Levels of Individualism across Two Cultures and Three Social Classes." *Journal of Cross-Cultural Psychology* 28.4 (1997) 490–95.

McCaffery, Lawrence J. "Irish Textures in American Catholicism." *Catholic Historical Review* 78.1 (1992) 1–18.

McCoy, Jennifer, Tahmina Rahman, and Murat Somer. "Polarization and the Global Crisis of Democracy: Common Patterns, Dynamics, and Pernicious Consequences for Democratic Polities." *American Behavioral Scientist* 62.1 (2018) 16–42.

Newson, Lesley, and Peter J. Richerson. "Why Do People Become Modern? A Darwinian Explanation." *Population and Development Review* 35 (2009) 117–58.

Newson, Lesley, et al. "Why Are Modern Families Small? Toward an Evolutionary and Cultural Explanation for the Demographic Transition." *Personality and Social Psychology Review* 9 (2005) 360–75.

Norris, Pippa, and Ronald Inglehart. *Sacred and Secular: Religion and Politics Worldwide.* Cambridge: Cambridge University Press, 2004.

Patterson, Colin. *Chalcedonian Personalism: Rethinking the Human.* Oxford: Peter Lang, 2016.

———. "A Constructive Approach to Secularism." In *God and Eros: The Anthropology of the Nuptial Mystery*, edited by Colin Patterson and Conor Sweeny, 123–35. Eugene, OR: Wipf & Stock, 2015.

———. "A Cultural Evolutionary Approach to Modernity: What Might It Mean for Christian Faith?" *Zygon: Journal of Religion and Science* 55.1 (2020) 52–72.

———. "What Has Eschatology to Do with the Gospel?—An Analysis of Papal Documents on Mission *ad gentes*." *Missiology* 47.3 (2019) 285–99.

———. "The World of Honour and Shame in the New Testament: Alien or Familiar?" *Biblical Theology Bulletin* 49.1 (2019) 4–14.

Pew Research Center. "The Future of World Religions: Population Growth Projections, 2010–2050." April 2, 2015. https://www.pewforum.org/2015/04/02/religious-projections-2010-2050/.

———. "Religious Belief and National Belonging in Central and Eastern Europe." May 10, 2017. https://www.pewforum.org/2017/05/10/religious-belief-and-national-belonging-in-central-and-eastern-europe/.

Pius XI, Pope. *Casti connubii.* December 31, 1930. https://www.vatican.va/content/pius-xi/en/encyclicals/documents/hf_p-xi_enc_19301231_casti-connubii.html.

Ratzinger, Joseph. *Eschatology: Death and Eternal Life.* Translated by Michael Waldstein. Washington, DC: CUA Press, 1988.

The Roman Missal. English translation of the third typical edition. Collegeville, MN: Liturgical Press, 2011.

Schierenbeck, Alec. "The Constitutionality of Income-Based Fines." *The University of Chicago Law Review* 85.8 (2018) 1869–1926.

Schultheiss, O. C. "Implicit Motives." In *Handbook of Personality: Theory and Research*, edited by O. P. John, 603–33. 3rd ed. New York, NY: Guilford, 2008.

Schultheiss, O. C., and C. Brunstein. "Inhibited Power Motivation and Persuasive Communication: A Lens Model Analysis." *Journal of Personality* 70.4 (2002) 553–82.

Second Vatican Council. "Dogmatic Constitution on the Church. *Lumen gentium.* 21 November 1964." In *Vatican Council II: The Conciliar and Post Conciliar Documents*, edited by Austin Flannery, 903–1001. Rev. ed. Northport, NY: Costello, 1988.

———. "Pastoral Constitution on the Church in the World, *Gaudium et spes*, 7 December 1965." In *Vatican Council II: The Conciliar and Post Conciliar Documents*, edited by Austin Flannery, 350–423. Rev. ed. Northport, NY: Costello, 1988.

Sidanius, Jim, and Felicia Pratto. *Social Dominance: An Intergroup Theory of Social Hierarchy and Oppression*. Cambridge, UK: Cambridge University Press, 2001.

Stark, Rodney. *The Rise of Mormonism*. New York: Columbia University Press, 2005.

Stefanou, Christina, and Marita P. McCabe. "Adult Attachment and Sexual Functioning: A Review of Past Research." *The Journal of Sexual Medicine* 9.10 (2012) 2499–2507.

Stillman, Tyler F., et al. "Alone and without Purpose: Life Loses Meaning Following Social Exclusion." *Journal of Experimental and Social Psychology* 45.4 (2009) 686–94.

Suomi, Stephen J., Roberta Delizio, and Harry F. Harlow. "Social Rehabilitation of Separation-Induced Depressive Disorders in Monkeys." *American Journal of Psychiatry* 133.11 (1976) 1279–85.

Taborsky, Michael. "Social Evolution: Reciprocity There Is." *Current Biology* 23.11 (2013) R486–R488.

Tappé, Mercedes, et al. "Gender Differences in Receptivity to Sexual Offers: a New Research Prototype." *Interpersona* 7.2 (2013) 323–44.

Triandis, Harry C. "Individualism-Collectivism and Personality." *Journal of Personality* 69.6 (2001) 907–24.

Trivers, Robert. "Parental Investment and Sexual Selection." In *Sexual Selection & the Descent of Man 1871–1971*, edited by Bernard Campbell, 136–179. Chicago: Aldine, 1972.

Twenge, Jean M., Kathleen R. Catanese, and Roy F. Baumeister. "Social Exclusion and the Deconstructed State: Time Perception, Meaninglessness, Lethargy, Lack of Emotion, and Self-Awareness." *Journal of Personality and Social Psychology* 85.3 (2003) 409–23.

Ueda, Peter, et al. "Trends in Frequency of Sexual Activity and Number of Sexual Partners among Adults aged 18 to 44 Years in the US, 2000–2018." *JAMA Network Open* 3.6 (2020) e203833–e203833.

Weaver, Rebecca Harden. *Divine Grace and Human Agency: A Study of the Semi-Pelagian Controversy*. Macon, GA: Mercer University Press, 1996.

Wellings, Kaye, et al. "Changes in, and Factors Associated with, Frequency of Sex in Britain: Evidence from Three National Surveys of Sexual Attitudes and Lifestyles (Natsal)." *British Medical Journal* 365 (2019) l1525.

Wilkinson, Gerald. "Reciprocal Altruism in Bats and Other Mammals." *Ethology and Sociobiology* 9 (1988) 85–100.

Wongsomboon, Val, Mary H. Burleson, and Gregory D. Webster. "Women's Orgasm and Sexual Satisfaction in Committed Sex and Casual Sex: Relationship between Sociosexuality and Sexual Outcomes in Different Sexual Contexts." *The Journal of Sex Research* 57.3 (2020) 285–95.

World Values Survey. "WVS Online." https://www.worldvaluessurvey.org/WVSOnline.jsp.

Zuroff, David C., and Sidney J. Blatt. "The Therapeutic Relationship in the Brief Treatment of Depression: Contributions to Clinical Improvement and Enhanced Adaptive Capacities." *Journal of Consulting and Clinical Psychology* 74.1 (2006) 199–206.

INDEX

Aksan, Nazan, 127n1
Ambrose (bishop), 222n1
Ambrosiaster, 222n1
Anthropology, theological. *See* theological anthropology
Aquinas, Thomas, 6n4, 99, 283–84, 284n1
Aristotle, 6n4, 87, 257n9, 283
Attachment (motive), 8, 49–73, 175, 280
  avoidant-insecure form of, 51, 55, 70, 115, 116, 247, 250
  and belief in God, 186–189
  changes in attachment strength, 119–20
  and conscience, 128, 134, 137–40, 142, 145, 154, 158
  cultural attachment, 73, 73n
  and death of spouse, 59
  description of, 51–59, 75–76
  and divorce, 53, 59
  and dominance, 74–82, 119–20, 158, 171–73, 185–87
  in the Scriptures, 78–79
  effects of low fertility rate on, 172–73
  and existential security, 65, 67, 70, 71–73, 73n11, 121, 187, 212, 215, 276–77, 281
  to God/Christ, 66–71, 280–81
  the group form of, 59–61
    and belief in hell, 219–220
    and Christian hope, 211–14
    and the church, 60, 69, 263–65
    and culture, 61
    hostility to out-groups, 61
    and idolatry, 275–78
  insecure-anxious form of, 55, 70
  through the lifespan, 53–59
  in marriage, 57–59, 229
  and Christian mission, 273–75
  in non-human animals, 49–50
  non-intellectual nature of, 81
  and oxytocin, 58, 58n7
  and pleasure, 169
  and politics, 245–47
  and prayer, 197–98, 203
  in the Scriptures, 62–65
  and sexual love, 57–58, 58n7, 115–117, 238
  to the state, 183–184
  unconscious nature of, 52–53
Augustine, 94–95, 95n10, 222n1

Barkan, Steven, 109n6
Barnabas, letter of, 214
Belief in God, 181–93
  and attachment, 186–89
  and attachment to the state, 183–84
  and conscience, 189–91
  effects of sociological processes, 184–85
  and an impersonal mindset, 187–88, 191–92
  and social reciprocity as justice, 191–92
  variations among nations, 182–83
Belief in hell. *See* hell, belief in
Benedict XVI (Pope). *See* Ratzinger, Joseph

INDEX

Birnbaum, Gurit, 116n4
Birot, Antoine, 97n11
Blatt, Sidney, 120n9
Bonaventure (theologian), 199–200, 199n2
Bonhoeffer, Dietrich, 43n4
Bowlby, John, 51, 59n8
Brunstein, C., 16n2
Bugental, Daphne, 8, 8n6, 37n2, 83, 83n1, 85
Buss, David, 104, 104n2, 110, 231n5
Butzer, Bethany, 116n4

Campbell, Lorne, 116n4
Cassidy, Jude, 49n1, 76n1
Catechism of the Catholic Church, 30n6, 99, 99n12, 99n13, 149, 149n8, 163, 163n3, 223n3, 252n5, 254n7, 256n8
CDC (Centre for Disease Control, USA), 227n2
Childcare, 54–55
Churchill, Winston, 163
Clark, Russell, 107, 108n4
Coalitional grouping (motive), 8
Competence, 13, 19, 25, 26–27, 30, 75, 77, 78, 129, 148, 149, 165, 263, 265
  and pleasure, 169
Conley, Terri, 108n5
Conscience (motive), 8, 127–63, 175–76, 195, 280, 281
  and attachment, 128, 134, 137–40, 142, 145, 154, 158
  and authority, 151–63
    God/Christ as authority, 151–52
    the Catholic Church as, 155
    human authority, 153–54, 157–60
    the leader-follower relationship, 161–63
  and marriage, 231–37
  parents as original authority, 151–52
  political authority, 154–55, 157–58
  in the Scriptures, 154–57, 158–60
belief in God, 189–91
  its development, 127–29
  distinctively human, 131–32
  distortions of,
  and the Catholic Church, 149
  conscience as "gut feeling", 130, 189–90
  conscience as utility calculation, 130–31, 190–91
  and dominance, 134–35, 136–37, 147–50, 148n7, 158
  and emergence of moral sense, 129
  and empathy, 128,
  God/Christ as transcendent moral authority, 130, 131, 141, 144–45, 151–52, 154–55, 190, 282
  language/reason necessary for, 132, 143
  as locus of freedom, 143–44
  guide for other motives, 133
  as moral authority, 130–31
  other-oriented, 129
  and pleasure, 169
  relational/personal, 130, 131, 142
  in the Scriptures, 137–43
  its simulacrum, 135–37
  and "the true self", 145–47, 182
Contraception, 22, 117, 171, 230
Convenience, the pursuit of, 166–68, 214n5
Conversion (to Christ), 144–45
Cortisol, 54–55
Curiosity, 164
Cyprian (bishop), 222, 222n1

Death, the problem of, 204–205
De Dreu, Carsten, 61
De Waal, Franz, 84, 84n3, 87n5
Doherty, Carroll, 243n2
Dominance (motive), 8, 10–48, 165, 175, 280
  in animals, 10–11
  and attachment, 74–82, 185–87
  in the Scriptures, 78–79,
  and awareness of mortality, 33–34
  and conscience, 134–35, 136–37, 147–50, 148n7, 158
  and conscious reasoning, 20–23

and the conscious self, 18–19
cultural influences on, 17–18,
    170–174
its development, 13–14, 75–76
distortions of thought, 23–24, 32,
    174, 187
effects of low fertility rate on,
    172–73
and the fall, 31–33
group form of, 36–48
    and belief in hell, 219–220
    and the Catholic Church, 42–44
    and Christian community,
        263–65
    and Christian mission, 272–73
    description of, 37–38
    in the Scriptures, 38–42
and human mating, 12
and human progress, 31–33
and an impersonal mindset,
    187–88, 192–92
its moral status, 29–30
and politics, 245–47
and prayer, 196–98, 203
in the Scriptures, 24–29
through attention-seeking, 15
through power, 15–16
through status, 15
the value of, 44–47
Drugli, May Britt, 55n6
Dunbar, Robin, 261n3

Empathy, 88, 128, 132, 244–52
Employer-employee relationship,
    90–91
Eternal life, 204–216
    hope of, 209–216
    and Catholic theology, 209, 213
    and Christian community,
        211–14
    in the Scriptures, 205–209
    and sociological processes,
        211–13
Evolutionary theory, 9, 10–11, 12
    and Christian faith, 282–83
Existential security, 65, 67, 70,
    71–73, 73n11, 121, 187, 212, 215,
    276–77, 281

Falkenström, Fredrick, 120n9
Feeney, B. C., 53n4, 53n5
Feeney, Judith, 115n2, 116n3
Fehr, Ernst, 84n2
Fellowship, 69, 70, 213–215, 259–267,
    278
    and attachment, 263–65
    and competence, 263–65
    description, 260–61
    and group size, 261–62
    and hope, 213–215
    and social brain hypothesis, 261–62
    and social reciprocity, 265–67
Fertility rate, 170–74
    effects on attachment motive,
        172–73
    effects on dominance motive,
        172–73
    effects of Industrial Revolution,
        171–72
    ideas for restoring, 174
Feynman, Richard, 167, 167n2
Fisher, Anthony, 145n4
Fiske, Alan, 8n6, 90n8,
Foa, Edna, 8n6
Foa, Uriel, 8n6
Freeloaders, the problem of, 86, 162
Free-will, 23, 143–44, 144n2, 208,
    221, 282
Friesen, Amanda, 251n4

Gallagher, James, 22n4
Gangestad, Steven, 107n3
Gender equality, 46–47, 124–26, 227,
    236, 237
Gintis, Herbert, 87n7
Grace of God, 79, 80–81, 144n3,
    148–49
Gregory the Great (Pope), 30n7
Groeneveld, Marleen, 55n6
Group-identity, description of, 35–36

Hare, Christopher, 243n2
Harlow, Harry, 50, 50n2
Harm avoidance. See self-preservation
Hatfield, Elaine, 107, 108n4
Hawley, Patricia, 13n1
Hell, belief in, 217–24

(Hell, belief in continued)
   and attachment, 219–220, 223
   and Catholic theology, 221–23
   and dominance, 219–220, 223
   Jesus' descent into hell, 222–223
   and social reciprocity, 218–19, 223
Henrich, Joseph, 6n3, 164n1, 184n5
Hsu, Ning, 225n1
Hudson, Nathan, 120n8
Hungary, government of, 183, 183n4

Industrial Revolution, 171–72
Inglehart, Ronald, 72, 72n10, 183n3

Jeremias, Joachim, 118, 118n5, 118n6, 123n10
Jerome, 222n1
Jewett, Robert, 39, 39n3, 261n2
John of the Cross, 222–23
John Paul II (Pope), 163, 233, 233n7, 254n7, 263
Joseph, husband of Mary, 111

Kant, Immanuel, 284
Kelly, J. N. D., 222n1
Kochanska, Grazyna, 127n1
Koinonia. *See* fellowship
Konrath, Sara, 120n7
Ksaizkiewicz, Aleksander, 251n4

Lambert, Nathanael, 87n4
Leighton, Ralph, 167n2
Lorenz, Konrad, 49
Louth, Andrew, 214n4
Luther, Martin, 80
Luttrell, L. M., 84n3

MacCrimmen, K. R., 8n6
Marriage, 111–12, 113–14, 115–17, 119–26, 225–41
   and attachment, 229, 237–40, 280
   authority in, 231–37
   complementarity in, 113–14, 124–26, 226–27, 234–35, 235–36, 237, 237–39
   convergence of genders, 225–26
   and dominance, 112–14, 231–32
   and mating, 228–29

   and pleasure, 169
   and psychological therapy, 120–21
   and sexual love, 57–58, 58n7, 115–117, 123, 238
   and social reciprocity, 121–26, 229
   See also mating
Marshall, Roger, 45n6
Mary, Jesus' mother, 69–70, 111
Mating (motive), 8, 101–26, 175, 281
   and attachment, 115–21, 238–39
      insecure attachment, effects, 119–21
   in the Scriptures, 117–19
   definition of, 101
   and dominance, 102, 112–14
   finding a spouse, 112–13, 231
   and the spousal relationship, 113–14
   the evolution of, 103–109
   its hidden aspects, 102–103
   its relative importance, 101–102
   in the Scriptures, 109–112
   sexual strategies theory, 104–109,
   and social reciprocity, 121–26
McCabe, Marita, 115n1
McCaffrey, Lawrence, 145n4
McCoy, Jennifer, 243n2
Messick, D. M., 8n6
Mission (Christian), 268–78
   and group attachment, 273–75
   and group dominance, 272–73
   and idolatry, 275–78
   and the lordship of Christ, 273–78
   and secular perceptions of Christians, 269–71
   and social desirability, 271–73
   and Christian attitudes towards the state, 273–75
Monin, J. K., 53n4, 53n5
Moral authority, 130–31, 151–63
   and attachment, 162–63
   changes in, 152, 157–58
   a Christian approach to, 157–62
   and the Catholic Church, 152n1, 155
   God/Christ as, 144–45, 151–52, 190–91
   human, 153–54, 157–60

husband/father, 156
other forms, 156
parents as original, 151–52
political, 154–55, 156–57, 157–58
Moral sense, 129
Motives, general, 4–9
  changes through history, 164–74, 282
  and cultural evolution, 5–6
  effects of low fertility rates on, 170–74
  and human reason, 8,
  and social motives, 7–8, 279–80
  comparison with non-humans, 4–5

Newson, Lesley, 170n4
Norris, Pippa, 72, 72n10, 183n3

Orbán, Victor, 183–84
Oxytocin, 58, 58n7

Patterson, Colin, xii, 87n6, 144n1, 170n4, 209n2, 211n3, 256n8, 284n2
Paul, apostle, 4, 28, 39, 65, 79, 94, 123, 149–50, 260–61
Pew Research Center, 181n1
Pius XI (Pope), 233, 233n6, 234, 234n8, 235n9
Pleasure, distillation of, 168–69
  and the Christian tradition, 169n3, 214n5
Political Authority, 154–55, 156–57
Politics, 242–58
  and church-state relations, 256–258, 257n9
  in its conservative-progressive dimension
    and attachment, 245–47
    and the Christian faith, 248–58
    description, 242–44
    and dominance, 245–47
    and idolatry, 249–51, 253, 258
    and libertarianism, 243n1, 244n3
    and the lordship of Christ, 255–58
    and subsidiarity, 254
    and taxation, 255
Poole, Keith, 243n2
Pratto, Felicia, 35n1

Prayer, 194–203
  corporate, 200–203
    attitude of the priest, 200–201
    the role of music, 201–203
  private, 195–200
Punishment (legal), 91, 98–100, 253
Purgatory, 222

Ratzinger, Joseph/ Benedict XVI (Pope), 180, 180n1, 205n1, 223n2
Reason
  as instrument of dominance, 21–22
Reasons for acting, 3, 6–7, 21–22
Reciprocity, social. *See* social reciprocity
Resurrection of Jesus, 207–209
Richerson, Peter, 170n4
Roman Missal, 194n1

Schierenbeck, Alec, 90n8
Schmidt, David, 104, 104n2, 110
Schultheiss, O. C., 16n2
Self-preservation, 7n5, 164
Sexual abuse (child), 145, 263
Sexual Strategies Theory, 104–109, 230
Shaver, Phillip, 49n1, 76n1
Sibling jealousy, 55
Sidanius, Jim, 35n1
Social Reciprocity, 8, 83–100, 175, 281
  and belief in hell, 218–19
  biological roots, 83, 84
  and Christian fellowship, 265–67
  and the Cross of Christ, 96–98
  cultural variations, 84–85
  description of, 83–84
  and dominance, 88–91
  as justice, 86–88, 98–100
    and belief in God, 191–92
    and politics, 245–58
  in relation to God, 87n6, 96–98
  and marriage, 121–26, 229
  and punishment (legal), 98–100
  in the Scriptures, 91–96
    justice, 92–96
    social relations, 91–92
  and social groups, 86
Stark, Rodney, 273n1

Stefanou, Christina, 115n1
Stillman, Tyler, 87n4
Subsidiarity, 254
Suomi, Stephen, 50n2

Taborsky, Michael, 84n3
Tappé, Mercedes, 108n4
Temple, William (Archbishop), 43
Theological anthropology, 179, 211, 283–84
Therapy, psychological, 120–21
Triandis, Harry, 45n6
Trivers, Robert, 104n2
Twenge, Jean, 87n4

Ueda, Peter, 230n3
Unconscious mind, 3–4, 4n2, 52–53

Vatican Council, Second, 146, 146n5, 147, 147n6, 259n1

Weaver, Rebecca, 95n10
Wellings, Kaye, 230n3
Wilkinson, Gerald, 84n3
Wongsomboon, Val, 230n4
World Values Survey, 182–3, 182n2

Zuroff, David, 120n9

www.ingramcontent.com/pod-product-compliance
Lightning Source LLC
Chambersburg PA
CBHW071233230426
43668CB00011B/1420